BIRTH OF A COLONIAL CITY

Long before Calcutta was "discovered" by Job Charnock, it thrived by the Hugli since times immemorial. This book, and its companion *Colonial Calcutta*, is a biographical account of the when, the how and the what of a global city and its emergence under colonial rule in the eighteenth and nineteenth centuries.

Ranjit Sen traces the story of how three clustered villages became the hub of the British Empire and a centre of colonial imagination. He examines the historical and geopolitical factors that were significant in securing its prominence, and its subsequent urbanization which was a colonial experience without an antecedent. Further, it sheds light on Calcutta's early search for identity – how it superseded interior towns and flourished as the seat of power for its hinterland and developed its early institutions, while its municipal administration slowly burgeoned.

A sharp analysis of the colonial enterprise, this volume lays bare the underbelly of the British Raj. It will be of great interest to scholars and researchers of modern history, South Asian history, urban studies, British Studies, and area studies.

Ranjit Sen is former Professor, Department of Islamic History and Culture, University of Calcutta.

BIRTH OF A COLONIAL CITY

Calcutta

Ranjit Sen

LONDON AND NEW YORK

First published 2019
by Routledge
2 Park Square, Milton Park, Abingdon, Oxon OX14 4RN

and by Routledge
52 Vanderbilt Avenue, New York, NY 10017

Routledge is an imprint of the Taylor & Francis Group, an informa business

© 2019 Ranjit Sen

The right of Ranjit Sen to be identified as author of this work has been asserted by him in accordance with sections 77 and 78 of the Copyright, Designs and Patents Act 1988.

All rights reserved. No part of this book may be reprinted or reproduced or utilised in any form or by any electronic, mechanical, or other means, now known or hereafter invented, including photocopying and recording, or in any information storage or retrieval system, without permission in writing from the publishers.

Trademark notice: Product or corporate names may be trademarks or registered trademarks, and are used only for identification and explanation without intent to infringe.

British Library Cataloguing-in-Publication Data
A catalogue record for this book is available from the British Library

Library of Congress Cataloging-in-Publication Data
A catalog record for this book has been requested

ISBN: 978-1-138-36678-7 (hbk)
ISBN: 978-0-429-02982-0 (ebk)

Typeset in Sabon
by Apex CoVantage, LLC

To Dr Snigdha Sen, my wife

and

The Myriad People Who Made Calcutta

the Glory of the East

CONTENTS

Preface ix
Acknowledgements xvi
Note on the text xviii

Introduction: an overview of the colonial origin of Calcutta 1

PART I
Scanning the context 29

1 Mapping the pattern of urbanization in history: the Calcutta Chapter 31

2 A comparative understanding of the growth of the three colonial cities: Madras, Calcutta, and Bombay 37

3 Revolution on the riverbank: a study of the creation of a mankind necessary for urbanization 46

4 Geopolitics of early urbanization in Calcutta 1698–1757 63

PART II
Early formations 79

5 Who was the real founder of Calcutta?: between two perspectives 81

6 How Calcutta superseded interior towns 110

CONTENTS

7	The logic of urbanization	138
8	Municipal administration	159
9	Making a pilgrim centre: Kalighat	170
10	Challenges of an urban growth	184
11	The city assumes form	205
12	The city in hindsight: some observations in conclusion	232
	Bibliography	242
	Index	258

PREFACE

Historians differ in their views about the origin of Calcutta. Some say that its origin was pre-British and its evolution was in the process when the British took over. In other words, its origin was entirely indigenous and a colonial growth pattern was imposed on it. This school of thought has a nationalist outlook in its thinking and it grew as a response to the claims of the British imperial school of thought which developed over the last three centuries. It objected to the view much prevalent at the time that 24 August 1690, the date of Job Charnock's third and final landing on the city, should be regarded as the date of foundation of the city and that Job Charnock should be regarded as its founder. Taking note of this objection the Honourable High Court of Judicature, Calcutta, consulted some eminent historians of the city and sought their opinion as to whether it could be said that the city owed its origin to the English and that Job Charnock could be treated as its founder. The historians were unanimous in their opinion that the city was pre-British because its early references predate the coming of the English. Accordingly, the verdict of the Honourable High Court was specific: the city had no date of birth and Job Charnock could not be regarded as its founding father.

Keeping this in mind, the present book has set as its aim the study of urbanization of Calcutta as an exclusive phenomenon which took place as a process of evolution in course of the last three centuries. This evolution was certainly in consistent with the growth of the Empire itself.

The Calcutta, it should be noted, which later became the capital of an empire, took its birth after a war and before a rebellion. The Mughal Empire under Aurangzeb and the English East India Company were locked in a war between 1686 and 1690. It was at the end of the war that Job Charnock set his feet on Sutanuti for the third time on 24 August 1690. This was the final arrival of the English in Calcutta

PREFACE

after which there was no retreat. In 1696 there was the rebellion of Shova Singh in western Bengal. That rebellion was a massive uprising which the Mughal power controlled and eventually crushed with great difficulty. This rebellion taught the English the first lesson as to how to curve the contours of a state in this part of the country. Territory and military might were the two major ingredients with which a mercantile body could build up their commercial base provided they had the backing of their own form of government and constant supply and guidance from their own home. In this they were amply supported by Madras which acted as the rear area of their advanced outpost in the region around Kolkata-Sutanuti-Govindapur. It was from Madras that Robert Clive set his sails in January 1757 and recaptured Calcutta from the *Nawab*. The open seaboard came to their assistance. In 1632 the Mughal Emperor Shahjahan drove the Portuguese out of the Bengal sea. Once the sea was made clear of pirates and a predominating aggressive power from the West it became an open corridor of transit for the English sailing from Madras. The Mughals had no powerful navy with which they could rule the waves. The result was that the sea provided an open gate for the English either for their advancement into the territory or for their retreat from here. Without the help of a navy and an open sea to their support, the English could not have built an empire here.

Calcutta was the outcome of geopolitics that had governed developments in south Bengal in the eighteenth century. A new kind of social change was taking place in this part of the country. This may be called an inquilab or a revolution whereby everything turned upside down. Money of the Indians was providing resource to the Europeans and the sword of the Europeans was providing security to the people. This was made clear when during the time of the Maratha invasions people flocked to Calcutta for security. For the first sixty years, Calcutta, which was slowly growing into a power base of the English, did not grow territorially because the Bengal *Nawabs* maintained a strict vigilance on the developments of the English in Calcutta. The city acquired territorial dynamism only after the battle of Palasi when the district of twenty-four Parganas was granted to the Company as their *zamindari*. During the half century since the battle of Palasi, the English in Calcutta did six major things. Firstly, they fleeced the *Nawabs* and appropriated a huge amount of money from the Bengal treasury. This was called the 'Plassey Plunder.' Secondly, they built a new fort in the city that kept both the *Nawab* and their European competitors at bay. Thirdly, they transferred all the major administrative, judicial, and financial institutions from Murshidabad to Calcutta

PREFACE

thus denying Murshidabad its functional bases of institutional administration. Fourthly, they changed the diplomatic protocol of the country. Previously the Governor or his agent had to go to Murshidabad to meet the *Nawab*. Now the protocol was changed. The *Nawab* or his agent had to come to Calcutta to meet the Governor and later the Governor General of the British possessions in India. Fifthly, the office of the Governor General was built into an office where the highest power of the country now came to be installed. Finally, they set up the Supreme Court to appropriate a jurisdiction which originally belonged to the *Nawab*. When this was the situation the *Nawabs* gradually surrendered their own marks of sovereignty to the English.

While the geopolitics helped the English to insulate and grow their city as their power base the city itself was undergoing a change from within. From the 1770s and 1780s the internal morphology of the city changed. It started taking slowly the shape of what later came to be known as the City of Palaces. Calcutta was now being steadily installed into power. The territorial revenue of the three provinces of Bengal, Bihar and Orissa was now converted into the sinews of the Company's commerce. While coming to Calcutta in the beginning of 1757 in order to retrieve the city from the *Nawab* Clive bombarded and destroyed the two cities of Chandernagore and Hughli thus removing from the scene two major competitors of the city of Calcutta. Immediately after the battle of Palasi the English started renovating the internal infrastructure of the city. The English came out of their cramped existence within the Fort. Now began a new sprawling life of the English in the city. The White Town began to grow very rapidly. From the beginning of the 1790s money was raised through lottery for the growth and development of the city and the boundaries of the city came to be rudimentarily defined in 1794. With this the nucleus of an empire was created. It was in this situation that in 1803 Lord Wellesley declared in his minutes that the British Empire in India could no longer be ruled from a shabby city or from the emporium of traders. His intention was that Calcutta was to be ruled from an imperial city. Thus the city of Calcutta came to be recognized as the base of a new empire in India. Calcutta now became an imperial seat of power relegating Delhi to the background.

In understanding this evolution of the city, as noted previously, the present study differs from other approaches to the subject common and prevalent, which till date have considered the growth of Calcutta as one of the most outstanding gifts of British colonialism in India. On the contrary, our emphasis is to show that Calcutta had grown not out of any deliberate and careful design on the part of the English and not necessarily as an outcome solely of British efforts. It grew as situations demanded, mainly in response to eventualities relying entirely on partnership with the natives. This happened in two distinct phases – the first being the one that synchronizes with the first century of the British rule in India. The second phase tends to be the trans-mutiny phase when the urbanization of the city needed to respond to the industrial, military and global needs of the British Empire. In the first phase it was native capital and native partnership which helped the Empire to bring the city into formation. The British capital came in the second phase.

At the beginning of its career the Empire was financially constrained to undertake the task of urbanization so much so that capital was drawn from the indigenous people through lottery. That was the phase when the native capital financed a mini-industrial revolution in the periphery of Calcutta. In the eighteenth century, the city grew first as a garrison town centring round a fort, then as a port city and finally at the end as an administrative centre. In totality, the city was, in its final form, an attractive halt for the east-moving Britons where away from their distant homes the British adventurers could find trajectories of their home-life recreated. As the city progressed through the first century of British rule in the nineteenth century it became an imperial city acting on the famous minute of Lord Wellesley in 1803 which for the first time defined the directions and dynamics of urbanization in Calcutta. It underlined the feeling that the British possession in India had assumed the shape of an Empire, which must not rest on an imperfect base. Consequent upon this dictum of Lord Wellesley two things happened. First, Calcutta got its basic infrastructure – drains and roads – and grew as what has been called the City of Palaces. Secondly, Calcutta became installed in power coordinating on the one hand the growth of the British Empire in India and on the other the trade potentialities of the British Asiatic trade with its global nexus in the continent and beyond. What we see as pre-mutiny urbanization was really a combination of these two elements of growth. Calcutta was eventually urbanized on a very narrow perspective on a limited scale mostly around the White Town of the city and completely at the cost of interior towns – Hughli, Chandernagore, Burdwan, Malda, Murshidabad, Dakha, Rajshahi, and Chittagong. But in the long run she could not fulfil her promise. Her urbanization had three components – firstly, those of a garrison town, then those of a port, and finally those of an administrative town – the seat of an empire. As a garrison town it lost its supremacy when Madras emerged as a competent base of power against both the French and Haidar Ali in the south in the middle of the eighteenth century and Bombay became

PREFACE

militarily independent enough to fight against the Marathas with occasional help from Calcutta. As a port it began losing its sway when the British Empire developed a ring of ports around Calcutta as a part of its measures to control the sea and the vast terrain of Asiatic trade that had flourished on the collapse of the French and Dutch trade in south Asia. These ports – Penang, Singapore, Chittagong, Madras, Colombo, Bombay, and Karachi – were the real competitors of Calcutta and also its cordon. Finally, Calcutta lost its charm as an administrative centre and the seat of power when the capital was transferred from Calcutta to Delhi in 1912. With the turn of the twentieth century, Calcutta turned into a tragic figure seething under discontent and looking for retrieving its glamour – this time not as a seat of power but as a seat of revolution.

From all that has been said previously, it is clear that the book is not on the origin of Calcutta. It is on the growth of a garrison town and a commercial city known to tradition as Kolkata and to the newly arrived mercantile community from the West as Calcutta. The origin of the city is confused and there are no reliable records with which we can construct its antiquities. The result is that, up till date, Calcutta has not known any authentic and full-fledged biography of its own which can be trusted as the real history of the city. This is true except the two initial attempts at writing a scientific biography of the city, first by Beverley in 1876 followed by A.K. Ray in 1901. Both wrote their books as parts of the census reports of their respective years. Unable to dispel the mist around the origin of the city the present work has taken as its subject the creation of a colonial town that was termed as the second city of the Empire – in rank next to London. Most of its urbanization was the outcome of British needs viewed from imperial interests. Imbued with the spirit to implant in the East the Renaissance culture of the West, the English built a city not only on utilitarian basis but also with a sense of manifest pride and exclusiveness so common in the psychology of an island people. The choice of the riverfront for the white city in the south had at its back the racist spirit of segregation from the native people of the north. Originating as a garrison town with a fort in the centre it eventually reconciled its military parameters with those of a port and an administrative centre so much so that in its ultimate city formation it could install itself to power coordinating the growth of the British Empire in India. In the process it presided over the decline of the regional power centre in Bengal, Murshidabad and the seat of a national power, Delhi. Its rise was majestic.

This story of the city has been the outcome of a thorough research for many years during which the city has revealed its aspects, crowning

PREFACE

and significant, which had hitherto remained unknown to any research. To say this is to underline the fact that all its chapters manifest dimensions of new and novel exploration of urban history in a south Asian context. It opens a global vista of an intellectual understanding of what may be called the most outstanding process of modern history, a combination of a city, property, and community rolled into one formation, called Calcutta. At heart it has the genre of a township that eventually metamorphosed three village habitations into a magnificent structure called The City of Palace. In practice this city eventually became the second city of the British Empire. This Empire gave rise to innumerable towns and cities in the world – Cape Town in South Africa, Penang in the north-west, and Singapore slightly off on the southern coast of Malay peninsula, Rangoon (Yangon) in Burma, Colombo in Sri Lanka on the Indian Ocean, Kingston in Jamaica in the West Indies, Durban in East Africa, Nairobi in Kenya, Lagos in Nigeria, Sydney, Melbourne, Perth in Australia, Toronto in Canada, and Christchurch in New Zealand. These are a few of the myriad cities that came up in four continents, Asia-Africa-America-Australia, in course of the three centuries of the colonial expansion in the world, from the eighteenth to the twentieth centuries. Among all these cities Calcutta assumed a distinction in being the one from where the British could map up their own Asian empire. How Calcutta was installed into power and how the adjacent cities of the country were dwarfed by her so as to make her own majesty paramount has been the thrust of the book. It is a book on colonial urbanization in south Asian context in which economics, sociology, and history have been mixed in a combination of trustworthy determinants of history. The book has parts; parts are divided into chapters and chapters are subdivided into sections. All these form the limbs of a body, the text of the book. This text has an inner integration born of facts which are drawn immensely from different records. The facts presented in the book have been marshalled through interpretations which work out the cohesion of the entire text on the rise of a city into power and prominence. The tool of interpretation is logic; the instrument of narration is language, simple and lucid attuned to the romance of the past. It is sensitive to the appropriateness of history. An appropriate history is frilled here with imagination so as to keep the story from degenerating into an arid narration of the past. Three things can be said to have been novel in the book: its contents, most of which were unknown to historians till date; its in-depth engagement with the subject; and, finally, its direction toward understanding the destiny of a people in whom the age had left its own manifestation. The book is thus an epitome of an age in which

PREFACE

the manufacture of one city became the prime mover of the history of an empire.

* * *

Writing on Calcutta is a challenge. In the absence of private papers and family records one has to depend entirely on government documents and official literature to know how the city was formed. Calcutta's history thus has an official mind at the back to give its own version. Mr. H. Beverley, c.s., while writing the first connected history of the rise of Calcutta as a part of his *Census Report* of 1876, advised all future historians to collect materials from domestic archives. When as a sequel to the *Census Report* of 1901 Mr. A.K. Ray wrote his excellent account of Calcutta – *A Short History of Calcutta* – he tried to follow Beverley's advice. But he failed. Knowing that failures very often are pillars of success I undertook an effort to hunt out domestic archives in the city and outside. My efforts, great in terms of my own capacity, were essentially too meagre to show me the light of success. This tryst with destiny I met thirty years ago when I started researching Calcutta's past. I knew from the beginning that my search had to coexist with colonial versions of the city which I could not verify and cross-check with versions of private and domestic experiences. I, therefore, raised questions which were essentially indigenous, native to my own thought. This was one way of making archival facts answer my own queries as they have been presented in the book. These queries, if properly answered, I believe, will unearth truth which otherwise hides its face in oblivion. Some of these queries are as follows: Who was the real founder of Calcutta? What geopolitics determined urbanization of the city? Did the riverbank have the adequate human potential that could ensure urbanization on land? How did Calcutta supersede interior towns? How did the city assume its own forms? Could the temple of Kalighat rally as a centre for urbanization? Was Calcutta's soul checkmated in the eighteenth century? These questions set the precincts within which the book has taken its shape. I have no pretension to provide to readers the final and the perfect version of the story as to how the city grew. My humble presentation in this book performs a single end. It allows facts to speak for themselves so as to make the story free of bias. Facts do often propound truth and truth propagates its own logic. That logic makes the story coherent. With coherence at the core the present book has turned out to be this at the end: a small and humble piece of writing in which city becomes an epitome of time.

Ranjit Sen

ACKNOWLEDGEMENTS

Writing the present book was apparently a solitary work of an individual man. But behind this there was the concern of a crowd who, as is common in history, remain in oblivion. The book would not have taken shape if the University Grants Commission had not sanctioned a University Project for Excellence at the University of Calcutta to pursue the colonial antiquity of the city of Calcutta. The real momentum for writing this book came from that. I remain beholden to the UGC for its support to me. Mr. Dibyendu Basu had typed my hand-written manuscripts and had given them the elegant shape necessary for a book form. The staff in the reading room of the National Library, Kolkata, had always been on their toes to satisfy my insatiable hunger for books. Mr. Indranil Mandal and Ms. Tanima Debnath, my students, had served me as project fellows in the aforesaid UGC Project on urban history in the Department of Islamic History and Culture, University of Calcutta. While being in the Project they were my assistants in hunting books, journals, records, and documents regarding Calcutta in the West Bengal State Archive and in other libraries in the city. My students in the classrooms in University of Calcutta and in the Aliah University, Kolkata, had raised questions and kept me alert ever in my quest for truth. The Institute of Historical Studies, Kolkata, had allowed me to present my researched papers in their seminars and occasionally printed them in their journal *The Quarterly Review of Historical Study*. They have also published my book *The Stagnating City: Calcutta in the Eighteenth Century*. With the permission of the Institute and its present Director, Professor Chittabrata Palit, I have drawn materials from my writings available in this journal and the book in the form of texts, excerpts, citations, and references. The Calcutta Historical Society like the Institute of Historical Studies has been equally generous to me in allowing me to use and incorporate in

ACKNOWLEDGEMENTS

my book articles either in full or in part published in their esteemed journal *Bengal Past and Present*.

Words of thankfulness to all persons and institutions stated here will be too meagre an expression to show my gratitude to them. Yet this book remains to be the visible monument of my gratitude to all of them. My friends working in the reading room of the library of the Asiatic Society, Kolkata, were of immense help to me. Without their support many of these pages would have remained unwritten. Whenever a new book on Calcutta appears on the market, the information is immediately passed to me by my young friend, almost of the age of my son, Shri Jayadewa Jayawardana of Mahabodhi Book Society, Kolkata. Without him some of my research visions would have remained un-resurrected. My son Shubhrajit Sen is one of my greatest inspirers. Knowing that a person of my age in India is not at home in electronic competence he provides me with technological assistance so that I may remain comfortable in my own academic station. Last but not the least there is the one whose existence proliferates to me in diverse roles – a partner in my academic pursuits, the custodian of my wellbeing, the healer of pains when my life loses its animation. She is my wife Dr. Snigdha Sen – the invisible bridge between this book and its destiny.

NOTE ON THE TEXT

The term "Calcutta" has been used in this book instead of its modern version "Kolkata" because the study concerns the colonial period of the history of Calcutta when the term 'Kolkata' was not in vogue. The place was originally referred to as "Kalikata" from which the English version of the term "Calcutta" has derived its origin. In all contemporary official documents till recent times, it has been referred to as "Calcutta." "The first mention of Calcutta spelt and written as it is," writes P. Thankappan Nair, "is to be found in the English language and not in Bengali" in a letter dated 1688 written from Burdwan. As a consistency with tradition we prefer using the word "Calcutta" in place of "Kolkata."

[Thankappan Nair, *Calcutta In The 17th Century*, Calcutta: Firma Klm Private Limited, 1986, p. 24].

INTRODUCTION
An overview of the colonial origin of Calcutta

Problems of origin and premising questions

The origin of Calcutta is shrouded in obscurity. It was certainly pre-British and if surmise is allowed in historical research, it may be said that it was also pre-Mughal. For a long time Calcutta had been a throbbing settlement which was essentially a weavers' centre with a vivacious thread-mart unmistakably denoted by the name of its adjacent territory *Sutanuti* (variously written as *Chuttanutty* or *Sutanutty*, *Suta* is from Sanskrit *Sutra* meaning thread; in Bengali thread is *Suta*). The weavers had settlements that spread from Sutanuti to Barahanagar. In India as elsewhere a riverside settlement had always been a populous settlement and Calcutta had never been an exception to this. Riverbanks harbour fisherman-colonies and a part of the early settlers in Kolkata was certainly fishermen. To what extent these men could grow the potentialities of early urbanization is not known. Urbanization is basically a response to challenge and Southern Bengal – which for a long time remained to be unprotected because of being in the margin of governance by any powerful ruler and also because of being always devasted by the incursions of the Arakans, Maghs,[1] and the Portuguese[2] – did not manifest such challenges. Elements of tradition – hearsay, myth, occasional references in administrative manuals and indigenous literature – make up the spirit in which notions about a settlement in Calcutta thrived and continued. Certainly Calcutta was a *Pithasthan* or pilgrim centre – *Kalikshetra* – which was hallowed by the presence of a *Kali* temple situated at a place called Kalighat. This pilgrim centre was then surrounded by jungles and it was inaccessible because of beasts and dacoits. Moreover the emergence of Kalighat to prominence was a colonial phenomenon and prior to the coming of the English it did not flourish as a routine centre of visits by pilgrims.[3] There has been an attempt

INTRODUCTION

to push back the antiquity of Calcutta (*Kalikata*) to the time of the *Puranas*. But, beyond conjecture, no historical authenticity can be ascribed to it. There has been speculation about the origin of the name of *Kalikata*, which was the original version of the modern name Kolkata. But since all these are wild surmises historical consensus cannot be reached on it.

Basing its opinion on the verdict of a group of experts, the Honourable High Court of Calcutta declared that Calcutta had no founder and, therefore, has no specific date of birth. This judgement stripped Job Charnock of his links with Calcutta as its originator: 24 August 1690, the date when Charnock set his feet finally for the third time at Sutanuti, lost its status as the date of the birth of Calcutta. The historians on whose advice the Honourable High Court of Calcutta acted must have been moved by an urge to find the original roots of Kalikata and to remove from the history of Calcutta's antiquity elements of colonial connection. This was one of the major official attempts in independent India to decolonize an important segment of Indian history, namely a nation's memory.

Admitting the necessity to keep oneself free from inhibitions of a colonized mind the present research has distanced itself from conjectural analysis of the antiquity of this great city of India. On the contrary it has addressed itself to the study of a colonial town, Calcutta – the town which was essentially an outcome of the growth of the British Empire in the east. After Magadha[4] in the sixth century BC, Calcutta became the only town in eastern India which could function as the seat of power of a great south Asian empire. One may argue that Mughal Kalikata provided the nucleus for the colonial town. But that would be a very far-fetched concept because, even at the end of the seventeenth century, Calcutta manifested no remarkable sign of an early urban take off. Even Job Charnock himself lived in a thatched house.[5] Urbanization depends upon the use of bricks. Stones were not available within a territory of at least a fifty-mile radius around Calcutta.[6] Therefore the urbanization of the city seldom depended upon stones. The use of bricks became rampant from the middle of the eighteenth century – the time when because of fire and white ants a search for an alternative of timber[7] as the most fundamental construction material was undertaken. Operating on this knowledge that the origin of Calcutta would be illusive to a researcher, the present book has from the beginning set its period of study between the two terminal dates 1698 and 1912 – the first date being the one when the three villages of Sutanuti, Kalikata and Govindapur were purchased by the English

INTRODUCTION

East India Company and the second date being the one when capital was transferred from Calcutta to Delhi.[8]

Given this, the axis of the present book is clear. It shuns conjectural approaches to history and refuses to tread in uncertain areas about which confidence cannot be built without knowledge of scientific records. The authenticity of scientific records is determinable through cross-examinations of other records. Therefore, where scientific records are not available this research has not set its vision.

A colonial town, a colonial period and a nearly two-century history of a colonial rule are the specific settings in which the present book tends to organize itself. It looks into Calcutta not as a town that grew out if its own momentum. It believes that Calcutta was manufactured by the British. It concerns, therefore, with the simple question as to how it was constructed through stimuli given by the Empire. What has marked the growth of Calcutta – an imperial stateliness? Or what has stunted its growth, the rulers' miserliness? This question will be discussed in the book. With the rise of nationalism the question arose in India, was the British Empire justified in all the experiments and expenses it made during the course of its rule in India? The answer was obviously a broad 'No.' Dadabhai Naoroji[9] showed that Indian poverty had proved the British rule to be a sham. Romesh Chandra Dutta[10] showed that the 'drain' of Indian wealth had destroyed the *raisond'etat* of the existence of the Empire itself. If an empire finds itself falsified in all its justifications of rule, it would be naïve to say that the building up a city in Calcutta represented the stateliness of a group of empire-builders who had no intention to stay here as permanent denizens of colonized settlements and who displayed all intentions to christen their historical duties as 'brown men's burdens.'

The focus of the research is thus clear. It looks into the question whether Calcutta suffered a stunted growth because of a lack of adequate political will to build it up into an eastern partner of London. Calcutta was the centre of the British Asiatic trade. But it was never given the status of a trade metropolis. Power, command, directions, and decisions were all controlled from London. The imperial soul had never invested its majesty to Calcutta and as a result Calcutta never did open up its intrinsic sources of growth and sustenance. Once the capital was shifted from Calcutta,[11] its glitters dimmed and what once seemed to be an eastern partner of London became a shrivelled city threatened with collapse under malafide pressures of the Empire.

INTRODUCTION

The central point: tracing the birth and not the origins of Calcutta: the operation of geopolitics

The origin of Calcutta, as has already been said, is shrouded in obscurity because it is pre-British in all sense of the term. It was certainly as old as the Mughal Empire because its reference is available in the *Ain-i-Akbari*[12] the administrative manual of the Mughal Emperor Akbar. Its mention is also found in the indigenous pre-British Bengali literature. Thus the origin-part of the history of Calcutta is in the realm of conjecture and virtually in obscurity. I have tried to unearth materials with regard to Calcutta's origin. But source materials are too scarce to crown my effort with success. My main effort was, therefore, to find out the imperial will and the imperial engineering that had gone into the construction of an imperial city. What I mean by "birth" in my book is the emergence of a Gangetic city – Calcutta – which sprang up in record time – say, within the first half of the eighteenth century – in less than six decades' time since the final arrival of Job Charnock in 1690.[13] In my study I found that this Calcutta was a product of an exigency. In its war with the Mughal Empire (1686–1690), the English East India Company needed a strategic place which would be away from the Mughal capital in Bengal at Murshidabad and the Mughal army headquarters at Dhaka and Hugli. The Company also needed a place which would be on the riverside so that a riverine base with an approach to the sea could be used as serving a double purpose – an English trade settlement and a garrison town of the Company. Given this, I engaged myself to look deep into the process of Calcutta's birth and eventually found that its emergence in the eighteenth century was basically as a garrison town. From this it metamorphosed into a port town and then into the administrative seat of power of a vast empire. Calcutta's birth in this sense was a strategic phenomenon. In this it had no novelty in itself because a fort-city or a garrison town recalls the aspects of medieval city formations that centred around castles[14] – both in Europe and in India. What was new in the case of Calcutta was a combination of three important characteristics of town formation. Calcutta as a garrison town lost its essential glamour to its aspects as a trade centre that performed the functions of a watch-centre as well for keeping a vigilance and maintaining an effective control over the seabourne trade of other European merchants. Also added to this was the newer and other more glittering role of Calcutta as an administrative town.[15] Its growth as the centre of the British Empire superseded its two other roles as a garrison town and a trade centre so much so that other Mughal cities in Bengal looked lustreless vis-à-vis its growing

INTRODUCTION

prominence. The first few chapters of my study will approach the historical process of the amalgamation of these three peculiar characteristics of the city so that what we discover in Calcutta's birth is the emergence of a composite city on the lower banks of the Ganga.

It should be noted that once the Empire started forming itself, Calcutta superseded Madras as the eastern halt of the east-moving Britons. Britons moving to the east was not rare after the end of the Napoleonic Wars.[16] There was blockage at many points in the British economy since the outbreak of the French Revolution, leading to the rise of Napoleon and the imposition of the Continental Blockade. Employment avenues were choked and many Britons, vagrants and respectable, moved to the east.[17] The result was that there was the need to build up an eastern city as a replica of London. The initial planning of the city deeply resembled that of London to give the newcomers from England a sense of confidence in an alien land.

Calcutta was kept insulated from the beginning. The fear that the *Nawabi* spies would infiltrate into the city kept its early administrators awake almost to the point of war-alert.[18] The result was that throughout the first half of the eighteenth century there was incessant conflict between the *Nawabi* administration in Murshidabad and Hughli and the Company's administration in Kolkata.[19] The Bengal *Nawabs* did not allow the English in Calcutta to expand their territorial possessions so that, till the Battle of Palasi, Calcutta's territorial limits remained confined within the three villages of Kalikata, Sutanuti, and Govindapur. In 1757 after the fall of Sirajuddaullah and the accession of Mir Jafar to the *masnads* of Bengal the English got 24 Parganas as their *Zamindari*.[20] This lifted the brake on English possessions in Calcutta and the city got a chance to build up its entity within a sprawling space spreading as far south as Culpee near the Sundarbans and the sea. In the north there was boundless freedom of expansion because, in no time, the *Nawabi* administration collapsed and the frontiers of Calcutta seemed to be dynamically proceeding far in the north towards Barrackpore. But the English were judicious and they kept the territorial area of the city strictly limited within the proximity of the Fort area so much so that the modern Chowringhee area encompassing the vast *maidan* (a sprawling meadow) between the Circular Road and the Esplanade came to form the real city at the time.[21] The real boundaries of the city were drawn in 1794[22] at the far end of the century.

This is in short the geopolitics out of which Calcutta grew. In the entire process of its geopolitical growth there were three major obstacles which the city had to overcome. The first was the *Nawabi* hostility. The vigilance of the Bengal *Nawabs*[23] set an invisible fence around

INTRODUCTION

the English territory in Calcutta. The second obstacle was the Maratha invasion in the 1740s. To ward off this invasion, a ditch was dug to the northern part of the city which was later called the Maratha ditch.[24] The soil that was raised out of this digging went to fill the low land in the east and south and the east, and out of this filling the present circular road was formed. The third obstacle was the competition of the French at Chandernagore.[25] This obstacle was removed at the beginning of the year 1757. Clive, in his journey from Madras towards recovering Calcutta, bombarded both Hugli and Chandernagore. Thus the *Nawabi* base that was working as the watch-post to keep vigilance both on the English activities in Calcutta and the movement of the seabound riverine trade was crushed. Likewise the potentiality of the French to develop Chandernagore as a centre of trade and military power was also destroyed. In 1632 during the time of Sahjahan, the Portuguese were driven out of the places around Hugli.[26] Now both Hughli and Chandernagore were crushed. No power thus remained in south Bengal to challenge the British might and the British domination of the Bay of Bengal. The entire seaboard between Madras and Calcutta now lay open to the control of the English. One can say that, with the battle of Palasi in 1757, the geopolitical issues that shaped Calcutta's emergence into prominence were settled once for all. From 1757 to 1772, when the company decided *to standforth as the Diwan*, was the period for the inner consolidation of the strategic aspects of Calcutta as a garrison town. The new Fort was built in the sixties and the early seventies of the eighteenth century and once that was done the position of Calcutta as a military base for the expansion of the Empire was assured. The Empire could take off now.

The Fort not only ensured an empire. It also guarded a port. Calcutta was the outcome of this: a combination of a fort and a port. Guns backed trade. Trade fetched an empire and empire created a city. This was how Calcutta was born.

The cosmopolitan crowd of the port city

Two things happened in the eighteenth century. Calcutta emerged as a port and the country's power-structure that had governed the entire area between Bengal and Delhi collapsed. Dhaka and Murshidabad sank. The tripartite combination of *Nawab* Mir Qasim of Bengal, Shujauddaullah of Awadh and the Emperor of Delhi, Shah Alam II was defeated at the battle of Buxar in 1764. The result was the Mir Qasim disappeared into obscurity; Shujauddaullah was humbled and the Emperor was pensioned off. The entire Mughal army that

INTRODUCTION

so long guarded the eastern flank of the Mughal Empire collapsed. One generation of administrators and warriors were wiped out.[27] This created a vast administrative vacuum in which new men stepped as collaborators of the English. Hastings admitted them into a new fraternity with the Empire.[28] Later on, Hastings also curbed Chait Singh of Banaras and the rugged Afghans of Rohilkhand. The Marathas who made themselves supreme in north India and brought the weak Mughal Emperor Shah Alam II under their control also retired after the death of Mahadaji Sindhia in 1794. The result was that the entire Jumna-Ganga basin of north India became, so to say, a politically free zone for the necessary emergence of this strategic area as the most productive and supportive economic hinterland for Calcutta port. The port had emerged into its status as a substitute of Hugli already in the first half of the eighteenth century. Its flourish came when in the second half of the eighteenth century the entire hinterland of the port became its supportive rear area. After the fall of the *Peshwa* in 1818,[29] there remained no opposition to the English either in west or in north India. The result was that a complete political vacuum was created in the heartland of India. It was here that the political thrust for empire-building was initiated by the English. The growth of the Calcutta port took place as ancillary to this formidable process of empire-building in India. The Calcutta port absorbed two things – the market-bound surplus commodities of the hinterland and the potentially surplus employment-searching man-power of the countries along the course of the river. Calcutta thus grew as an amalgam of two powerful trends of city-formations. On the one hand there was the urge of an island people to build up their possessions in Calcutta as an eastern halt for the out-moving Britons who would find here a unique resemblance with London. On the other hand there was the native mass who tended to exchange their old-world misery for a new-world solvency available in Calcutta. The town morphology at the initial stage was patterned after London with the Esplanade and the Chowringhee *maidan* serving to be the sprawling middle around which palaces, mansions, and edifices of the White Town could be built. The core of the White Town was kept insulated from the beginning to preserve its interior privacy from the interference of the *Nawabs*. This meant that Calcutta was to be an exclusive settlement where the aristocracy of the empire-builders could be preserved. The second trend was completely different from this exclusiveness of the early Britons in Calcutta. It was its growth towards cosmopolitanism. Calcutta was after all the town that served to be the base of a mercantile community – the people of the English East India Company.

INTRODUCTION

Traders needed commodities and production centres. Textile products being the major article of Company's trade in Bengal, in no time it opened its doors to the weavers from the native production centres of the country.[30] In the broad aftermath of the Palasi Calcutta witnessed a massive spate of civil construction mainly around the heart of the White Town. This needed labour and bands of workers drawn mostly from the peasants of the interior were allowed to flood in. in addition to this the port needed workers to cushion its ever-increasing functions as the most effective commodity-outlet of the hinterland. Sturdy men from the central and northern India flocked in Calcutta. Moreover the Europeans needed the services of the native menials and the compulsions of their lifestyles forced them to open the city to the lowly people from places around.[31] Moreover almost every Englishman had a comrade-in-arm – a *banian*[32] – a skilled and efficient Bengali who supplied him cash at times of need and acted as his secretary and liaison man in all his private and public business. In all sense he was the Englishman's secretary who functioned as the keeper of his master's secrets. Such men – *banians* – had their own agents and attendants who arrived in the city and added to the slowly swelling crowd of the town. Men from various other callings also landed at the city. Those who found their treasures unsafe in the countryside transferred them to the city and shifted with their families to the native quarters of the town. The kidnapping of young girls in the countryside was very rampant during the rule of the *Nawabs*. To escape from such hazards, solvent Hindu families migrated to the city. Out of this, the town assumed its cosmopolitan character.

What is significant is that the Company's government in Calcutta had no money to build the infrastructure necessary for the upkeep of a swarming population. As a result, in the vicinity of stately structures, there invariably grew a belt of lowly dwellings of the native work force which often took the shape of slums. Land was needed to provide living space to the people. Trees were felled and forests disappeared in the process. An urban settlement needed bricks and bricks were made by burning clay. Therefore, for the making of bricks fuel was required and trees were cut to supply the need of timbers. This affected the ecological balance of the country. Fields were dug to procure mud for brick kilns. This created gutters and holes which caused great inconvenience to the people.[33]

Calcutta thus from the beginning balanced two antithetical humanity – rich Englishmen and affluent Indians around them and a miserable mankind consisting of somewhat destitute Indians who lived from hand to mouth. The middle tier between the two – a prosperous

INTRODUCTION

middle class – was long conspicuous by its absence in Calcutta. Its emergence took place from the end of the first quarter of the nineteenth century.[34]

During the first hundred years of Calcutta's emergence as a colonial town in the eighteenth century it acutely suffered the pangs of a capital-short economy.[35] Whatever revenue could be raised from Calcutta was spent for maintaining the Company's establishment in the city. A trading community on becoming rulers had the propensity to convert territorial revenue into sinews of commerce. This meant that little money was left for Calcutta's growth in the eighteenth century. For the promotion of the city infrastructure fund was raised through lottery in the last decade of the eighteenth and in the first three decades of the nineteenth century. All important city roads were built with the fund thus raised mainly from residents' contributions.

As a matter of fact from the middle of the eighteenth century to the middle of the nineteenth money flowed from the interior to Calcutta. This was because every *zamindar* in the countryside wanted to possess their own estates in Calcutta. Banking houses and business communities transferred their allegiance to Calcutta so that in the immediate aftermath of the Palasi Reza Khan lamented that business in Murshidabad was like a drop of water while in Calcutta it was like a river. Our evidences show that all the big *zamindars* in the districts transferred their capital to Calcutta from the middle of the eighteenth century. The Indians who hovered around the various European companies in Calcutta and places around and acted as the liaison men of the East India Companies of the English, the French and the Dutch amassed money. Jadunath Sarkar says that a capitalist class formed by the Indians grew in Calcutta so that a wealth of native capital found its shelter in the city.[36] One reason behind this was that Calcutta as a cosmopolitan settlement gained the confidence of the Indians. In the 1740s when the Maratha invasions took place the scared population of the neighbouring areas rushed to Calcutta for shelter and protection.[37] The British gun assured them a security which the *Nawabi* administration was unable to provide. Moreover the people had enough experience of the chaos of the decaying Mughal rule and they preferred the settled order prevailing within the English territory to the chaos outside. The flight of Krishnaballav (alias Krishnadas), son of Raja Rajballav, *diwan* or the finance minister of Dakha to Calcutta with a huge wealth,[38] only showed that the leaders of the Bengal *Subah* had developed a direction towards Calcutta. After the battle of Palasi, the Company's administration extracted £10,731,683 from a shaky *Nawab* Mir Jafar. Much of this wealth went into personal appropriation and a bulk of

9

it was used to fill the deficit of money required for the official trade of the Company. A part of the wealth lost in personal appropriation was spent in purchasing lands and constructing garden houses in and around the city. The spirit for promoting Calcutta thus gained ground. A new rallying point was now opened to the people.

For an escape from the functioning chaos which the *Nawabi* administration at Murshidabad then was, people turned to Calcutta where order had settled as a powerful attribute of the Government. For long the people of Bengal had not experienced the kind of a rule of law that the English had been able to establish here in Calcutta. Thus what Calcutta presented to the people at least in the eighteenth century was a picture of administrative confidence vis-à-vis the Mughal decadences around. One thing that the British might had assured to the people was a safe life within all available parameters of a secured existence. It will be wrong to think that Calcutta throughout the course of the eighteenth century or at least in the second half of it was free of dangers and afflictions. It was not, for it was going through a transitional phase of its life in the eighteenth century. The Mughal rule was slowly heading towards its end yielding place to the British. Between the Battle of Palasi and the appointment of Hastings as the first Governor General of the British Empire in India in 1773 Bengal was steadily being converted into a protectorate.[39] Although there were *Nawabs* on the *Masnads* of Bengal power virtually shifted to a new centre – Calcutta. Governors of Calcutta up to 1772 became masters in an emerging pattern of power that was alien in its character and sudden in its thrust. Truly speaking the thrust became crushing in its impact since the time Clive re-conquered Calcutta at the beginning of 1757.[40] Calcutta was recovered by the application of force and a resisting *Nawab* suffered a disastrous defeat at the hands of the English. The *Nawab* was entirely at the mercy of the English and was forced to sign the Treaty of Alinagar (Calcutta) on 9 February 1757. He had to surrender many marks of his sovereignty under pressure from the English. But what was more fundamental than a written agreement was the fact that a body of the *Nawab*'s subjects – some alien traders – functioning not above the status of local *taluqdars* demonstrated their superiority in arms. So long Calcutta was held by the English as a purchased territory subject to the control of the *Nawab*. Now in 1757 they held it as a conquered territory. It was good of the English that the right of conquest was not proclaimed in 1757. Nor was it formally applied in 1764 when, at the battle of Buxar, the Emperor of Delhi was defeated and had to bend his knees before the English. In any case, the status of Calcutta in 1757 had undergone a revolution. From a purchased property it turned into

INTRODUCTION

a conquered one. With this, the status of Calcutta as a colonial town was formally over. The phase when Calcutta was manufactured as an imperial town had now begun.

Calcutta assumes a new career

During the first century of British occupation, Calcutta had a checkered story of a rise into prominence. In 1698 it was one among the three purchased villages in south Bengal along the bank of the river. In 1726 the Mayor's Court was set up[41] in Calcutta. This for the first time gave the city a kind of judicial and jurisdictional enclave to the city. Theoretically the Indians were not subject to the jurisdiction of the court, but, in all practical sense, the court became a centre around which the judicial pretensions of the city grew and eventually it vied with the *de jure* authority of the *Nawab* as the ultimate dispenser of justice. This judicial pretension was reinforced by territorial acquisition in 1757 when because of Clive's victory over the *Nawab* it became a conquered city under the control of the English. A series of changes then set in. The new Fort was raised and power was consolidated. The *diwani* was received in 1765, making possible the union of revenue with trade, and territory with power. The combination of revenue and army cushioned this transformation and Calcutta became second to none in the British Empire in the world. A few years later in 1773 it became the seat of an imperial administration with the foundation of two important institutions that eventually determined the character of city – the office of the Governor General and the Supreme Court. The *Sadar Nizamat* and the *Sadar Diwani Adalats*[42] were also transferred from Murshidabad to Calcutta. Calcutta became the core of a new paradigm – empire-building. The office of the Governor General dwarfed the station of the *Nazim* or *Nawab* at Murshidabad – the Mughal viceroy in the east – and eventually laid the basis for putting forward the pretension that the governor general was equal to the Mughal Emperor if not in rank, at least in *de facto* position of power, so that he would not be under any obligation to act as a subordinate vassal of the Emperor.[43] This had relentlessly hurt the status of the Mughal Emperor. As in all times the Emperor's stipend was regulated from Calcutta and Delhi remained under the will of the new rising city of the east.

As these happened some other imperceptible changes took place ensuring Calcutta's rise to prominence and power. Four important Mughal cities – Patna, Hughli, Murshidabad and Dhaka – passed into eclipse.[44] The gravity of the English power shifted from Madras to

INTRODUCTION

Calcutta for the time being only to be retrieved later. The port character of the city[45] and the garrison character of the town now merged together in the status of a capital city that became the nucleus of an emerging empire in the east. This was a revolutionary phenomenon. No Indian Empire which could properly be called all Indian in character and extent had emerged from the east in the past save the Magadhan Empire[46] in the sixth century BC. After a long 2,500 years, the English were the first who, basing their power in Calcutta in the east, had introduced themselves as real contenders of an all-Indian empire in direct confrontation with the Marathas in the west, the Rohillas and the Sikhs in the north, and Mysore in the south. The foundation of Calcutta had, therefore, an intrinsic historical importance in it. The English power was entrenched in the city just as the Muslim power was centrally entrenched in Delhi and locally first in Gour and then Dhaka and in Murshidabad. Calcutta became with the English one major centre in the map of conflicting power-distribution in India. Who would inherit the Mughal state? That was the greatest political question that had haunted all pretenders to power in India in the eighteenth century. Calcutta's potentiality provided the English to be a pretender in this. The momentum to act for pretension was also a gift of the city – in the best of as also in the worst of its times.

Politically Calcutta in the eighteenth century emerged as this: a base from which the English could commission their pretension into a large all India effort to inherit the Mughal state.[47] This political character of the city also matched the character of its planning as an urban centre. The English wanted to model the town as a replica of London so that it could serve as a halt to the east-moving Britons in the eighteenth century. In effect Calcutta did not shed off the characteristics of a congested Mughal town either of contemporary age or of any earlier time. The morphology of Calcutta certainly assumed the apparent getup of an English town but at heart it remained steeped in the pattern of a tradition-bound Mughal urban settlement. It was in this queer combination of an Anglo-Mughal urbanity that Calcutta throughout the course of colonial history found itself being shaped. Within the structure of a paradox a new phenomenon arose. The indigenous people, the native Hindu Bengali race, promoted their own renaissance in the city. Calcutta thus became a centre of a new cultural upsurge. The people indigenous to the soil built up their own pattern of culture which was essentially Indian in spirit revitalized only by the touch of the west. From the core of this new culture a new Calcutta emerged. It was this Calcutta – the Calcutta of Indians – which was made a base of nationalism. This nationalism was logically the outcome of the Bengal

INTRODUCTION

renaissance inspired by European nationalism in the nineteenth century. Socially and politically it was the outcome of a civil society that took shape under the inspiration of the university age that came into being in the middle of the nineteenth century.

Spiritually shaped by its own renaissance, Calcutta at the end was only this: a city with a soul unmatched with the spirit of the British Empire. How this un-matching city was born is part of the substance of this book. Everywhere in the book we have stuck to the expression "Calcutta" instead of its modern name "Kolkata." This is because we have discussed the city neither in its pre-colonial nor in its post-colonial perspectives. Our thrust has always been on the growth of a city patterned by the Empire. The Empire had imposed its will on the city. The city balanced its own will antithetically to that of the Empire. This dialectic of the growth of the city has not been traced in its proper perspectives till now. We do it only to show that a city manufactured by the Empire had its own tryst with destiny. The Empire gave it its own momentum. Its mood was its own. This mood was the only lasting phenomenon in the city, all other parameters being transitory. Her promises of an urban growth were not fulfilled in the long run.

The regime of governance

In the eighteenth century the main motive behind town planning in Calcutta was security. The creation of the new Fort in the 1760s (which ended in 1773) underlined the compulsive direction towards which Calcutta could grow. In the course of three decades from the fall of Mir Qasim, the Bengal *Nawab*, in 1764, to the defeat of Tipu Sultan in 1799 in the south, the English in Calcutta had dwarfed the neighbouring powers, contained the Emperor, outdistanced their trade competitors, and triumphed over their local sources of fear. Being entrenched in territory and with command over revenue of three eastern provinces in India they now ceased to be mere merchants. Mastering the regional finance of the declining Mughal Empire they now lorded over a wide territory as an absolute satrap whose main concern was now governance necessary for both trade and consolidation. The nineteenth century thus dawned in Calcutta with a new regime charged with governance. Three associate things surfaced as parts of governance: finance as economics of governance, infrastructure as policies of governance, and health ensuring life as missions of governance. All these were outcomes of a dire necessity. But they made in substance what may be called in short the municipal governance of the city. The Charter Act of 1793 gave the municipal governance its

INTRODUCTION

statutory basis for the city for the first time and with it the first modern municipal administration dawned in colonial India. After a trial for a few years, people's representation seemed to be necessary. In 1838 Raja Radhakanta Deb and Dwarakanath Tagore were appointed Justices of Peace. The native assistance in municipal governance was thus formalized. Promotion of infrastructure and incorporation of native assistance thus came hand in hand, showing the new orientation of the city. The Lottery Committee came into existence in 1817 twenty-four years after the city was first initiated into lottery. Its tenure was over in 1836. With it the period of intense activity for urban uplift was over. Roads were constructed, ditches were filled, city squares were formed, parks were created and ponds and water bodies were managed. In a word, Calcutta was dressed for a new take-off. Incorporation of native assistance came at this stage. It was invoked with the turn of new situation – that is after the initial phase of city's urbanization was over. A new era was being promulgated now with the appointment of the committee for fever and hospital – called in short the Fever Hospital Committee – as a successor to the Lottery Committee. This was indeed a transitional moment in the history of the city. From urban constructions emphasis now shifted to urban health. Hospitals now dominated city plans – names floated in official literature such as Native Hospital, Fever Hospital, Police Hospital, General Hospital, and finally Medical College. Existing and proposed institutions of health thus crowded planning manuals of the time. Some of these hospitals were as going on concerns taking positions along with asylums meant for the lunatics and lepers. The medical topography of the city was being worked with new zeal. Crossing over the phases of security and infrastructure, the city now entered a new phase where the primary concern of the government was health. The lottery phase of urban growth in Calcutta was ushered in within the semi-urban space of Calcutta and the first signs of globalization of European architecture and urbanism. The thirties of the nineteenth century – the Fever Hospital Committee phase – similarly saw the implementation of the globalized versions of medical ethics and other functional aspects of science of healing that had come into vogue in the west. With new reforms in the offing, more cooperation from the natives seemed to be a necessity, and wealthy and influential men in the society were invited to take seats in various committees that were formed to promote the sanitary configuration and health of the city. Drawing the Indians in western reforms was not an easy task and the thirties of the nineteenth century saw a tussle between the British effort at persuasion and the Indian stamina to hold back.

INTRODUCTION

The Fever Hospital Committee seemed to be concerned with the real uplift of life in the city, but no plan in this seemed to be beyond meeting eventualities which could be called an outcome of sustainable state-planning. Miasma, filth, drain, cleanliness, habitation, removal of thatched huts, and even the fire-proneness of the city were constant parts of deliberations or even reports of the Lottery Committee and the Fever Hospital Committee, but state-level determination to impose decisions to change was absent. The public will with which Wellesley had steered the city into a career of urban modernism seemed to be lacking in all subsequent efforts once the Lottery Committee had ceased to exist. One reason for this was that the state had never achieved the economic solvency under the influence of which condition it could plan for long-term economic investment in the city as the state in England had done. The result was that all plans in city development for three decades after the winding of the Lottery Committee were patch works being parts of a ramshackle philosophy of public welfare. The continuous embellishment of the white city certainly led Calcutta to glitter as an imperial seat of power but, as Pradip Sinha says, it also led to "further accentuation of the physical differences of the European and Indian parts" of the city.[48] It should be noted that the most intensive effort to town planning was made during the period of the Lottery Committee and the Committee's "work of Calcutta," in Pradip Sinha's words, was "the most systematic work in the 19th century."[49] In any case one may note that, from the time of Wellesley's Minute in 1803 to the winding up of the Lottery Committee in 1836, the will of the state to introduce reforms in urban morphology was most effective. The fall of Tipu Sultan in 1799 brought about a new flush of pride for British victory and under Wellesley the pride was twisted into a new diplomatic pattern of control under the name "Subsidiary Alliance." The spirit of the state was now absorbed in the glitters of a new vision of an empire. Old Calcutta was not in keeping with this spirit of the state. Calcutta had to be changed and the change was ushered in the three decades following the drafting of Wellesley's Minute. The pride which the rule of Warren Hastings had caused to instil in British dominations in India created in the aftermath a situation in which the change in the city's status could be suggested. This was done by the drawing of the boundary of Calcutta and the first raising of finance for the urbanization of the city in 1793. From 1818 a period of peace for thirty years graced the British rule in India. It was in this phase that the first major attempts were made to urbanize the city and propel it to the direction where it could assume its new role as the seat of power.

INTRODUCTION

The result was that "admirable professional considerations" were brought into force for all planning programmes of the time.[50] Two things happened as a result of the activities of the Lottery Committee. Prices of lands escalated[51] and the European influx into the city increased. Lottery Committee observations were categorical to this end.[52] While the White Town was gradually being filled by new waves of white immigrants, the Black Town was steadily passing under the control of rich Indians. One thing the Lottery Committee did was to create a long north-south axis along the present linear thoroughfares of Wellington Square – College Street – Cornwallis Street – Shyambazar (largely made up of ancient Shovabazar).[53] In the wide mass of territory between the riverfront and this central axis of the city, large properties were purchased by opulent Indians so that as time went on it became difficult for the government to acquire land for the creation of new roads and for the expansion of lanes and by-lanes that had given the city a look of a congested countryside transplanted into a new urban set-up. In any case the Lottery Committee did a yeoman's service to the city which no previous government could do. A concept of improvement it had instilled into the minds of the Indians. This is where the British Empire fulfilled its role as a modernizer and distinguished itself from any of the earlier empires of the past. The awareness of improvement occasionally reflected in contemporary journals. A passage in *Jnanannesan* as late as 1837 tried to draw public attention to the changes around.[54] It said that diseases had been beaten and three reasons were at the root of it. The town had been improved by the Lottery Committee. An immense progress had been made in Medical science and a change had been contemplated in people's food habit. It was clear that by the end of 1830s a large part of jungles in and around Calcutta had been cleared and the British Empire set into motion aspects of sanitized living which were absent in medieval Indian town planning. As noted earlier, four parameters were thus visible in making sanitized living a possibility. Firstly, the town was made free of jungles and was properly dressed up. Its roads and drains were created, water bodies were taken care of, parks for relaxation outside cramped households were in the process of being built, and thatched mud huts were replaced by tiled roofs, wooden structures, and finally by brick constructions. A dressed town made urban living an enjoyable experience. Secondly, medical science was improved and hospitals were created. Health care became a part of urban living. Efforts to beat miasma were undertaken during the auspices of the Hospital Committee. Thirdly, the food habit and the diet system of the people were influenced, and, finally, an effective policing of the

INTRODUCTION

whole order was imposed from the top, much to the relief of some and disgust of many who preferred living in a traditional world. The Indian world around Calcutta had been in a state of change in the first thirties of the nineteenth century. This was the singular achievement of the Lottery Committee.

It is not very clear as to why the Lottery Committee was snapped. Certainly the money market was getting stringent and may be that people's contribution through lottery in making the city worthy of living was showing signs of decline.

Agency Houses began to collapse and there was a run on the money market. The Company's government was drawn increasingly into conflict with its own subjects who were now raising protests either for increase in taxations or for more compensation for lands acquired in the name of improvement of the town. The Lottery Committee had truly exhausted its functions. All the preliminaries of town planning had been served and there was no concern for public health. One may say that the first phase of planned uplift of Calcutta was over with the Lottery Committee. The second phase, according to A.K. Ray, began "with the establishment of the Corporation of the Justices in 1871, under Act VI of that year."[55] Between 1836, when the tenure of the Lottery Committee was over, and 1871, when the second phase of town uplift began, a period of thirty-five years intervened during which emphasis had shifted from town planning to more strategic things for the Empire. By the beginning of the 1840s the role of native capital in promoting trade, industry, and banking had come to an end. The fall of the Union Bank in 1848 had ruined the fiscal aristocracy of the city. Within one decade British capital started flowing into Bengal. The age of the steamship was ushered in. Coalfields had been discovered in Bengal. The age of the railways, telegraphs, and universities was in the horizon. With all these imperial economics were changing and with that also changed the metropolitan mind of the people. Calcutta was left to progress with the century – not very much in tune with the forces of the age – in its own way.

Notes

1 Throughout the course of the first half of the eighteenth century the south-eastern part of Bengal was under the threat of Magh incursions. It was a legacy from the seventeenth century. Three sets of people led deep incursions into Bengal in the seventeenth century and carried men and women as slaves to be sold to the Europeans either at the coasts of Madras or Orissa or in the neighbourhood of Calcutta. Occasionally slaves were clandestinely sold in Calcutta also. These marauders and lifters of men

INTRODUCTION

and women were the Arakans (the half civilized tribes of the Chittagong hills and the Burmese of the fringe territories of Burma called Arakan which was then under the rule of a Burmese king), Maghs (the sea-faring rugged people from Chatgaon or Chittagong) and Firingis (the Portuguese). Jadunath Sarkar writes:

> "The deep channel parting from a bend of the Ganges some distance east of Tamluk and running eastwards to Dacca and Chatgaon was called by the English merchants in that age as the Rogue's River, because 'the Arakanese used to come out thence to rob and sailed up the river Ganges.'"- Jadunath Sarkar, *History of Bengal*, Vol. II, Dakha University Publication, 1948, second impression 1972, Dakha, p. 378. The statement quoted by Sarkar above was from Streynsham Master's Diary, i. 321, map in i.507.

> "The Arakan pirates, both Magh and Feringi used constantly to plunder Bengal. They carried off the Hindus and Muslims they could seize, pierced the palms of their hands, passed thin strips of cane through the holes, and threw the men huddled together under the decks of their ships. Every morning they flung down some uncooked rice to the captives from above, as people fling grain to fowl – They sold their captives to the Dutch, English and French merchants at the ports of Deccan. Sometimes they brought their captives to Tamluk and Balasore for sale at high prices. . . . Only the Feringis sold their prisoners, but the Maghs employed all whom they could carry off in agriculture and other occupations or as domestic servants and concubines." – cited by Sarkar, *History of Bengal*, pp. 378–379. Sarkar adds: "It was Shaista Khan's task to put an end to this terror." – *History of Bengal*, p. 379. For further details see A.K. Ray, *A Short History of Calcutta Town and Suburbs Census of India, 1901*, Vol. VII, Part I, 1902, RDDHI-India edn, Calcutta, 1982, p. 259.

2 The Portuguese were known in contemporary literature as the 'feringis' and the 'harmads'. How the Arakanese, the Portuguese and the Maghs were extirpated from Chittagong, the base of their activities and mobilization, has been beautifully described by Sarkar, *History of Bengal*, pp. 377–381.
3 For details, see Ranjit Sen, *A Stagnating City Calcutta in the Eighteenth Century*, Institute of Historical Studies, Calcutta, 2000, Ch. VI, entitled "A Pilgrim Centre: Kalighat"
4 Magadha in the sixth century BC embraced territories around modern Patna and Gaya. It "could boast of powerful chieftains even in the days of the Vedic Rishis and the epic poets" – writes the historian H.C. Raychaudhury in R.C. Majumdar, H.C. Roychaudhuri and K.K. Datta, eds. *An Advanced History of India*, Palgrave Macmillan, London, p. 55. The pre-Aryan people that lived here were called the Kikatas 'who were noted for their wealth of kine.' In the sixth and fifth century BC, the throne of Magadha was occupied by the rulers of Saisunaga dynasty. According to the Buddhist writers this dynasty was split into two; the earlier one was called by them as Haryanksa. The most important ruler of the Haryanka line was Bimbisara.

INTRODUCTION

5 Straw houses persisted in the city even in the second half of the nineteenth century. It was because of this straw huts Calcutta became a fire-prone area. See Ray, *A Short History of Calcutta Town and Suburbs Census of India, 1901*, p. 161. Even in the white town, straw huts could be seen hinding behind mansions and palatial buildings. In general such mud and thatched houses came under control from 1837. The Act XII of that year enjoined people to provide an outer roof with incombustible material.
6 Stones in Calcutta were normally brought from Rajmahal.
7 Timber necessary for hardy constructions were brought from the foothills of the Himalayas. It came by the Ganges via Munghyr. See Rev. J. Long, *Selections from the Unpublished Records of Government from 1748–1767 Inclusive*, Calcutta, 1869, Second edn. Edited by Mahadevaprasad Saha, Firma K.L. Mukhopadhyay, Calcutta 1973, No. 808, p. 544.
8 Calcutta remained the capital of British India from 1773 to 1911. From the first day of 1912, capital was transferred to Delhi.
9 Dadabhai Naoroji was a Parsi businessman and one of the founders of the Indian National Congress. He was elected to the House of Commons to speak for Indian interests in the 1890s. His famous book was *Poverty and Un-British Rule*, London, 1901.
10 Romesh Chandra Dutt was a Bengali litterateur of the highest calibre. He was an ICS officer who resigned his job "to pursue," writes B.R. Tomlinson, "his attacks on the revenue administration of Bengal, focused on the distortions to the Indian economy brought about by British rule, and by the impoverishment of the mass of the population through the colonial 'drain of wealth' from India to Britain over the course of the nineteenth century." – B.R. Tomlinson, *The Cambridge History of India III.3: The Economy of Modern India 1860–1970*, Cambridge University Press, Cambridge, First South Asian Paperback Edition, 1998, p. 12. R.C. Dutt's famous book in which his 'drain' theory was unleashed is *The Economic History of India in the Victorian Age*, London, 1906. His Economic History consists of two volumes. Dutt's argument was that we produce surplus and that it went to benefit England. We raised clouds, he said, but it rained elsewhere.
11 The shifting of capital, it is generally believed, was because of the rise of nationalism in Bengal. Calcutta was the hub of nationalist culture and was giving leadership to both the moderate and the rising radical wings of the Indian National Congress. It should be noted that after the government's failure to keep up the partition of Bengal in the face of massive agitation by the people of the land the whole show of government had become a sham. Calcutta had emerged as a different city much away from what the British wanted it to be. Calcutta did not participate in the revolt of 1857 but in the immediate aftermath of the revolt it became the centre of a new radical culture which did not seem compatible with the nature and philosophy of the British rule. The coming of the revolutionary terror from 1906 onwards and the use of bomb as an instrument for the radical uplift of revolution created a new atmosphere in which Calcutta lost its *raison d'état* to remain as the capital of the British Empire.
12 In a recent writing, the pre-British source of reference to Calcutta has been recorded as follows: "The three villages of Sutanuti, Kalikata and Gobindapur figure in the maps of Vanderbrooke (1600), Valentine (1656),

INTRODUCTION

Thomas Bowrey (1687) and George Herron (1690). The name Kalikata found mention in Manasamangal of Bipradas (1595) and in the rent-roll's of Akbar, the Mughal emperor. The colonial city, which certainly was the product of the English settlers, grew out of its own environs." – Subhas Ranjan Chakraborty, "Kolkata" in Ranjan Chakrabarti, ed., *Dictionary of Historical Places Bengal, 1757–1947*, Primus Books, New Delhi, 2013, p. 365.

13 See Ray, *A Short History of Calcutta Town and Suburbs Census of India, 1901*, pp. 32–37.
14 The urbanization which Europe experienced in the tenth and eleventh centuries was in many ways influenced by the need for security. Lewis Mumford observes: "Five centuries of violence, paralysis, and uncertainty had created in the European heart a profound desire for security when every chance might prove a mischance, when every moment might be one's last moment, the need for protection rose above every other concern, and to find a safe haven was about the most one asked from life." – *The Culture of Cities*, p. 14. Because of this need for security, in most cases, the cities in the west were castle-centric.
15 Calcutta's real role as an administrative town began in 1773 when Warren Hastings became the Governor General and Calcutta became the major seat of administration for the three British Presidencies in India.
16 On 9 March 1792, the Girondists, who were the war party in France during the time of the French Revolution, formed a ministry, and, on 20 April, France declared war against Austria. This triggered a war in Europe. In July, Prussia joined Austria by declaring war against France. Britain joined later. This war situation did not stop altogether all through the revolution and continued even when Napoleon became the Emperor of France. In May 1804 he "adopted the rank of Emperor of the French" and thereafter used the title "Napoleon." In May 1803 Britain declared war on France and European wars continued intermittently till Napoleon's defeat at the battle of Waterloo on 18 June 1815.
17 Amales Tripathi in his Trade and Finance in the Bengal Presidency wrote that the highest influx of the east-moving Britons in Bengal took place in the year 1822–1823.
18 "In 1733 some persons who were 'lurking about the town' of Calcutta were suspected to be spies and robbers. The zamindar was ordered to 'turn them out of the town and if they returned again they were to be whipped out'. In 1734 the in[n]keepers of Calcutta were asked not to entertain any strangers in their taverns without giving timely notice to the Company. The innkeepers failing to comply with this order would themselves be 'sent directly to Europe'." – Sukumar Bhattacharya, *The East India Company and the Economy of Bengal from 1704–1740*, Firma K.L. Mukhopadhyay, Calcutta, 1969, p. 172. Such vigilance was very frequent in Calcutta in the first half of the eighteenth century.
19 For detail see Bhattacharya, *The East India Company and the Economy of Bengal from 1704–1740*, Ch. II.
20 For details of this aspect of the English position in Calcutta, see chs. I and II under the titles "Conquest and Sovereignty" and "The Company becomes 'zamindar'" in W.K. Firminger, *Historical Introduction to the Bengal Portion of the Fifth Report* (1917), Reprint, Indian Studies Past and Present, Calcutta, 1962.

INTRODUCTION

21 See chs. viii and ix under the titles "Town and Suburbs" and "Population and Revenue" in Ray, *A Short History of Calcutta Town and Suburbs*.
22 "By the Proclamation of 1794, the boundary of the town was fixed to be the inner side of the Mahratta Ditch." Ray, *A Short History of Calcutta Town and Suburbs Census of India, 1901*, p. 110, also see Appendix I, pp. 116–119.
23 The vigilance of the Bengal Nawabs was maintained till the time of Siraj Uddaullah. This vigilance broke down when there was sabotage from within. For the attitudes of the Bengal Nawabs toward the English and other foreign Companies see (i) Bhattacharya, *The East India Company and the Economy of Bengal from 1704–1740*, Ch. II; (ii) K.K. Datta, *Alivardi and His Times*, The World Press private Ltd., Calcutta, 1963, Ch. V; (iii) Brijen K. Gupta, *Sirajuddaullah and the East India Company, 1756–1757: Background to the Foundation of the British Empire in India*, Photomechanical Reprint, E.J. Brill, Leiden, 1966, Ch. III.
24 "Between 1742 and 1753 the development of the town constituted chiefly in the rapid increase of native Indian houses, both cutcha and pucka – mostly cutcha, in the outlying parts of the European town within the Mahratta Ditch." –Ray, *A Short History of Calcutta Town and Suburbs Census of India, 1901*, p. 99. The Maratha ditch was thus the boundary of the town of Calcutta.
25 Chandernagore (Chandannagore) is situated 30 kilometres north of Calcutta. See Chakrabarti, *Dictionary of Historical Places Bengal, 1757–1947*, pp. 133–135.
26 Once the Portuguese were driven out of Hughli the entire seaboard of the Bay remained exposed to the English navy operating from Madras. Their command over the seaboard helped the English to maintain their sway in Calcutta. The removal of the Portuguese also helped the country in another way. The slave trade was reduced. Kidnapping of human beings, particularly of women, by the Portuguese, Mags, and Arakans had become a menace in the country. Once the fear of being kidnapped was removed, a brake was lifted from the economy of the country. For about 100 years, the economy of Bengal enjoyed stability so far as its man-power potential was concerned. In the 1740s when the Maratha invasions began to take place the country's economy once again suffered a jolt. There was a mass exodus from the western part of Bengal to its eastern part. The population of Calcutta increased because it was a safe sanctuary for suffering mankind.
27 For further details, see Ranjit Sen, *New Elite and New Collaboration: A Study of Social Transformation in Bengal in the Eighteenth Century*, Papyrus, Calcutta, 1985, Ch. I, pp. 18–19 and Abdul Majed Khan, *The Transition in Bengal 1756–1775: A Study of Sayid Muhammad Reza Khan*, Cambridge University Press, 1966, pp. 104–105. About the vacuum on the English side because of the death of English officers after the wars with Mir Qasim, Majed Khan writes: "So many losses left too few men even to run the commercial offices properly, especially as those remaining were often junior and inexperienced, heavily dependent on their banians" (p. 105).
28 "In his dual government Clive envisaged a model of broad Anglo-Mughal partnership under a shrinking canopy of Timurid sovereignty. With this sovereignty waning in a situation that saddled the English in supremacy,

INTRODUCTION

such partnership lost its raison d'etre. Hastings understood this and he invited the Indians in subsidiary collaboration with the English, thus, superseding the pattern of Indo-British alignment highlighted by Clive. Clive, the author of all British successes in the south was co-opted into partnership by the power elite of Bengal. After 1765 that elite had dwindled into insignificance. Now it was for the English to co-opt partners. Towards that end, Hastings estimated the worth of friendship with lower men and lesser beings with whom he had many years of intercourse." – Sen, *New Elite and New Collaboration*, p. 17.

29 The last Peshwa Baji Rao II surrendered to Sir John Malcolm on 3 June 1818. He was defeated in two battles – at Koregaon on 1 January 1818 and at Ashti on 20 February 1818. After his defeat, writes K.K. Datta, "The Peshwaship, which served as the symbol of national unity among the Marathas even in the worst days, was abolished; Baji Rao Ii was allowed to spend his last days at Bithur near Cawnpore on a pension of eight lacs a year; his dominions were placed under British control; and 'British influence and authority spread over the land with magical celerity.'" Majumdar, Roychaudhuri and Datta, *An Advanced History of India*, p. 702. Percival Spear wirtes: "It is incorrect to say that the Maratha confederacy was crushed (in 1818), because it had been in dissolution since 1802 and largely by its own act. What really happened in 1818 was the substitution of British authority in central India for no authority at all, and the expansion of paramountcy over the ancient Rajput states." Percival Spear, ed. *The Oxford History of India by the Late Vincent A. Smith*, At The Clarendon Press, Oxford, 1958, reprinted 1961, p. 572.

30 A letter from the Court of Directors, Dated 31 January 1755, paragraph 54 says:

> It has appeared to us as very extraordinary that so exceeding populous a place as Calcutta is, and no doubt inhabited by great numbers of weavers, should be of so little immediate benefit to us; the merchants have employed those useful people, and have hither too run away with the advantage which we might with equal ease have obtained. But thanks to the conduct of those merchants which have drove you to expedients which might other ways have been thought of; you now find manysorts of goods are fabricated within our bounds, cheap and of good qualities, and may be had at the first hand as it is evidently for our interest therefore to encourage not only all the weavers now in our bounds, but likewise to draw as many others as possible from all countries to reside under our protection, we shall depend on your utmost efforts to accomplish the same; and shall hope the time is not far off wherein we shall find a great share of your investment made under your own eyes. – Mahadevprasad Saha, ed., The Revd. J. Long, *Selections from the Unpublished Records of Government from 1748–1767 Inclusive*, No. 170, p. 79 under the title "Weavers to be encouraged to settle in Calcutta."

31 The English officers in Calcutta developed the lifestyles of a Nabob. Their domestic households were packed with servants of various kinds together with their business asssistants. All of them lived around their residential

INTRODUCTION

dwellings so that behind and around the splendid edifices on the Chowringhee and the riverside areas mud and thatched houses raised their heads. The Calcutta Committee proceedings of 27 April 1767 contained the following note:

> Mr. Russell, as Collector general begs leave to represent to the Board that of late years the street by the river side to the northward of the Custom House has been greatly encroached upon by a number of golahs, little straw huts and boutiques that have been indiscriminately reared.
>
> He would further propose that no golahs whatever should be suffered to remain to the southward of this spot, which will relieve the inhabitants from the apprehensions of fire, and of their houses being entirely undermined by rats.
>
> The straw huts, everywhere dispersed throughout the white town, is (are) another grievance, and an innovation of very late, which he would also recommend to the consideration of the Board. – Long, Selections, No. 945, p. 659.

32 Every European who was engaged in private trade had his own native business assistants and partners. They were called *banians*. It was a general practice that at the outset of their career young English officers opened their trade with funds provided by rich Indian traders who had amassed money by trading with the European Companies. These Indians lent their money to the English officers and the latter in return provided them with protection, official support and political influence. Thus being under the umbrella of men of political authority, these Indians acted as secretaries, accountants, market-surveyors, record-keepers, trustees and primary agents in all practical transactions of business of the Europeans in general and the English in particular. The three volumes of N.K. Sinha's *Economic History of Bengal* are replete with references to *banians*. It was the money of the *banians* which financed whatever little industry Bengal had till the middle of the nineteenth century. For this reference may be made to Sabyasachi Bhattacharya's article in *Cambridge Economic History of India*, Vol. II, ed. By Dharma Kumar, (pp. 270–295), See Sinha *Economic History of Bengal*.Vol. II, pp. 24, 25, 27, 30, 31, 70, 75, 76, 78, 81, 82, 83, 124, 148, 178, 192, 220, 221, 225, 279. In Bengal, *banians* were not all from the *bania* class. Upper Class Hindu Bengalis, even Brahmins, acted as *banians*. N.K. Sinha defines the term *banian* as one derived 'from bania or merchant, a term used to designate the Indian who manages the concerns of the Europeans.' – Sinha *Economic History of Bengal*, Vol. II, p. 233. See Somendra Chandra Nandy, *Life and Times of Kantoo Baboo: The Banian of Warren Hanstings*, Allied Publishers, 1978.

33 Mud huts and thatched cottages required earth, wood, and bamboos for their construction. Since such huts were increasing in the city because of infiltration of lowly men pulled from the peasant societies of the countryside to provide labour for civil constructions soil digging had become a routine phenomenon in the city and around in the eighteenth century.

34 The middle class in Bengal emerged from three elements. Firstly, the *banians* and traders who amassed money in course of the eighteenth century settled themselves in the city of Calcutta and the neighbouring towns to

INTRODUCTION

provide the basis of a money elite. Secondly, the Permanent Settlement created a landlord class that had a tendency to reside in Calcutta so that a class of absentee landlords appropriating the wealth of the interior created the base of a new propertied elite in the society. The third element was an educated mankind produced by the Hindu College and the new education that was coming into shape in the first quarter of the nineteenth century. For the economic origin of the Bengali middle class see Sinha *Economic History of Bengal*, Vol. II, pp. 222–229.

35 It is a paradox that, in spite of concentration of capital in Calcutta throughout the course of the eighteenth century, capital seemed to be in short in the city. This shortage of capital was manifested in public activities of the government, and not in private enterprises. Both the Court of Directors and the city administrators showed a spend-thrift and miserly mindset in addressing themselves to any public work during the first one century of the British rule in Bengal. There was a real dearth of money in the interior. This was because the last dreg of social surplus was squeezed out from the cultivating people in the form of rent and from the zamindars in the form of revenue without any equivalent return. From 1765 the English East India Company ceased to import bullion from England as the entire territorial revenue of Bengal, Bihar, and Orissa was at their disposal. The Sarrafs, the country banking houses, which acted as credit institutions for rural Bengal, were relegated to the background and the house of the Jagat Seths, the biggest banking house of the country and bankers to the state, were made non-functionary. The result was that, while in the city of Calcutta, there were *banians* and other trader-collaborators to ensure supply of fund there was no house in the interior to provide credit necessary for the economy to be going. All big zamindars syphoned their wealth to Calcutta and this growing metropolis did not benefit the country hinterland in any major way. In spite of this capital concentration in the city there was little fund to promote its urbanization as a public enterprise. A relief to this stringency came only when the lottery system was enunciated in the nineties of the eighteenth century.

36 Sarkar, *History of Bengal*, p. 418.

37 This was the first major influx of population into the city and the first major event through which Calcutta proved itself to be a sanctuary for the people. This was also the first important situation in which people learnt how superior the British arms were to that of the Nawab. The latter had no money to build up the defence of the state. Sir Jadunath Sarkar writes (*History of Bengal*, p. 461): "In his financial distress Alivardi put pressure upon the European Companies trading in Bengal. He complained that the English 'carried on the trade of the whole world; they formerly used to have but four or five ships, but now brought 40 or 50 sails which belong not to the Company'. He expected the rich merchants and refugees in Calcutta to assist him with a large contribution for meeting his army bill. The English at last settled his claim by paying 3½ lakhs of rupees, besides Rs. 43, 500 for his courtiers. The French at Chandernagore paid Rs. 45, 000." [Italics ours] About Calcutta's rise as a sanctuary of distressed people K.K. Datta writes: "the ready offer of shelter by the English to some of the ravaged and runaway inhabitants of the plundered areas of Bengal within the bounds of the Company's settlement in Calcutta, engendered

INTRODUCTION

in the minds of these people a feeling of sympathy for, and faith in, the English Company. The English were able to raise a volunteer army, and a certain amount of subscriptions, from the native, the Armenian, and the Portuguese inhabitants of Calcutta, to defend that city against threatened encroachments of the Marathas. This shows that the people reposed some amount of confidence in the support of the English." – *Alivardi and His Times*, p. 94.

38 For the Krishnadas affair see Gupta, *Sirajuddaullah and the East India Company, 1756–1757*, pp. 48–50.
39 To know how Bengal became a protectorate, see Ranjit Sen, *Metamorphosis of the Bengal Polity (1700–1793)*, Rabindra Bharati University, Calcutta, 1987, Chs. I–III.
40 For details as to how power was slowly clamped on the *Nizamat* in Bengal see the following books: (i) Sen, *Metamorphosis of the Bengal Polity*; (ii) Gupta, *Sirajuddaullah and the East India Company, 1756–1757*; (iii) Benoy Krishna Roy, *The Career and Achievements of Maharaja Nanda Kumar, Dewan of Bengal (1705–1755)*, Calcutta, 1969; (iv) Atul Chandra Roy, *The Career of Mir Jafar Khan (1757–65 A.D.)*, Calcutta; (v) K.M. Mohsin, *A Bengal District in Transition: Murshidabad 1765–93*, Dacca, 1973; (vi) N. Majumdar, *Justice and Police in Bengal, 1775–1793: A Study of the Nizamat in Decline*, Calcutta, 1960; (vii) Majed Khan, *The Transition in Bengal 1756–1775; A Study of Saiyid Muhammad Reza Khan*.
41 The Mayor's Court has been discussed at length in Firminger, *Historical Introduction to the Bengal Portion of the Fifth Report*, Ch. V, titled 'The Mayor's Court.'
42 The Sadar *Diwani* and the Sadar *Nizamat* Adalats were superior courts. One was "a court of appeal in civil cases." And the other was for "revising and confirming sentences." See Majumdar, Roychaudhuri and Datta, *An Advanced History of India*, p. 788.
43 The transforming status of the Emperor vis-à-vis the Governor General has been discussed by Percival Spear in *A History of Delhi Under the Later Mughals*, New Delhi, 1988, pp. 39–71.
44 The fall of Patna was indicated by the fall of population in the city in the nineteenth century. The fall has been recorded in the census report thus:

Census of 1872	population of Patna was 1,58,900
Census of 1881	population of Patna was 1,70,654
Census of 1891	population of Patna was 1,65,192
Census of 1901	population of Patna was 1,34,785

"The reasons for the decline in population are obvious. The frequent famines (1866–67, 1873–74) and epidemics coupled with inadequate relief measures and medical aid were responsible for the waning population. Further, no major economic opportunities emerged to attract new people." – Surendra Gopal, *Patna in 19th Century a Socio-Cultural Profile*, Naya Prokash, Calcutta, 1982, p. 18.

Patna began to slide into eclipse since the second half of the eighteenth century. It started when Mir Qasim with the help of Vansittart removed Clive's protégé at Patna, Ramnarayan and possessed the resources and treasures of Bihar. Then he shifted his capital to Monghyr thus forcing Patna into a zone of shadow. He spent the resources of Bihar in his wars

INTRODUCTION

with the English. In 1759 Ali Gahar (later Emperor Shah Alam II) laid a siege to Patna. He hoped to strengthen his claims to Delhi by acquiring Bihar and Bengal. Ram Narayan successfully defended the city till such time as Clive could send his army. This event opened the eyes of the English who henceforth built up Patna and Bihar as buffers against the turmoil of the west. The fall of the major cities of eastern India indicated a process of de-urbanization. But de-urbanization affected the great cities like Dakha, Murshidabad, Burdwan, Patna etc. and not the smaller ones like Bhagalpur, Monghyr, Khirpai etc. See Dharma Kumar, ed. *The Cambridge Economic History of India*, Vol. 2: c. 1757-c. 1970, Orient Longman, 1982, 1984, pp. 277–279.

45 For the development of Calcutta as a port see Ray, *A Short History of Calcutta Town and Suburbs Census of India, 1901*, Ch. XIII.
46 Note that of the sixteen Mahajanapadas in the sixth century B.C. four emerged powerful. They were Avanti, Vatsa, Kosala, and Magadha. Out of these Magadha, which embraced the districts of Patna and Gaya, emerged triumphant.
47 The successor states of the Mughal Empire, those of Oudh, Bengal, and Hyderabad and also the Sikh empire in the north-west and the kingdom of Mysore in the south had inherited much of the Mughal Empire in their own forms. But the real contest was between the English emerging both from the east and the south and the Marathas from the west. The French effort to curve an empire from the south and those of the Afghans under Ahmad Shah Abdali from the north-west seemed to be abortive. The Marathas and the Afghans exhausted themselves through their mutual fights as the French had collapsed because of their conflicts with the English unsupported either by their authorities at home or by any local support like immense control of revenue which the British had in Bengal. The Mughal Empire in providing the *diwani* of Bengal, Bihar, and Orissa to the English had selected its own successor within the frame of Mughal constitution. As the British Empire succeeded the Mughal Empire from being within the ranks of a talukdar (of the three villages of Sutanuti, Govindapur, and Kalikata in 1698) and the zamindar (of the twenty-four Parganas in 1757) one might say that the Mughal Empire saved itself from being subverted by any non-Mughal power by force. The English could build their constitutional position from being absorbed in the administrative partnership of the Mughal elite.
48 Pradip Sinha, *Calcutta in Urban History*, Firma KLM Private Ltd., Calcutta, 1978, p. 29.
49 Ibid.
50 Ibid.
51 Proceedings of the Lottery Committee (henceforth referred to as PLC), 20 July 1820.
52 The Officers of the Lottery Committee individually and also collectively noted this development. Early planners' concerns and speculations were manifested in their observations. Here are some examples:

"I have already stated that the value of ground in Calcutta generally rises in proportion to its contiguity to a great thoroughfare and that upon this circumstance rested the possibility of effecting the improvement I proposed." PLC, 3 February 1820

INTRODUCTION

"Adverting to the increasing European population of this Town we cannot doubt but the greatest part would be purchased in its improved state for the erection of Dwelling Houses at rates which would more than repay previous expenditure." PLC, 4 May 1820. See also letter to John Trotter, Esq., Secretary to the Lottery Committee, April 20, 1820

53 Bordering on the ancient trade route of Chitpur, a pilgrim thoroughfare, leading first to the then Sarvamangala Devi temple and then far beyond it to Halishahar, the entire territory between modern Shyambazar and Bagbazar seemed to be very strategic. On the one hand, it connected the old Nawabi military station at Dum Dum (subsidiary to the faujdari of Jessore) and the ancient trade route to Kapasia (region around Dhaka where Karpas or cotton was grown), and on the other it provided passage to the newly developed British military stronghold at Barrackpore. Therefore, improving links between this part of the city with the white town where the fort was situated was to the interest of the British rulers in Calcutta.

54 "Lottery Committee O Byadhi O Taar Protikaar" (Lottery Committee and Disease and its Remedy), Jnanannesan, 21 October 1837 reprinted in Suresh Chandra Moitra, ed. *Selections from Jnanannesan*, Prajna, Calcutta, 1979, p. 59 (Bengali section).

55 Ray, *A Short History of Calcutta Town and Suburbs Census of India, 1901*, p. 221.

Part I

SCANNING THE CONTEXT

1
MAPPING THE PATTERN OF URBANIZATION IN HISTORY
The Calcutta Chapter

An unsure identity

Urban history, it is said, is unsure of its identity.[1] Its forms, methodology, and discipline as well as its concepts and procedures have not yet been developed. It had borrowed freely from external sources, geography, topography, demography, economics, sociology, and many other such subjects. The result of this is that although we have chroniclers of towns we seldom have historians of urbanization. In the west urban history took its shape as a discipline only around or after the World War II when it became a formidable component for the growing American nationhood.[2] India is an agglomeration of villages and more than 70 per cent of its population lives in the countryside.[3] Hence the writing of urban history has taken a backseat in comparison to agrarian history writings. From time immemorial India's history has accommodated within its fold a queer paradox. It is abound with the story of foundations of towns, but towns here could never shake off relics of villages from their core. As a result, towns in India had always been only developed villages with some callings of life other than agriculture and rural crafts. The total disjuncture from rusticity could rarely become a stable phenomenon in India. Its effects had been serious. The concept of town as sovereign in itself with no organic attachment with villages except those of the basic subsistence relations had thus never grown in India. It was a singular misfortune for India that her earliest civilization, the Harappan civilization, having originated as a potential centre of urban growth, eventually relapsed into an infinite monotony of an agricultural one. The sort of urbanization which Europe experienced in the high middle ages when towns at the crest of a commercial revival after the tenth and eleventh centuries raised their heads as break-away units from feudal manorial system was unthinkable in the

Indian context. Thus, when Europeans came to India they concerned themselves not with towns, which were absent in their broad experience, but with village communities, rural land tenures, revenue from agriculture, and agrarian relations. In this context urban history did not grow effectively in India. Long before the Europeans came to India the people of this country had their own ways of writing history.

That was mostly narrative history that revolved around rulers. Cities had no great role to play as subjects of history.[4]

Indifference to urban history was in fact a global phenomenon. Attention to towns grew in Europe only when consequences of the Industrial Revolution were felt very acutely in the continent. Marx's *The Communist Manifesto* for the first time ushered in the epoch-making theory that, because of the rise of the bourgeoisie, towns and cities overwhelmed villages. But understanding of urban history stopped at that only. Interests in the history of towns remained lulled for some time and were revived many years later when F.W. Maitland published his work *Township and Borough* in 1898. Following his lead, Henry Pirenne in the 1920s published his work on medieval towns.[5] Then there was a wait for many years before a landmark work on urban history could be produced. In 1963 was published Asha Briggs *Victorian Cities*. Even then institutional formalization of urban history writing did not gain momentum. Such formalization took rest of the twentieth century to crystallize itself.[6]

In India urban history had never been a popular theme of writing for historians. The British historians who wrote on India were mostly panegyrists of British exploits in the east. To them the history of India was coterminous with the history of the emergence and expansion of an empire which was replete with wars and the exploits of the Governors General or the history of civilizing missions from the west that involved stories of wars against oriental misrule through a steady process of reform and regeneration. For many British historians writing for India an imperial undertone seemed to be unavoidable. Their works prepared the minds of future British civil servants in India and, therefore, quite naturally and also a little surreptitiously they imparted the message of the empire. This was the compulsive logic under which many British historians found themselves commissioned to write. Under such circumstances political and administrative history got precedence over economic and social history where the city could serve as the most convenient unit of analysis. From the beginning the Imperial government in India was concerned mainly with two things, the problem of governance and the means of governance, i.e. revenue. When the nationalists emerged a new set of problems called for definition – famine, poverty, deindustrialization, drain of wealth, rural indebtedness, the railways versus canals, and irrigation and finally degeneration of Indian life. Industrialization and urbanization are concurrent events and the absence of the one automatically obliterates the importance of the other. When these problems filled the nationalist discourse it was logical that urban history would have no place in Indian historiography.

Uncongenial for colonial historiography

Thus urban history could not find a congenial soil in the colonial historiography of India. Could a pre-industrial urban history be possible in this situation? The answer would be broadly "no." Such a discipline did not grow in the free societies of the west.[7] How could it flourish in the inhibited colonial settings where incentives for change manifested little? W.H. Moreland many years ago laid his hands on the subject and wrote a masterful account of India towards the end of the sixteenth century.[8] With the judgement of a true investigator Moreland scanned the economic forces that prevailed in India at the time of Akbar's death. He discussed the condition of important cities of the time but none of his discourses did form the principal focus for urban history. His intention was to show what India was like at the end of the best of the Mughal rule so that it could be compared to the condition of the Indians under the rule of the British in modern times. The result was that in spite of being a primary study of the economic condition of the Indian society in pre-colonial era it failed to become the starting point of a productive from of urban history in India.

In this situation, writing on Calcutta is not only to be an effort to restore Calcutta to history, but perhaps, more importantly, also to restore history to Calcutta. A town history for Calcutta became an administrative necessity when the census operations started in India. Thus Mr. H. Beverley, c.s. wrote a history of the city as a part of his Census Report of 1876. In later years A.K. Ray followed suit writing a detailed history of Calcutta as a necessary part of the Census Report of 1901.[9] "It is a pioneer venture in Calcutta study." This is how the book has been rated by historians.[10] But unfortunately the work was never followed by another of its kind. The growth of Calcutta was a phenomenon in urban history and its complexities were seldom analyzed.[11] From the coming of A.K. Ray's book down till the end of the colonial era in India Calcutta remained in quest for a sound historian.[12] In course of the rest of the twentieth century a school of urban history did not grow in Bengal or India at large. Seven decades passed since A.K. Ray's history in the Census Report of 1901 before new ventures could be made toward understanding Calcutta.[13] Nearly another two decades more had to go by when a well-documented study of Calcutta's morphology manifested itself.[14]

Notes

1. "As a historical discipline, urban history has always been peculiarly unsure of its own identity. H.J. Dyos, the father of British urban history, described it as a 'portmanteau subject,' 'a field of knowledge' rather than a discipline as traditionally defined. Much of the history of towns and cities is written outside the confines of the academy, merging into the genres of 'local history' or topography. Although it would claim a greater degree of historical rigour than such writings, urban history has never established its own identifiable theories and methodologies, being instead a promiscuous borrower of concepts and procedures from other fields of history and from disciplines of the social sciences" – Martin Hewitt, "Urban History" in Kelly Boyd, ed., *Historians and Historical Writings*, Vol. 2 (M-Z), Fitzroy Dearborn Publishers, London (Chicago), 1999, p. 1246.
2. "The sense of urban history as a discipline emerged first in the United States in the years around World War II, prompted by the works of Arthur Meir Schlesinger and Richard C. Wade which integrated the city into Turner's frontier thesis, and thus made cities central to the development of American nationhood" (Ibid.).
3. India's estimated population in July 2007 was 112,98,66,154 (112 crores, 98 lakhs, 66,154). Of this more than 70 per cent of the population alive in 5,50,000 (five lakhs and fifty thousand) villages. The remainder lives in 200 towns and cities. India covers 2.4 per cent of the world's land area but supports more than 15 per cent of its population.
4. "The peoples of south Asia who came under the British colonial rule from the middle of the 18th century had various traditions of history writing. Most accessible from the point of view of the conquerors were the narrative histories written in Persian that chronicled the reigns of Mughal emperors or other rulers. Eighteenth century British scholars eagerly translated such works and indeed commissioned a by no means uncritical history of the transition to British rule in eastern India by Ghulam Hussain Khan, published in translation in 1789 as View of Modern Times (modern reprints available). British people also began to write histories to chronicle their own doings in India, Robert Orme's *History of the Military Transactions of the British Nation in Indostan (1763–78)* being the first of such books." – Peter Marshall, "India since 1750" in Boid, *Historians and Historical Writings*, Vol. I (A-L), p. 580.
5. Henri Pirenne authored a book titled *Medieval Cities: Their Origins and the Revival of Trade* (1927). This book was based on some lectures he delivered in the United States in 1922. His main contention in the book was that in course of two centuries, from the tenth to the twelfth, Europe recovered control of the Mediterranean from the Muslims. This helped them to open up sea routes to the Orient. This in its turn resulted in the formation of a merchant cum middle class who steadily built up their

characteristic abode, the city. From this Pirenne moved to his logical next step. He argued that out of this revolutionary development capitalism originated in Europe and cities became the birth place of capitalism in the continent. Out of capitalism grew democracy, the basis of Europe's modern way of life. Pirenne's theory of a commercial renaissance in towns in the eleventh century had since remained to be the hallmark of standard interpretation of Europe's rejuvenation and eventual emergence into the modern world.

6 "Even then, institutional formalization occurred only hesitatingly. In North America, an Urban History Newsletter was published form the 1950s, eventually superseded in 1974 by the Journal of Urban History. But it was not until the establishment of the Urban History Association in 1988 that urban historians could claim an associational base. In Europe it was not until the mid 1970s that the first urban history journals were established, and not until the early 1990s that the European Association of Urban Historians was formed; in Britain, it took 20 years to convert the Urban History Newsletter into a semi-annual journal, Urban History, and in the mid-1990s there was still no formal urban history association. Outside these two continents, although it has been possible to trace an increasing amount of urban history research, little or no progress towards the institutionalization of the discipline has taken place."

7 "However, as political and purely economic approaches were challenged in the 20th century by broader social perspectives, the pre-occupations (and limited sources-bases) of pre-industrial urban history came to be seen as increasingly restricted, despite Pirenne's attempt to develop a more socio-economic framework for the study of medieval cities. From the 1950s through to the 1980s pre-industrial towns were marginal to urban historians. Only in the 1980s, often through the creation of a new generation of networks of urban historians, such as the Early Modern Towns Group in Britain, were there signs of a lessening of this imbalance." – Boyd, *Historians and Historical Writings*, Vol. II. p. 1247.

8 W.H. Moreland, *India at the Death of Akbar: An Economic Study* (London, 1920), Indian Reprint, Delhi, 1962.

9 "The first connected history of the rise and growth of Calcutta was written by Mr. H. Beverley, c.s., as a part of his Census Report for 1876. In paragraph 109, page 36, of that report, he recommended the future historian of the town to draw for his materials upon the domestic archives of the leading Native families in the town, besides official records and the notices of the Eastern travellers. When, therefore, at the instance of the Census Commissioner of India, I was asked last November, by the Deputy Chairman of the Calcutta Corporation, to undertake the task of writing a short history of Calcutta, in connection with the Census Report for 1901, I applied to a great many native Indian families for assistance, besides soliciting the help of Government for the loan of old books, papers and periodicals dealing with ancient Calcutta." – A.K. Ray, *A Short History of Calcutta: Towns and Suburbs, Census of India*, 1901, Vol. VII, Part I, (published in 1902, Rddhi edition 1982), RDDHI-INDIA, Calcutta, Preface.

10 Nisith R. Ray's, "Introduction", in Ray, *Calcutta Town and Suburbs* (Rddhi edn.), p. vii.

SCANNING THE CONTEXT

11 "No other city in India has perhaps evoked more curiosity and yielded more harvest in historical literature than Calcutta. The story of the city has been told over long years. But, on the whole, barring a few exceptions, the process is generally repetitive. They tell the story of how Charnock 'a block of rough British manhood' bodily, as if, lifted a city from out of a marshy unhealthy place on the river, how the Settlement grew to be the centre of a mighty empire and a city of palaces, how successive British rulers adorned the city with splendid edifices, on the models imported from their homeland, how the city grew to be the busiest trade emporium, east of Suez, how streets and squares were laid, and above all, how it grew to be the nerve-centre of cultural activities. Behind the entire façade built by the British writers, and following them the Indian authors, there lurks, dim and distant, the shadow of the Indian town in Calcutta and its inhabitants. Not only authors, but artists too, treated the Indian town as out of bounds. The picture which thus emerge in largely that of a colonial city par excellence – exotic and even bizarre." – Ibid, pp. vii–viii.
12 Bombay was more fortunate in this regard. She could meet her historian in 1920, the year when S.M. Edwards published his book *The Rise of Bombay: A Retrospect*.
13 In 1977 was published S.N. Mukherji's book *Calcutta Myths and History*, Subarnarekha, Calcutta and in 1978 Pradip Sinha's book *Calcutta in Urban History*, Firma KLM Private Ltd., Calcutta.
14 In 1994 was published Soumitra Sreemani's work *Anatomy of a Colonial Town Calcutta 1756–1794*, Firma KLM Private Ltd., Calcutta.

2
A COMPARATIVE UNDERSTANDING OF THE GROWTH OF THE THREE COLONIAL CITIES
Madras, Calcutta, and Bombay

Born in turmoil

Calcutta was born in turmoil. It was born in the midst of a war. The English East India Company was engaged in a war with the Mughals which lasted from 1686 to 1690. It was in course of this war that Job Charnock, popularly known as the founder of the city, arrived at Sutanuti, a village which eventually formed the nucleus of future Calcutta. Hardly was the war over when a revolt broke out against the Mughals in western Bengal. This was the revolt of Shova Singh and Rahim Khan which took place in 1696. The English purchased the three villages, Kalikata, Govindapur, and Sutanuti in 1698. This was when the revolt was just suppressed but its members were still there. The rebels in western Bengal carved out a state for themselves although it was a short-lived one. This was an eye-opener for the English. They learnt that, in India of the time, the logic of might provided the most significant source of right. After the revolt the Company was invited by the Mughal Government in Bengal to return to this country. They returned but this time with an advantage. They secured the right to purchase property. They purchased the three villages at a nominal sum of Rs. 1,300 only. Thus within eight years since the termination of their war with the Mughals the English purchased their property in Bengal. The site of Madras was purchased by the Company in 1639. Thus the founding of colonial Madras took place nearly sixty years before the founding of Calcutta.[1] The logic of the foundation of Calcutta and Madras was nearly the same – trade and security. The turmoil of a revolt in Bengal taught the English the lesson that they needed their own foothold in order to escape the blast of state vicissitudes like a war or a revolt. Their trade in Bengal did not assume any great proportion about this time. Therefore acquisition of land in Bengal was not a compulsive urge in their trade aspirations. They were invited by the Mughal provincial government here and they responded with hesitation. But once they did they extracted an advantage from the Mughal Government. The western flank of the Mughal Government was shattered and the economy of the interior collapsed totally. The war and a revolt left their sequel. A new kind of money-short economy was created. Since the European Companies brought bullion with them, the Mughal Government wanted to ensure their return at any cost. The price they paid for this was to allow the Company to purchase property in Bengal. Thus the colonial town of Calcutta emerged only as a property of the English. They began to call this property their 'estate.'[2] Madras and Bombay also began their career as a property of the English. The logic of their growth was the same – security and trade exploration.

The foundation of a property around Madras was a necessity for the English. "Business at Masulipatam and Armagaon was hampered by the exactions of local officials, and experience showed that the piece goods required for export to Bantam and Persia were to be had at cheaper rates farther south."[3] Thus in order to escape the exactions of local officials the English sought an escape into a new territory close to the area from where they could procure their supply of piece goods. In Bengal they were urged not by a motive of escape but by a motive of exploring new fields for commercial expansion. The acquisition of property in Bengal was an adventure. In Madras it was a necessity.

> The chief at Armagaon, Francis Day, therefore secured from a local Hindu chief the grant of a strip of land just north of the friendly, decaying, Portuguese settlement of San Thome. The grant was afterwards confirmed by the raja of Chandragiri, the representative of the old sovereigns of Vijayanagar; by it the English were permitted to erect fortifications and the revenues were divided between them and the Nayak. Thus England acquired her first proprietary holding on India soil, and the foundation of the Presidency of Madras was laid. A fort was quickly built (to the dismay of the thrifty directors at home) and named Fort St. George. This gave to Madras its

official designation as the Presidency of Fort St. George. In 1647 the district fell into the hands of Golkonda, but happily the English were on good terms with the general, Mir Jumla, and secured his confirmation of their position.[4]

The right to construct fort was a unique right which the English were denied in Calcutta till the middle of the eighteenth century. The Bengal *Nawabs* were so sensitive to the construction of a fort by the English on any part of the territory ruled by them that they did not hesitate to put the whole issue to the arbitrament of force in the middle of the eighteenth century. Thus, throughout the course of eighteenth century, the British mind was bent on securing the same privilege as they enjoyed at Madras namely the right to fortify their own settlement. The result was that the construction of the town was not their immediate objective any time in the first half of the eighteenth century. They settled down to town planning only in the second half of the eighteenth century when the right to fortification and the right to mint coins did not keep them preoccupied. In their immediate pursuits security was an overwhelming end. They always wanted to keep their settlement in Calcutta insulated and free of the spies of the *Nawab*. Beyond this preoccupation they had other incentives. "The destruction in the 1660's of Portuguese and Arakanese pirates, who had infested the head of the Bay of Bengal, by Shayasta Khan opened a new area of trade to the Dutch and the English. Bengal offered new products such as silk and saltpetre, and trade in these rapidly grew."[5] The eighteenth century was a century of warfare in India and Europe. Saltpetre was therefore in great demand. The Bengal silk was also a prime commodity in demand in European market. Once the Portuguese were removed from Bengal the entire seaboard lay open to British and Dutch adventurers. Now the combination matched British aspirations. The Portuguese were gone and there was none to tap the resources of saltpetre and silk so profusely available in eastern India. In this trade vacuum the English stepped in.

> In 1688, however, Sir Josiah Child's foolish war with Aurangzeb ended in the expulsion of the English. When the *Nawab* Ibrahim Khan invited them back, they chose not Hughli, the Mughal centre of commerce, but a mud-flat with a deep-water anchorage, the site of Calcutta. As at Madras the choice was dictated by the need for security. There the delta of the evil-smelling Cooum, here extensive swamps,

provided protection. So Job Charnock, turbulent, masterful, but "always a faithful man to the Company," doggedly set to work to build and fortify the settlement of Calcutta. In 1696 was built Fort William – so named after King William III – and the Presidency of Fort William or Bengal was established.[6]

The vacuum created by the removal of the Portuguese offered space for expansion of the English trade. Trade and arms moved together. Calcutta was purchased in 1998 and the rudiments of the Fort were started two years before that. Madras and Calcutta thus shared the same nature in their birth as a garrison town. They were basically fort-settlements garrisoned for the protection of trade.

Career begins as a property

Like Madras and Calcutta, Bombay also began its career as a property of the English. Originally a possession of the Portuguese it was gifted to the British Crown as a part of the dowry of Catharine of Braganza, Queen of Charles II. "The cession was made by the Portuguese in order to secure English support against the Dutch. A few years later the king, who had failed to appreciate the value of the acquisition, granted the island to the East India Company in return for the trifling sum of ten pounds a year."[7] It is thus clear that neither the Portuguese nor the British Crown could anticipate the future greatness of Bombay. Operating in south Asia, the British mind was riveted on Madras, Calcutta, and Chittagong. In Bengal their main attraction was Chittagong and not Calcutta. Throughout the course of the first half of the eighteenth century several times they tried to get hold of Chittagong but they failed. Chittagong had a natural port and was away from Murshidabad, the seat of the administration of the Bengal *Nawabs*. Moreover from Chittagong they could maintain a watch on the movement of the Dutch operating on the waters of south-east Asia. Calcutta was within the reach of the Murshidabad government and was closely watched but the faujdar of Hughli. Bombay suffered the same disadvantage as Calcutta being within the vicinity of the Mughal seat of administration at Surat. But then Bombay had an unrestricted passage to the sea which Calcutta did not have. The future greatness of Bombay was never anticipated by the Portuguese. Likewise it remained unappreciated by any agency of supreme governance of the British Crown. This was because many people in Europe and elsewhere at that time had a "misty notion" that the "Island of Bombay with the towns and castles therein ... are within a very little distance from Brazil."[8] Only the Portuguese Viceroy of Goa, DeMello de Castro, shed tears when Bombay was transferred to the British. In a final letter to the King of Portugal he wrote in January 1665:

> I confess at the feet of your Majesty, that only the obedience I owe your Majesty, as a vassal, could have forced me to this deed (i.e., the cession of the island), because I foresee the great troubles that from this neighbourhood will result to the Portuguese; and that India will be lost on the same day in which English nation is settled in Bombay.[9]

Commenting on this, Edwardes wrote:

> There is something pathetic in this last appeal of the Viceroy, who fully recognised the possibilities of world-greatness which underlay "the inconsiderableness of the Place of Bombaim" and knew by instinct that his race could never be the dominant power in western India, if once "the poor little island", as Pepys querulously termed it, were handed over to the men of England.[10]

Removal of the Portuguese: a boon

The removal of the Portuguese from the Arabian Sea and the Bay of Bengal eventually helped the rise of both Bombay and Calcutta. The Dutch had never been the competitor of the English either in western India or in Bengal. Hence the passing away of the Portuguese control over the high seas meant that henceforth the movement of English vessels in the coastal water would be free and unhindered. In the eastern side on the seaboard between Bengal and Madras the English Company could easily build up their link systems. The fact that in the beginning of 1757 Clive could sail from Madras in his mission to rescue Calcutta from the control of the Bengal *Nawab* only shows what benefit the English could gain from the expulsion of the Portuguese from the Bengal scene in 1632. In the west the English gained another advantage which they did not enjoy in the east. The Calcutta possession of the English was under a strict watch from the Bengal *Nawabs* so much so that between 1698 when Calcutta was purchased and 1757 when the battle of Palasi was fought the Company's government was not allowed to add even a small strip of territory to their original possession in Calcutta. This was in spite of the fact that the Delhi

Emperor had granted them, by a farman in 1717, fifty-five villages around Calcutta. Bombay was free from this Mughal vigilance. The Portuguese had been able to crush the Arab trade dominance in the western seas and in doing that they kept Bombay much removed from a major zone of global Muslim predominance. C.R. Boxer writes:

> the Portuguese were able to deprive the Muslim traders of the Indian Ocean of a large share of the trade in Indian textiles and piece-goods, Persian and Arabian horses, gold and ivory from East Africa, as well as from spices from Indonesia, Ceylon, and Malabar. Moreover they extended their carrying trade into the China Sea, where Arab merchants had not penetrated since medieval times, save in insignificant numbers. Voyages between the principal ports in these areas (Macau-Nagasaki; Malacca-Siam; Ormuz-Goa, for example) were much shorter and easier than the long haulround the Cape of Good Hope. Money and goods invested in such "ventures" brought in quicker and safer returns than did cargoes shipped to Europe. The comparative value of gold and silver in India, China and Japan varied in fluctuating ratio which enabled the Portuguese at Goa and Macau to make a handsome profit by acting as bullion-brokers trading in these precious metals.[11]

Within this network of Asian and global trade Bombay was fitted in. Neither Madras nor Calcutta was from the beginning so much a part of the global maritime enterprise in the east. Much of the English enterprise in Calcutta was absorbed in the process of adjustment with the *Nawabs* of Bengal. Madras from the beginning tried to curb out a space for itself in south Indian politics. Thus in the eighteenth century it turned out to be a rear area for the English steeped in territorial and political ambitions in Bengal and in the Carnatic. This robbed both of them of the growth potential Bombay had. In Goa and Bombay and other Portuguese centres of the east the demographic policy of the Portuguese created new techniques of man-power mobilization.

> The national militia of Portugal was no basis for the army in India. And while the population of Portugal was actually declining, and while another great Portuguese empire was being opened up in Brazil, forces for India could only be maintained by recruitment in India. Some troops with officers of noble blood did come out in the annual fleets, but in the main reliance was placed in those who had settled in the Indies and

married there. Albuquerque, recognizing the strength which such settlers represented, had encouraged mixed marriage. The stubborn resistance of so many settlements to the Dutch, who early became masters at sea, testifies to the valour of the *casados* and their slaves.[12]

As a result of all these a cosmopolitan society was already in the offing in western India. This demographic setting helped Bombay in its later growth. The population of mixed descent was called Indo-Portuguese whom Edwards called "a people of Mixed European and Asiatic descent," generally speaking, "a degenerate and debased race, 'the hybrid product of the Union of Portuguese with the native women of low-class, possessing the good qualities of neither.' "[13] After the cession these men were enlisted as soldiers and subsequently they formed "the original nucleus of the Bombay Amy." Calcutta never had the man-power reserve which Bombay had, and, in the absence of this reserve, Calcutta had to suffer in 1756 when *Nawab* Sirajuddaullah invaded Calcutta and captured it.

Challenges of Competition: Calcutta and Madras

In Bombay the English were somewhat free from the competition of any western power. In Calcutta and Madras they were not. In both these countries they were challenged either by the Dutch or by the French. Calcutta's emergence as an English city was made possible by two things. At the beginning of 1757, Chandernagore, the French settlement in Bengal, was destroyed by Clive. In no time Murshidabad and Hugli sank and Calcutta absorbed the glory lost by these two cities. Hugli was a Shia colony and Murshidabad was dominated by the Sunni Muslims. With the going down of these two centres of Muslim culture the emergence of a cosmopolitan Calcutta became possible. The second event which helped the growth of Calcutta in the eighteenth century was its conquest by Clive in the beginning of 1757. It changed the status of Calcutta. It was now a conquered city. It did not give the English *de jure* sovereignty but their mastery was now free from encumbrance. Henceforth the political will of the English could be applied in all matters promoting the city. It was this political will which blossomed into its full majesty under Lord Wellesley who decided that the British empire in India ought not to be ruled from an emporium of commodities for trade but from a city of imperial dignity. This provided the pace for urbanization in Calcutta, which was broadly a phenomenon of the nineteenth century.

SCANNING THE CONTEXT

The British choice to settle at Madras was dictated by their desire to avoid competition from the Dutch. At a very early stage of their coming to the east, they tried to settle somewhere in the territories of southeast Asia. But their ventures in this direction was baffled by the Dutch. "The English Company had discovered," writes N.S. Ramaswami,

> that south-east Asia was not a good market for its manufactures. Captain James Lancaster of the first voyage had sold iron, tin and lead in south-east Asia and brought spices. But his woollen goods found no purchasers in 1808 the English factors at Bantam wrote to London that there was a big market for Indian calico cloth. A trading centre in India, therefore, became necessary.[14]

Thus, repulsed from south-east Asia, the English sought their permanent station in south Asia. Madras, or as it was called Madraspatam in those days, was not their first choice.

> It was decided that the third [English] voyage [to the east], on its way to Bantam, explore trade possibilities at Aden and Surat. The English faced much hostility from the Portuguese at Surat, but Jahangir permitted them, in 1608, to build a factory there. However, it was not until four years later that they could do so. Their cause was helped by a resounding naval victory that Captain Best, though heavily outnumbered, gained over the Portuguese off Swaly. This was the first blow Portuguese naval supremacy suffered The Mughals considered naval warfare beneath their dignity and had, in consequence, to put up with Portuguese hectoring at the sea. Sailors of another nation were found who could rout those who had hitherto been invincible.[15]

In the west the English factories had been set up at Surat, Agra, Ahmedabad, and Broach. This was in 1619 when Tomas Roe returned to England. On the east coast they were still looking for areas where they could properly settle down. They set up a factory at Masulipatam, the greatest trading centre in the south in September, 1611. Yet situations were fluid for them. They were haunted by the competitions from the Dutch.

> The Dutch were increasingly becoming aggressive in southeast Asia. The massacre at Amboyna, which rankled in English minds for generations, occurred in 1623. Ten Englishmen and

nine Japanese were arrested on the charge of attempting to seize the Dutch Fort and murder the Governor, tortured and executed with great barbarity. Amboyna marked the virtual expulsion of the English from south-east Asia. They had only India to look to.[16]

The English were moving around. They moved to Petapoli, Armagaon, Pulicat, and areas on the Nellore coast. But nowhere could they settle down. Ultimately they found Madras and Calcutta, situated on a linear axis on the seaboard, as places where they could build up their settlements in the east. From here, these two harbour settlements, they could now administer their twin drives, one for territory and the other for maritime supremacy and commerce.

Notes

1. For details, see Ranjit Sen, *A Stagnating City: Calcutta in the Eighteenth Century*, Institute of Historical Studies, Calcutta, 2000, pp. 2–4.
2. For details of this point see Ranjit Sen, *Metamorphosis of the Bengal Polity, 1700–1793*, Ch. 1 & 2, Rabindra Bharati University, Calcutta, 1987.
3. J.B. Harrison, *Oxford History of India*, The Clarendon Press, Oxford, 1958, 3rd edn, reprint 1961, p. 333.
4. Ibid, pp. 333–334.
5. Ibid, p. 334.
6. Ibid.
7. Ibid.
8. S.M. Edwardes, *The Rise of Bombay: A Retrospect* (Volume X of the Census of India Series 1001, by order of the Government of Bombay), *Times of India Press*, Bombay, 1902, pp. 90–91.
9. Ibid, p. 91.
10. Ibid.
11. C.R. Boxer, in *Portugal and Brazil*, ed. H.V. Livermore, p. 223.
12. Harrison, *Oxford History of India*, p. 330.
13. Edwardes, *The Rise of Bombay*, p. 97.
14. N.S. Ramaswami, *The Founding of Madras*, Orient Longman, 1977, p. 13.
15. Ibid.
16. Ibid.

3

REVOLUTION ON THE RIVERBANK

A study of the creation of a mankind necessary for urbanization

The river

The Ganga has witnessed innumerable revolutions on its banks. Sparks of small revolutions combined to create conditions of big revolutions. The expulsion of the Portuguese from the bank of the Ganga in 1632 was necessary for the effective foundation of the Mughal rule in Bengal and then also for the growth of the British Empire in India with its seat of power in Calcutta. Likewise the breaking up of the French power in Chandernagore in 1757 through English bombardment was a pre-requisite for the creation of Bengal as a protectorate of the English, the nucleus of the future Empire. Between 1632 and 1757 Hugli was sacked thrice in 1632, 1686, and 1757) and that made the foundation and the consequent emergence of Calcutta as an important colonial town possible. Meanwhile the Mughal Empire in the north broke down and, in the first half of the eighteenth century, a line of almost independent *Nawabs* set up their autonomous rule in Bengal. The flow of up-country and central Asian administrators to Bengal ceased. This facilitated the rise of indigenous people and their infiltration into the administration. The Mughal Empire in Bengal set up a new bureaucracy of local origin. Meanwhile there was a very powerful drive to maximize revenue.[1] This arose out of the need both to explore and guard the interior. A new landed aristocracy was created in the process. A new bureaucracy and a new aristocracy thus emerged long before the battle of Palasi took place. After the Palasi, new experiments were attempted at by the English. In the process, they retained the aristocracy and discarded the bureaucracy. Hastings went into new collaborations – this time with base men.[2] A new service elite was created. Dhaka and Murshidabad sank. The old power elite of the Mughals also sank with them. Now emerged a new money elite, a typical representative of which was Raja Nabakrishna. Political revolutions and social revolutions went hand in hand and the result was the creation of a nucleus around which the modern Bengali race could grow.

This was a total revolution in which the Ganga played a very important role. The river provided a line of military mobilization for whosoever had the need of it. It affected an axis for commerce without which Bengal's participation in Asiatic trade would have been difficult. It was an escape route for the Portuguese in 1632 and for the English in 1686 and 1756. But by the eighteenth century it became clear that the incoming power from the west would stay in Bengal and that it had the nautical superiority necessary for the management of the sea. The Mughals in Bengal were certainly weak on the river and the sea. They built a structure of a vast land-army, but they failed to take the sea and the rivers into confidence. Thus when they tried to drive the Portuguese out of Hugli they brought heavy cannon from Dhaka. The Portuguese in their turn could not hold on to their posts in Hugli because their reinforcements from Goa could not reach them in time. But then the question arises: why did the Mughals fail to establish a proper connection with the river? This may be due to the fact that the Mughals were obsessed with the concept of land invincibility – a lesson they imbibed from the military experiences of Muslim rulers of the past and also of rulers in west Asia. There might be other reasons. The Ganga changed its course very often and they were uncertain about their naval headquarters.[3]

"The river's fluctuations," a commentator observes:

> remain unpredictable over any short length of the delta. The History of Rajmahal illustrates Ganga's power over the people of the littoral. In medieval times, the Muslim rulers moved their capital to Rajmahal. In the seventeenth century, it was filled with people and every kind of merchandise. Its port was jammed with vessels.[4] Toward the end of the century, the river shifted its course three miles eastward, whereupon the government and merchants abandoned it for Dhaka, almost two hundred miles away.[5] During the next century, the Ganges resumed its earlier course, and Rajmahal sprang to life once more. Again, in 1863, the channel shifted further east, and the city became "a mere aggregate of huts surrounded by ruins."[6] In 1880, the river returned to its old bed and the city regained its prosperity.[7]

There is no reason to believe that the English negotiated the river very well. Steven G. Darian writes: "Throughout the nineteenth century, British efforts to maintain a steamer channel from Calcutta north beyond Rajmahal met with repeated failure."[8] Darian's observations is supported by a surveyor's report of 1835. It says: "The extraordinary deviations annually occurring in the course of the Ganges, affecting as they did all the streams that flowed from it, rendered it impossible to lay down any fixed rule of guidance or plan of operations by which the navigation of Nadiya rivers could be permanently maintained."[9] Even at the beginning of the nineteenth century incredible changes were taking place in the course of the Ganga. Writing in 1803, H.T. Colebrook observed: "there are few places where a town, or village, can be established in the Ganges with any certainty of long retaining the advantage of such a situation."[10] Colebrook further reports: "In one part of the channel . . . where I expected to have met with the first shallows, I found from twenty to sixty feet in the very place where there had been a ford but two years before."[11] Then, in less than two years' time, further changes took place:

> A considerable portion of the main channel, which . . . had contained nearly the whole stream of the Ganges, was at the time I saw it so completely filled with sands that I hardly knew myself to be in the same part of the river. The sands, in some parts, rose several feet above the level of the stream, and the people had already begun to cultivate . . . rice, in the very spot where the deepest water had formerly been.[12]

L.S. O'Malley, who served as a district officer at the turn of the last century, vouchsafed the unpredictability of the Ganga's course. He reported that, during the rainy season, the river assumed a devastating form. It could then wash away an acre of land in half an hour.[13] The volume of water rises and sweeps away its banks. On the authority of O'Malley Darian writes: "As to mock its image as an eternal river, some of the islands in the Ganges, become inhabited, cleared, and cultivated; the population increases, large villages start up, the land revenue is collected for ten or twelve years, and then the whole fabric will disappear within one rainy season."[14]

The renaissance

This was then the river by the side of which the Bengali speaking people grew up in course of the last one millennium. In 1201[15] Muhammad

Bakhtiyar Khilji captured Nadia. In 1757 Clive defeated Siraj at the battle of Plassey. During this long period of 556 years, Bengal passed through various stages of political development under the rule of the west Asian, east African, and central Asian sultans. During these years Bengal was exposed to inner Asia and her cultural links were established with the core of the Muslim world. Yet this was the age that has been regarded as medieval in Bengal's history. Jadunath Sarkar commented: "On 23rd June, 1757, the middle ages of India ended and her modern age began."[16] Therefore, to him the battle of Palasi marked a watershed in Bengal's history. It marked the moment that ushered in a new age. He wrote in a very memorable passage his own feeling about this moment of change:

> When the sun dipped into the Ganges behind the blood-red field of Plassey, on that fateful evening of June, did it symbolize the curtain dropping on the last scene of a tragic drama? Was that day followed by "a night of eternal gloom for India," as the poet of Plassey imagined Mohan Lal foreboding from the ranks of the losers? Today the historian, looking backward over the two centuries that have passed since then, knows that it was the beginning, slow and unperceived, of a glorious dawn, the like of which the history of the world has not seen elsewhere.[17]

This dawn was the consummation of a process that had been working down the ages which Sir Jadunath summed as the "Middle Ages" of Bengal. The historian was not unaware of this. He wrote:

> Has not Bengal, unknown to herself, been working through the ages to reach this consummation? Her storied past . . . shows how the diverse limbs of the country and warring tribes and sects of the people were fused into one by the silent working of time and a common political life till at the end of the Muslim period a Bengali people had become a reality. But not yet a Bengali *nation*, for the pre-requisites of a nation were then wanting. Two centuries of British rule and the neighbouring example of British society have now ground down large sections of the Bengali people to that uniformity of life and thought which alone can create a nation. It is for the future to perfect this good work.[18]

Thus the achievement of the Middle Ages is the creation of an articulated existence of the Bengali people. The historian was visualizing a journey from the articulation of a people to the formation of a nation. To this end he wrote:

> In June, 1757, we crossed the frontier and entered into a great new world to which a strange destiny had led Bengal. Today in October 1947 we stand on the threshold of the temple of Freedom just opened to us. May the course of the years 1757 to 1947 have prepared us for the Supreme stage of our political evolution and helped to mould us truly into a nation. May our future be the fulfilment of our past history.[19]

Sarkar's view was thus clear. What sank in 1757, he thought, was not Bengal's independence but simply Bengal's Middle Ages. This means that the British age that seems to have started that year must be thought of not in the immediate perspective of foreign occupation, but in a broad and long-term historical perspective as a process of growth. Throughout the last 1,000 years the Bengali people had been growing and in the process of its growth it experienced foreign invasions, underwent foreign rule, and yet maintained their own distinct existence by observing all their abiding ethos. The art historian Percy Brown once said that "the country, originally possessed by the invaders, now possessed them."[20] Bengal was conquered by the Turks, the Arabs, the Afghans, and the Habshis, but at the end she conquered them all in her own turn. In this story of conquest and reconquest the Ganga played a part. Most of the capitals of kingdoms in Bengal perhaps barring one, Dacca, were situated on the Ganga. Ghulam Hussain Salim[21] says that Sulaiman Karrani found that Gaur's climate was unhealthy. It was unsuitable for large and growing populations. Hence he transferred the capital to a nearby place called Tanda (the Afghan Capital) which was 15 miles south-east of Malda towns.[22] Tanda, Gaur, Monghyr (a temporary capital during the time of *Nawab* Bir Qasim), Murshidabad, and Calcutta were all situated on the bank of the Ganga. The nucleus of empire-building and kingdom-formations in Bengal mostly began on the banks of the Ganga. The Indo-Turkish rule in Bengal was based at Nadia, the Mughal rule first at Tanda and then at the moment of rejuvenation at Murshidabad and the British at the outset in Calcutta.[23] It is because of this that the historian uses the dipping of the sun at the Ganga as a symbol for the passing away of the Middle Ages.

The Middle Ages in Bengal's history long before its symbolic sinking into the Ganga sent signals of the forthcoming Renaissance in Bengal's history. These signals were transmitted from the time of the Mughal conquest of Bengal. The historian writes: "Mughal conquest opened for Bengal a new era of peace and progress."[24] This peace was the precursor of the English renaissance. The historian adds further: "The renaissance which we owe to English rule early in the 19th century had a precursor, – a faint glimmer of dawn, no doubt, – two hundred and fifty years earlier. 'These were the fruits, the truly glorious fruits, of Mughal peace.' "[25]

Apprenticeship in governance

Thus the renaissance in Bengal was a process of more than 400 years. How did this renaissance come about? It came through an administrative grinding and religious awakening.

> Todor Mal's organization of the State revenue service had forced the Hindu clerks and account-keepers to learn the Persian language, in which all records of this department had henceforth to be written. In Bengal Todar Mal's elaborate land system (*zbati*) was never applied; but ambitious local Hindus and Muslims (of both of whom the mother tongue was Bengali) were now forced to learn the Persian language in order to get some share in the vastly extended secretarial work of the Mughal provincial administration. In Bengal, the State revenue was collected through middlemen or *zamindars* in the lump (and not as in upper India from the cultivators directly): hence the accounts were kept in Bengali (the sole language of the peasantry and of the army of local revenue underlings), and therefore, before the Mughal conquest very few Bengalis had any occasion to learn Persian. Under Mughal rule the higher posts in the revenue, accounts and secretariat departments were reserved for Muslims and Hindus from upper India, such as Khatris from the Punjab and Agra and Lalas from the U.P. It was only when Murshid Quli Khan established a local dynasty in Bengal that these high posts passed into the hands of Bengalis, many of whom were Hindus well versed in Persian composition. Unlike the independent Sultans of Bengal, the constantly changing subahdars of the Mughal times had no occasion to learn Bengali, and hence the agents (*Vakils*) of the local *zamindars* at their Courts had to be masters of Persian. Gradually (and notably in the 18th century) Persian culture infiltrated from the Subahdar's Court to that of the great Hindu Rajas – such as those of Nadia

and Burdwan. This is best illustrated by the varied learning of Bharat Chandra Ray Gunakar, the Court poet of Nadia.[26]

In the seventeenth century thus the up-country *khatris* and *baniyas* came to Bengal. The eighteenth century was the period of the rise of the Hindu Bengalis. This rise of the Bengalis truly speaking began from the late seventeenth century. The Mughal Empire in Bengal was consolidating itself. After Shova Singh's revolt in 1696, this consolidation became all the more necessary. The Portuguese had become ineffective in Bengal politics, but the age had ushered in new activities for the French, British, and the Dutch. Revenue was to be overhauled. The *faujdaris* had to be harnessed. The revolt of Shova Singh[27] could become devastating because there was no *faujdar*[28] to maintain the security of western Bengal. The *faujdar* of Jessore had to mobilize his forces to suppress the revolt. Later on Bengal was divided into innumerable *faujdaris* or military districts. Thus in the eighteenth century there were *faujdars* at Midnapur, Malda, Hughli, Chitpur, Sylhet, Chittagong, Jessore, Rajmahal,[29] and so on. The flotilla was to be vamped and zamindaris had to be readjusted. In the age of the Sultanate the demand for administrative personnel was not so great.

> But the Mughal provincial administration was so much more developed than that of the foregoing Sultans and ramified into so many branches with the advance of civilization, that an adequate number of hands could not be imported from upper India, and a large number of Bengalis had to be employed in its middle ranks, and these had to master the Persian language as a qualification for office. Thus Persian literature and a special school of Sufi poetry spread in Bengali Hindu society no less than in Muslim.[30]

From trade to land via corridor of power: creation of the seat for a new capital

This was how a community came to grow on the bank of the Ganga. From the sixteenth century to the nineteenth, this community consisting of the people of the Bengali speaking race showed a particular trend of growth. This was a trend from trade to land through the media of power. Towards end of the sixteenth century, the Bengalis lost their sea-faring initiatives – their maritime trade ventures to the upcountry people[31] – the people from Rajasthan who gradually formed the most influential capitalist class in the whole of eastern India, particularly in the Bengal *Subah*. The Jagat Seths, the state bankers in the

REVOLUTION ON THE RIVERBANK

days of the *Nawabi* administration, came from this class. Throughout the seventeenth till the middle of the eighteenth century, the *sarrafs*[32] who supplied credit to the agrarian world of Bengal came from this stock of mankind in Bengal. As the Bengalis lost their command over the external trade of the country to the people of Rajasthan, they developed their skill in different other directions – first as an effective bureaucracy under the Mughals, then as power brokers in the age of the formation of the British Empire in eastern India starting with the pre-Palasi conspiracy, acting further as native capitalists represented by the *banians*, growing eventually as entrepreneurs under the leadership of men like Ramdulal De and Dwarakanath Tagore, recoiling after the fall of the Union Bank in 1848 as landlords and real estate owners and finally emerging as nationalist agitators at the end of the nineteenth century. In this evolution they helped the city of Calcutta grow as a full-fledged urban settlement comparable only to London.

From the foundation of the Hindu College in 1817 to the upsurge of 1857 there intervened a peace of four decades during which two developments had concurrently occurred on the river banks – an educated Bengali literati grew and native capital selected Calcutta as its seat of accumulation. The second event became the subject of a celebrated book *Kalikata Kamalalaya* by Bhabani Charan Bandopadhyaya. Published in 1823, this book celebrated the rise of Calcutta as a seat of capital formation in the days of the early advent of capitalism in India. The Bengali community that had been assuming shape on the bank of the river turned out to be the early suppliers of capital to the first generation of Englishmen who were busy articulating the configuration of the Empire. N.K. Sinha writes: "So long as the agency houses did not develop, the *banians* acted as agents and middlemen for the East India Company's servants and British free merchants."[33] S. Bhattacharya says that they continued to be the suppliers of capital till the middle of the nineteenth century.[34]

The point to be noted here is that a community was steadily growing on the bank of the river that adjusted itself with the twists and turns of the river on the one hand and, on the other, it adapted with its whole spirit to the revolutions of the state and time.

A competent capitalist class diverted from industry to land: a new urbanism of property and wealth

Without the growth of this community the rise of Calcutta would not have taken place. Cornwallis was aware that a very competent class of capitalists had grown on the banks of the Ganga who might finance the industrial revolution that was taking place at Fort Gloster Budge Budge. Thus a new competitor of the Industrial Revolution of England was in the offing at the bank of the river Ganga that could have posed a barrier to the influx of capitalism in India. To prevent this growth he introduced the Permanent Settlement in 1793 thus converting the Mughal *zamindars* into prototypes of British landlords. He himself confessed: "There is every ground to expect that the large capitals possessed by the natives which they have no means of employing when the public debt is discharged will be applied to the purchase of landed property as soon as the tenure is declared to be secured."[35] Commenting on this N.K. Sinha writes: "He (Cornwallis) gradually closed all other avenues to this class of capitalists who naturally turned their attention to land. This was the 'new productive principle' which he brought into operation."[36]

The Permanent Settlement was thus used as a supportive base for the foundation and growth of Calcutta. Once zamindari became a very profitable unit of property wealthy persons of the Bengali community rushed into invest their prosperity in land. In the first twenty-five years of the Permanent Settlement, innumerable zamindaris broke down because of large revenue pressures from the state. Their splinters were put on sale so that a very big land market emerged in eastern India in course of the nineteenth century. Splinters of truncated zamindaris became new attractions for Bengali capitalists and as zamindaris proliferated there was a rush among all successful *zamindars* and merchants in the interior and the city to purchase real estate properties in the city of Calcutta.[37]

This was how a new city grew on new property orientations set by the state. Land legislations and capital deployment thus became two complementary parameters of city formation. The early fishermen and weavers who were the original inhabitants of the city had little potentiality to match themselves with the change of time. The Seths, the Basaks, and the Malliks who had once provided the mercantile leadership to the community now gave way to Ram Dulal De on the one hand and Raja Nabakrishna on the other – men who had represented the crest of the Bengali community at the beginning of its colonial ascendancy. In *Kalikata Kamalalay* a visitor from rural Bengal interrogates his urban host as to the new *achara* – the new way of life – the Hindus were practising in the city. The traditional Hindu code of conduct, he argued, had become a matter of indifference in the city.

> How is it, he (the rustic visitor) wonders, echoing rumours circulating in the outback, that they all dress like foreigners

in Calcutta, eat meals prepared for them by Muslim cooks, drink brandy on ritual occasions, ignore shastric literature published in Bangla, and read nothing other than what is available in English and Persian.[38]

The Bengali society living in the villages looked with a sense of awe at the changes the urban Bengali society had gone through. The townsman's response to the queries of the village guest was a fatuous attempt at self-defence:

> The resident townsman tries to allay these fears as best as he can. Villagers have been misinformed about life in the city, he suggests. Yes; there are some Hindus who have been affected by those new ways, he admits, but by and large the older tradition is still in fact amongst the higher castes.[39]

The clash of culture was thus manifestly clear. The city of Calcutta was building up a world of new culture where it was said that *Kamaladevi*, the goddess of wealth, resided. A temporality had emerged which was commensurate with the ideology of a new urban uplift of the city. Ranajit Guha comments:

> In reassuring his interlocutor thus, he (the townsman) was no doubt voicing the opinion of the conservative elements amongst the city elite, of whom the author was himself a leading representative. But the fact that such reassurance was at all called for is important. It speaks of changing times, indeed of changes indexed in popular perception, with the advent of a new temporality rivalling one that was habitual and sanctified by custom.[40]

Birth of a collaborating humanity

Man, mind, and the city were thus moving as the three clustered parts of one process that was ushering in an urbanity in the eastern bank of the Ganga. Calcutta was not only a city emerging out of the complex of three villages, the human mind of this transforming habitation also changed from the inhibitions of customary social life bred in the bounds of Bengal's rusticity. From the middle of the eighteenth century, mud huts and thatched cottages were giving place to brick-built houses. The change was slow but perceptible. The officers of the company were switching over to Garden houses at far-flung areas of the city. The process started immediately after the battle of Palasi. That was also the time when the Company's personnel were trying to get rid of their cramped living in a fort-centric existence and were moving much beyond the rampart of the fort called Esplanade to explore new habitations along the Chowringhee. The city was opening its space to absorb a bigger flow of humanity from the countryside. With populations shifting from the villages to the city here in Calcutta business burgeoned to allure more and more men from outside – this time not only from interior villages but also from distant places in the west in a continuous stretch along the river. This helped the city to become cosmopolitan. The population of the city thus presented a peculiar admixture – on the one hand it was cosmopolitan because white men along with Indians of various places and diverse callings got merged in a confluence while, on the other, men from various strata of life varying from *zamindars* and rich merchants to destitute workers and domestic menials added to the heterogeneity of the city crowd.

This was the crowd fit to provide the human base for a city to take off. The city regulators in this crowd were the *banians* whose economic solvency placed them at the core of an upcoming mankind that had suffered a metamorphosis. The Bengali race which the city found in its midst at the time of its inception was not a poor humanity. *Zamindars*, rich merchants, and *banians* had settled here with their supportive agency personnel. They formed the upper crust of the society which acted as cushions to all efforts toward urbanization. The colonial city also had at its formative phase a lower human base consisting of domestic menials, construction workers (termed as *coolies* in the records), fishermen, weavers whom the Company's administration had settled in the city and so on. They provided the work force which the city had immensely utilized for its own uplift. These men eventually were kept in native ghettos and slums where they lived as humanity marooned within the structures of affluence around. With all these the composition of the city habitation was changing slowly toward a heterogeneity and cosmopolitanism without which the metropolitan character of the city would not have manifested. It took nearly 100 years since the battle of Palasi to streamline this population as a composite humanity to be in the service of the city. In the *Kalikata Kamalalaya* the urban entity of the population was still a little shaky vis-à-vis the interrogation coming from the amazed mind of a villager. By the middle of the nineteenth century, this phase of shaky confidence was over and the city could switch over to new ethos of life. Ranajit Guha says that the language of *kalikata Kamalalaya* showed elements of

> a judgemental, reticent prose still not fully involved in the life of a colonial city at its formative phase. With the phase decisively over by the middle of the century, Calcutta was to celebrate its coming of age in writing adequate to the surge of its urban ethos. Far from holding back, it would spill over into the streets, join the crowds, and defy the over-Sanskritized sensibilities of the literati by adopting the mode of every day speech as its vehicle.[41]

The text which brought the city ethos into literary prominence was *Hutom Pyanchar Naksha* published in 1861[42] – thirty-eight years after *Kalikata Kamalaya* saw its light. In course of these thirty-eight years a revolution had taken place. Persian had been replaced by English as the official language in the country. The language of the colonial masters had now become the vehicle of the new regime. It was both 'an instrument of dominance and an agency of persuation'[43] and was used very successfully to transform a people emerging from their village shelters into the openness of a city life. A powerful international medium of expression, the English language was transforming a localized people into a mass exposed to a global culture, which fit in their mentality to receive the incoming parameters of capitalism from the west. This was a revolution in true sense of the term. Capitalism from the west came on the crest of imperialism and vice versa and imperialism created its own culture through the medium of its own language.

"As the language of the rulers," Ranajit Guha writes,

> it [English] stood for all that set them conspicuously apart from the mass of their subjects, who spoke only in the local tongues. Yet, at the same time, as the principal medium of an officially sponsored education (which had, by then, come to mean English style education, according to Bankimchandra Chatterjee), it was the means used by the Raj to induce a very small, but affluent and socially powerful, minority amongst the colonized to favour collaboration.[44]

What is significant is that, in the first century of British rule in India, the people at the riverside transformed itself into a mature humanity so as to adapt its capacity and functions to the role of collaborating promoters of the new age. When a city comes up, it requires its human foundation without which it cannot grow. In the case of Calcutta, the growth of its human potential was indeed a revolution manifesting in stages and perfecting itself with every experience of change.

Trade, market, and artisan economy

In a recent writing, the indigenous origin of Calcutta has been traced in some appreciable detail, but nowhere in the essay is a reference made to a riverside humanity which had the potentiality for urban uplift and growth.[45] A wide region in south Bengal, it has been asserted, had been growing with potentiality of markets originating out of long distance riverine and overseas trade. The growth of this trade-based market regions, our author says, had been a phenomenon taking shape between the fifteenth and the eighteenth centuries. This was the time when the internal and foreign trade of Bengal was being linked to the wider vistas of the expanding Asian trade. Bengal's greatest export commodity of the time was cotton goods and articles of textile. Centring around the Bay of Bengal, the coastal and the oceanic trade created conditions for market-based towns in the region. These towns were truly a speaking outgrowth of some villages where an artisan economy had begun to predominate over agriculture. Kalikata, Sutanuti, and Govindapur were three such villages where weavers and their textile yields created momentum for urban growth.[46] Trade, market, and artisan economy have thus been considered as propelling factors behind the rudiments of urban growth that some parts of southern Bengal had been experiencing between the fifteenth and the eighteenth centuries. This might have created a mercantile humanity who had stakes in trade deployment. Such a mankind has not been credited with attachment to internal governance, so much so that, in the long run, it could emerge as a power elite transforming eventually into a money elite as it did in the eighteenth century. It finally into a collaborating humanity coordinating and cooperating with a new historical paradigm, namely empire-building. This transformation of a riverside took place when the sleepy world of the traditional interior crashed at the approach of ships, navy, crew of merchants, and rush of bullion from the west that had exposed the agrarian economy of Bengal to the winds of global maritime and mercantile changes. Uttara Chakraborty, our author, tried to trace the antiquity of the Calcutta region to a shadowy past – to the time of the Greek treatise *Periplus of the Erythrean Sea*, to the writings of Ptolemy and to Dhoyi's Sanskrit text *Pavanadutam*. With a great stretch of imagination, the expression 'Ganga' used by Ptolemy as a port,

REVOLUTION ON THE RIVERBANK

Chandraketugarh (Berachampa) thirty-five kilometres to the north of present Kolkata, and *Badudya* (modern Baduria near Basirhat in the North twenty-four Parganas) referred to in *Manasavijaya* by Bipradas Piplai have been clubbed in one running narrative story to indicate the indigenous past of Calcutta and its surrounding region. References to settlements in ancient texts do not provide us with substantial historical evidence about the potentiality of the urban origin of a region. True, lower Bengal being the site of the confluence of the Ganga with the ocean saw the growth of many settlements where trade thrived as a potentially functioning factor of growth. In any case with the changes in the course of the river the rise and decline of settlements had been a common feature in the changing history of riverine Bengal. But in no settlement in the past has history witnessed, at any given time, the rise of a community that could act as the human base for an empire. This happened in the region consisting of the three villages of Kalikata, Sutanuti, and Gobindapur with territories adjacent and around.

The growth of a community with human potential necessary for urban growth is a work of history processed through time. The growth of the Bengali community in and around Calcutta was an outcome of history unfolding over the last five or six centuries and culminating into the creation of a people that could perform in a double role as a functioning elite in governance and a collaborating partner in the process of empire-building. The emergence of the Bengalis as a humanity attached to governance was an outcome of the Muslim rule in Bengal. From the time of Murshid Quli Khan, the Bengalis started manning the bureaucracy, and consequently they emerged as a power elite sharing governance in the corridor of power. The power elite was essentially groomed as a service elite which, being inducted into partnership with the rulers, eventually turned into a power elite. As time went on the Mughal rule in Bengal degenerated into a functioning chaos so that the military aristocracy that had always found itself stationed at the core of the Mughal governing system turned out to be a broken reed on which it was difficult to rely. The Indo-Islamic partnership which was so uniquely orchestrated during the rule of the Sultans and the early Mughals came to be distorted and disorganized under the later *Nawabs*.

Hindu Bengalis that had so long manned the administration were now suddenly called upon to balance a precarious *Nizamat*[47] with the demands of change. Pressing hard on the land and land-revenue system of the country that had already gone to disarray, the forces of change had ruined both agriculture and finance of the country.[48] Out of this crisis of governance, a Bengali mankind had emerged as the only stable element of human force on which the transformation of the age could find its new foundation. From the time of the Sultans to the time of Murshid Quli Khan's *Mal Zamini* system (1722), this human force had steadily adapted itself to the ethos of governance and the etiquette of the rulers. Away from the military way of life in which the Muslim rulers were so adept, the Hindu Bengalis had developed their own context to grow as a Civilian population uninterrupted in their position as partners to rulers. Some years ago, I wrote: "Adapting for centuries to the culture of their masters the Bengalis had learn the art of adaptation very well. Martial vigour was never a curriculum in this art of adaptation. Warfare had never been in their ways. Techniques of battle they had never learnt. The result was catastrophic."[49] In 1905 when Bengal was partitioned, the partnership between the state and the society came to an end. The humanity that had evolved over centuries from the community of fisherman to a very powerful makers of a civil society collapsed into an ineffectual house of nationalist agitators. Within a decade, the capital was shifted from Calcutta to Delhi. The city which was destined to parallel London began to decay.

Notes

1 For details, see Ranjit Sen, (i) *Economics of Revenue Maximization in Bengal 1757–1793*, Nalanda Publication Pvt. Ltd., Calcutta, 1988, and (ii) *Property, Aristocracy and the Raj*, Maha Bodhi Book Agency, Calcutta, 2010, and also see Jadunath Sarker, ed., *History of Bengal*, Vol. II, University of Dacca, Dacca, 1948.
2 For fuller exposition of the point, see Ranjit Sen, *New Elite and New Collaboration: A Study in Social Transformation in Bengal in the Eighteenth Century*, Papyrus, Calcutta, 1985.
3 See K. Bagchi, *The Ganges Delta*, University of Calcutta, Calcutta, 1944, pp. 39–40; Steven G. Darian, *The Ganges in Myth and History*, The University Press of Hawaii, Honolulu, 1978, pp. 135–136, Radhakamal Mukherjee, *The Changing Fate of Bengal*, Calcutta, 1938, pp. 79–80; S.C. Majumdar, *Rivers of the Bengal Delta*, University of Calcutta, Calcutta, 1941, pp. 123–124.
4 Sebastian Manrique, *The Travels of Sebastian Manrique*, London, 1926–27, Vol. 2, p. 135.
5 Jean Tavernier, *Travels in India*, London, 1925, Vol. I, p. 102.
6 Elisee Reclus, *The Earth and Its Inhabitants*, Vol. 3: India and China, London, 1884, p. 226.
7 Darian, *The Ganges in Myth and History*, pp. 136–137.
8 Ibid, p. 137.
9 W.W. Hunter, *A Statistical Account of Bengal*, London, 1875, Vol. 2, p. 27.
10 H.T. Colebrook, "On the Course of the Ganges Through Bengal", *Asiatick Researches* 8 (1803): 2 quoted in Darian, *The Ganges in Myth and History*, p. 137.

11 Ibid, p. 21.
12 Ibid, p. 20, quoted in Darian, *The Ganges in Myth and History*, p. 137.
13 Darian, *The Ganges in Myth and History*, p. 137.
14 Ibid, pp. 137–138. Darian quotes from Observation by Captain Sherwill recorded in L.S.S. O'Malley, *Bengal District Gazetteers: Murshidabad*, Calcuta, 1914, p. 6.
15 This date has been given by Dr. Kalika Ranjan Qanungo in Jadunath Sarkar, ed., *History of Bengal*, Dacca, second impression, 1972 of the first 1948 edn, pp. 4 & 32, Richard M. Eaton (in his *The Rise of Islam and the Bengal Frontier, 1204–1760*, Oxford University Press, New Delhi, 1997, p. 23) gives the date as 1204.
16 Sarkar, *History of Bengal*, p. 497.
17 Ibid.
18 Ibid, pp. 498–499.
19 Ibid.
20 Percy Brown, *Indian Architecture, Islamic Period*, 5th edn, D.B. Taraporevala, Bombay, 1968, p. 38 quoted in Eaton, *The Rise of Islam and the Bengal Frontier 1204–1760*, p. 70.
21 In his *Riyazu-s-Salatin: A History of Bengal*, trans. by Abdus Salam, 1903, Reprint, Idarah-i-Adabiyat-I, New Delhi, 1975, p. 152.
22 See Sarkar, *History of Bengal*, pp. 181–182 & Eaten, *The Rise of Islam and the Bengal Frontier 1204–1760*, p. 142.
23 The history of Bengal's capitals has not been written till date. See Utpal Chakraborty, *Vilupta Rajdhani* (Thw Lost Capital), Amar Bharati, 8-C, Tamer Lane Kalkata 9, 1978.
24 Sarkar, *History of Bengal*, p. 188.
25 Ibid, p. 189 Akbar defeated Daud Karrani in 1575.
26 Sarkar, *History of Bengal*, p. 223.
27 For the revolt of Shova Singh, see Sarkar, *History of Bengal*, Vol. II, Muslim Period 1200–1757, University of Dacca (1948), Second Impression, July, 1972, pp. 391–396. How this revolt helped the rise of Calcutta has been discussed in Ranjit Sen, *A Stagnating City Calcutta in the Eighteenth Century*, Institute of Historical Studies, Calcutta, 2000, pp. 2–4, 8, 11, 48–50, 56, 89–90.
28 For *faujdars* in Bengal, see Ranjit Sen, *Metamorphosis of the Bengal Polity, 1700–1793*, Rabindra Bharati University, Calcutta, 1987, pp. 162–165.
29 For Rajmahal, see Eaton, *The Rise of Islam and the Bengal Frontier, 1204–1760*, Oxford University Press, Delhi, Calcutta, Chennai, Mumbai, 1997, pp. 138, 148, 149, 150, 167, 171.
30 Sarkar, *History of Bengal*, pp. 223–224.
31 Blair B. Kling, discussed this point in "Economic Foundations of the Bengal Renaissance" in Rachel Van M. Baumer, Vikas Publishing House Pvt. Ltd, New Delhi, pp. 26–42.
32 For Sarrafs in Bengal, see Sen, *Metamorphosis of the Bengal Polity, 1700–1793*, pp. 209–235.
33 N.K. Sinha, *The Economic History of Bengal*, Firma K.L. Mukhopadhyay, Calcutta, 1965, Vol. I, p. 101.
34 S. Bhattacharya in Ch. III, section 2, sub-section I in Dharma Kumar, ed. *Cambridge Economic History of India*, Vol. 2, c. 1757–c. 1970, Orient Longman in association with Cambridge University Press, 1982, 1984 Reprint.

35 Cited in Sinha, *Economic History*, Vol. I, p. 5.
36 Ibid.
37 This point has been thoroughly discussed in Pradip Sinha in his *Calcutta in Urban History* Firma KLM Private Ltd., Calcutta, 1978, pp. 140–159. There he has given in detail the real estate properties of opulent Bengalis of the time.
38 This is how Ranajit Guha paraphrases the queries of the rural interrogator in his book *The Small Voice of History: Collected Essays*, ed. and with an introduction by Partha Chatterjee, Permanent Black, Ranikhet, 2009, pp. 411–412.
39 Guha, *The Small Voice of History*, pp. 412.
40 Ibid.
41 Ibid, pp. 412–413.
42 Hutom Pyanchar Naksha, written by Kaliprasanna Sinha, has been translated by Swarup Roy under the title *The Observant Owl*, Black Kite, New Delhi, 2008.
43 Guha, *The Small Voice of History*, p. 413.
44 Ibid.
45 Uttara Chakraborty, "Gram Govindapur, Kalikata, Sutanuti: Shahar Kolkatar Upakhyanmala" (village Govindapur, Kalikata, Sutanuti: Anecdotes of City Calcutta) in Saumitra Sreemani, ed. *Kalikata Kolkata*, Bangiya Itihas Samiti, Calcutta, 2015, pp. 88–106.
46 Chakraborty, "Gram Govindapur, Kalikata, Sutanuti", pp. 91–92. For understanding the general model of commerce-based towns see Om Prakash, *European Commercial Enterprise in Pre-colonial India*, Cambridge University Press, 2000, pp. 8, 12–13, 18, 21, 22; C.A. Bayly, *Rulers, Townsmen and Bazars*, Oxford University Press, pp. 55–56.
47 The Mughal provincial administration was divided into two parts – *Nizamat* and *diwani*. The *Nizamat* had two departments – the criminal justice and army. Dewani was made of civil justice and land and land-revenue departments. Thus the Nazim or the Nawab had an army but no money. The Diwan had money but no army. Hence neither of them could revolt against Delhi. This system of cheeks and balance was maintained under the Mughal provincial administration.
48 For changes in the Bengal land and land revenue system, see Sinha, *Economic History of Bengal*, Vol. II, Calcutta, 1968; F.D. Ascoli, *Early Revenue History of Bengal and the Fifth Report*, Oxford, 1917; B.H. Baden-Powell, *The Land System of British India*, 3 vols. Oxford, 1892; Rai M.N. Gupta Bahadur, *Land System of Bengal*, University of Calcutta, Calcutta, 1943.
49 Ranjit Sen, "Anatomy of a Pensive Momen : 1905", in *The Quarterly Review of Historical Studies*, Vol. XLIII, October 2003 to March 2004, Nos. 3 & 4.

4
GEOPOLITICS OF EARLY URBANIZATION IN CALCUTTA 1698–1757

Understanding the nature of geopolitics

The selection of Calcutta[1] as a site for the settlement of the English East India Company in Bengal toward the end of the seventeenth century and its urbanization as the imperial city of the east in the eighteenth century were determined by geopolitics.[2] The Company's authority from the beginning wanted Calcutta to grow in three major aspects. Firstly, Calcutta was to grow, though not in its intrinsic capacity as a port town because its potentiality as a port had not been explored then. It was to grow as a garrison town[3] which would provide security to the English factories and trade engagements around and function as an outpost for Madras, the major British centre of power in India and the fort settlement from where a direct and uninterrupted seaboard connection with Calcutta could be maintained. Secondly, it was to grow as an English estate insulated from *Nawabi* interference from Hughli, the greatest of the *faujdari* power centres in western Bengal situated on the other side of the river which also acted as the greatest *Nawabi* custom house overseeing the seabound commerce in southern and western Bengal.[4] A garrison town and an insulated estate with territory and power Calcutta later developed for itself the necessary parameters of a port.[5] This is how the configurations of an imperial town and the future capital of an empire grew. Thirdly, Calcutta was to grow as a replica of London so as to serve as the effective eastern halt for the east-moving Britons. To this last aspect almost all the governors-general in India up to the revolt of 1857 directed their attention.

The geopolitics of Calcutta's urbanization was determined by two things: the situation around Calcutta[6] of the *faujdaries* of Chitpur,[7] Hughli,[8] Murshidabad,[9] Malda,[10] Balasore,[11] and Rajmahal[12] on the one hand, and the close vigilance imposed by the *Nawabs* of Bengal on the activities of the English Company in this part of the country on the other.[13] The *Nawabs* maintained two watch-posts on Calcutta – one was the *faujdari* at Chitpur adjacent to Calcutta on land on the same bank of the river as Calcutta was situated, and the other was at Hughli on the west bank of the river at a site almost opposite of Calcutta that was easily communicable by river. The result was that the English in Calcutta was almost quarantined. All their attempts to acquire land around Calcutta was thwarted by the *Nawabs*, and Calcutta could not grow territorially for nearly sixty years since the first acquisition of the three villages of Kalikata, Sutanuti and Govindapur in 1698.[14] The English urge to build up their Calcutta possessions as an acquired land-estate failed. An estate was necessary for stationing a garrison and, in an age of turmoil, a garrison was a prerequisite for consolidating their commercial position vis-à-vis other European companies and the interference from the *Nizamat*, which was the most dreadful thing to the English. They started building their fort very early in their career in Bengal,[15] but that was also interrupted by the opposition of all *Nawabs* from Murshid Quli Khan to Sirajuddallah. The Bengal *Nawabs* were determined to impose their prohibitions on the military and territorial ambitions of the Company whereas the latter was adamant not to succumb to the restrictive wills of the *Nawabs* that would paralyze their potentials for military and territorial growth. The geopolitics of urbanization grew out of these two antithetical forces of the time.

The *Nawabs* of Bengal were always under the suspicion that, under the pretext of urbanizing Calcutta, the English Company would promote their fortification. In 1720 a friction arose between the Government and the Company on the score of urbanizing the city. The *faujdar* of Hughli brought to the notice of the *Nawab* that the English had secretly undertaken some constructions in Calcutta. "The real ground of this complaint," went the English version of the case,

> is nothing more than a handsome road we were designing to make on the southernmost part of our bounds, on a direct line so as to keep the country open and clear for levelling of which we were obliged to make a small ditch for the earth which they out of disgust or ill nature have termed an entrenchment though nothing more than what a horse may leap over, this being a general benefit for the free passage of the air through the whole town would have been made at the expense of our merchants etc. inhabitants.

The *Nawab*'s fear was that, reports an English consultation, "we were building outworks and casting up trenches round our towns."[16] Under order from the government the Company's administration had to stop the work and fill up the trenches which were dug up. Instead of digging trenches the Company now adopted separate defence measures. It built barracks made of bamboos and straw and this was done, they wrote, to keep "out guards to secure our inhabitants" and also to "show the government we are fixed in our defence"[17] This was where the geopolitics had come to play to retard Calcutta's urbanization. The English were is no mood to submit tamely to the caprices of the *Nawabs* and the latter were in no mood to allow their over-mighty foreign subjects to overshadow their sovereignty.[18] Between these two irascible moods there was no compromise.

In order to diversify their business, the Company's administration in the second and third decades of the eighteenth century were trying to open new factories in the interior or to renovate the old ones, particularly at places like Dhaka, Malda, Lakhipur [Lakshmipur] and so on. This caused a drain on the Company's exchequer. The more the Company geared its activities the more was the fear of the *Nawabs* that the Company was clandestinely extending its enclaves in the country. From this arose the tendency on the part of the *Nawabs* to squeeze the English so that a part of the profit they reaped from their expanding business might be extracted as a price of the protection they received from the Government.

Under stress of geopolitics town planning was secondary

The whole attention of the Company's administration in Calcutta was, therefore, riveted not on town planning as a deliberate measure for urbanizing the city but on measures necessary for meeting eventualities. The Company addressed itself to twin aims – commerce and defence so much so that the internal promotion of the city as a place of human habitation suffered. A town planning required a solvency on the part of the town administration which the Company's Government in Calcutta did not have at this time. The bullion market in Bengal was then controlled by the Jagat Setts and the Company was dependent on the house of these *sarrafs* for the supply of bullion they required for minting money. Moreover the *Setts* were the custodians of the royal mints. The Company was trying to gain an access to the mints outside the control of the Setts. This they failed to achieve. Thus in 1724 when the *Nawab* demanded a huge sum of money from the Company the latter informed the *faujdar* of Hughli that they would pay Rupees 40,000 to the *Nawab* provided he allowed them a free use of the mint and a permission, to build their house at Hughli and settle their factory at Malda.[19] These were all strategic bargains in the geopolitics of the time. Mint, bullion, factory, and commercial houses – all thus became entangled as stakes in issues of governance on the one hand and power, politics, and business rolled into one on the other.

The Company's insistence on strategic installations and other security measures including the building of a fort and digging trenches was prompted by three major experiences. The first experience was one of belligerence: the war between the Mughals and the English Company, which took place between the years 1686 and 1690. The vicissitudes of the war drove home the lesson that the English were no match for the Mughals in land war. Therefore, they needed to take the sea into confidence and build up a command over the river that provided passage to the sea. The English were still unstable in Calcutta and they needed their connection with the rear command at Fort St. David at Madras to remain unsnapped. Calcutta having been situated nearly at the mouth of the sea, it required building its own capacity to thwart any offensive from Hughli which might take place in the event of a breakdown of relations with the Government. This urge to create in Calcutta an advanced strategic base for Madras left no room for the Calcutta Council to go for a planned undertaking of urbanization of the town.

The second experience which came as an eye-opener to the English was the revolt of Shova Singh in 1696–1698. This revolt took place over a vast area of west Bengal including Midnapur, Burdwan, and adjoining places. At that time the *Nawabi* defence in west Bengal was weak. Only one single *faujdar* from Jessore looked over the entire security of the area. Taking advantage of this weakness of the government, Shova Singh, a local zamindar of Midnapur, threw off the *Nawabi* yoke and carved a small but an independent kingdom for himself. This lesson of might being the logic for justifying action was never forgotten by the English, and ever since they acquired their foothold in the Calcutta territories they tried, heart and soul, for promoting their might which, they knew, alone could ensure survival in an age of turmoil. In the early years of its career, Calcutta's fate thus became inextricably tied up with this mood of strategic policymaking at the cost of its infrastructural development.

The third experience grew out of a relation of endemic bitterness between the government of the *Nawabs* on the one hand and the administration of the Company on the other. The *Nawabs* complained of the routine abuse of *dastaks*[20] by the merchants of the Company, while the latter complained about the routine harassment of the Company's agents on flimsy grounds born mostly of greed and suspicion. On one occasion the Council threatened the *Nawab* that if their men "are plundered in Patna, we will take satisfaction in Hugly."[21] This was the immediate aftermath of the death of Aurangzeb when signs of chaos were visible all round. The Company was under the fear that there would be "a revolution in the country and confusion in their business." In April and May, the panic ran high.

> [The Calcutta]council ordered all their factors to come back to Calcutta with as much of their effects as possible. All investments by out-factories were stopped. They arranged for the purchase of five thousand mounds of rice and of one thousand mounds of wheat to provide for the garrison. Sixty native soldiers were recruited to guard the town and factory at Calcutta.[22]

The security of the English settlement in Calcutta did not bring any peace to the English. Their interior settlements had not taken shape. In Calcutta the settlement had double functions to discharge. On the one hand it was to act as a forward outpost for Madras while on the other it was to function as the headquarters for its networks in the interior. Such networks were necessary for their penetration into the hinterlands of the port that was steadily coming into being in Calcutta. Rice, cotton piece-goods, salt, saltpetre, *Chunum* (lime), and timber were to be brought from the sources of their production. At times the interior stations were also used as centres for necessary man-power recruitments – weavers in particular – for the English factory in Calcutta and also for developing the infrastructure of the city itself. That was the time when the English factories at Dhaka, Kasimbazar, Hugli, Malda, Murshidabad, Lakhipur (Lakshmipur), Rajmahal etc. had not gone into their full-fledged operations so that they were still being geared up from their headquarters in Calcutta as its resource-procuring centres at the interior. They also acted as interior watch stations necessary to keep a watch on the activities of the *faujdars* in the districts. The *Nawabi* interference was a dreadful experience for the English in the early decades of their settlement in Calcutta.[23] In spite of its occasional and apparent gestures of benevolence, the *Nawabi* Government did not refrain from exercising very harsh sovereign measures on the Company. The invariable tendency had always been to extract money from the foreign traders in order to save the *Nizamat* from an endemic financial crisis. This mentality to fleece traders was partly due to the financial greed of the *Nawabs* and partly due to their unwillingness to trust a Company that had a few years ago gone into a war with the imperial authority in India and had tolerated the clandestine private trade of its employees. The reciprocal fear of each other's activities had been the most abiding factor in shaping the relation between the Company and the country government throughout the first half of the eighteenth century. Fearful of the English might and their intentions, the *Nawabs* seemed to be cautious in allowing the English to proceed deep into the countryside. As a result the English were disturbed that their district stations were not in the shape they were expected to be. Calcutta could flourish only on a growing feedback from these distant stations where investment would be made for commodity procurements for Calcutta. In 1727, a little before Murshid Quli Khan's death, the Calcutta Council advised the Chief of the Kasimbazar factory to wean over the *Nawab* with a handsome money tribute so as to get his permission to resettle their factories at Dhaka, Malda, and Hughli.[24] In the event of his not complying with the English request, it was decided to stop all their business in Bengal.[25] The *Nawabs* were constantly under the apprehension that the English were defrauding revenue due to the government and hence the practice developed to squeeze out money from the English by imprisoning their agents and putting a stop to their business in the districts. This *Nawabi* hostility kept the English in a state of alert so much so that, throughout the first half of the eighteenth century, the authorities in Calcutta found little time to pay attention to the question of promoting the urban uplift of their settlement in the three villages of Sutanuti, Govindapur, and Kalikata. The task before the Company was great. They had to give shape to formless habitations that grew here and there either as village markets around Sutanuti or as hubs of very lowly, destitute people like fishermen. This was not the place where a great many rich men, apart from the Seths and the Basaks, would like to settle. They had to keep the settlement free of the spies of the *Nawabs* and keep it insulated from criminals and vagrant Europeans who very often broke the moral fabric of the city life. The security and the upkeep of the settlement were also to be maintained at a level where it could stabilize its role as the core chapter of the British Asiatic trade of Bengal. Thus in the first half of the eighteenth century the English Company in Calcutta had very powerful geopolitical callings which superseded the urge to grow a ramshackle settlement in properly defined urban configurations.

Strong political will for urbanization absent

Under stress, urbanization needed a strong political will to promote itself and that was absent in the first half of the eighteenth century. Till such time as the Battle of Palasi, the English mind was upright in satisfying two very strategic needs of the Company – an expansion of territory to create more space on a sprawling and integrated landmass[26] and the acquisition of a "consolidated farman ensuring free movement of their trade over the whole country."[27] As early as 1708 Thomas Pitt, President and Governor of the Fort St. George, in a letter to Ziauddin Khan, Lord High Steward of Shah Alam's Household, "urged the necessity of having one document which would remove the impediments in the way of the trade of the Company and ensure for it better facilities."[28] Pit articulated the demands which the English wanted to satisfy and none of these demands showed any aspiration for growing the village settlements in and around Calcutta into an effective urban centre. He demanded mint rights near at home so that the Company's money supply could improve and ensure the necessary sinews of trade in Calcutta.[29] This defined the basic targets to which the Company directed its efforts from the beginning of their land acquisition in Calcutta. Acquisition of territory, a permission to increase the fortification of the city, a right to commission their stations in the interior, and access to mints[30] at their own place – these were all strategic considerations that overshadowed any desire for the urban improvement of the city. In the first half of the eighteenth century, the *Nawabi* administration displayed all signs of an erratic government. The *Nawabs*' leniency at the top[31] had always proved to be a feeble gesture for accommodation because, at the subordinate levels, hungry officers tightened their squeeze on the slightest pretexts. To fight this pressure back, the Company always had to remain militarily prepared, so all its surplus income from land was drained in extravagant defence measures. Diplomatic overtures from the side of the Company were not absent and they always contained a pack of lucrative fiscal gifts to the *Nawabs* without which they would not move. A tug-of-war between the *Nawab*'s men and the Company's agents on the value and weight of the gift was a regular phenomenon that always kept the Calcutta Council in a state of unmitigated worries.

These were, therefore, the tensions that marked the years of the colonial foundation of the city. Strategic planning was on the forefront. Taking advantage of the chaos, the English constructed two regular bastions in the fort. They acted on an empirical logic: "the emperor being dead, and now being the properest time to strengthen our fort, whilst there is an interregnum and no one likely to take notice of what we are doing."[32] Clandestine efforts of fortification had been a persistent practice with the Company's government in Calcutta up to the year 1756. That year *Nawab* Sirajuddaullah, in his youthful vigour and impetuosity, tried to stop this practice once for all by invading the city and inflicting a crushing defeat on the English. But the whole action eventually turned out to be a rash adventure without any follow-up measure to consolidate the achievement. In no time Clive came from Madras at the head of a powerful navy, bombarded both Chandernagore[33] and Hugli[34] and smashed the French and Mughal bases on the river so that Calcutta's military supremacy at the mouth of the Bay became ensured for all time to come. Calcutta was recovered from the control of the *Nawab* and the English henceforth held it not only as their purchased estate as before but also as their recovered power base with its unproclaimed status of a conquered city. The *Nawab* was forced to sign a derogatory agreement with the English in Calcutta surrendering many a mark of his *de facto* sovereignty to the English. Henceforth none of the important dignitaries of the Calcutta Council or their agents was found to be at the beck and call of the *Nawabs* at murshidabad. On the contrary the agents of the *Nawab* shuttled to and fro between Calcutta and Mursidabad to serve the mandates of the English and their governors in Calcutta. The centre of gravity in the geopolitics of the region had shifted from Murshidabad to Calcutta. The age was now ushered in for the proper foundation of a colonial city in Calcutta.

Calcutta grows as a garrison town

From 1698 to 1757, Calcutta grew mostly as a garrison town[35] and its fort-centricity was the most characteristic feature of its urbanization. The English were constantly haunted by the fear that the spies of the *Nawab* would infiltrate into the city in order to keep a watch over the internal development of the city itself. Afflicted by a psychology of fear throughout the course of the first half of the eighteenth century, the English in Calcutta had always kept themselves in a state of war-preparedness so that their power to retaliate might not suffer in a time of crisis.[36] Living in and around the fort within a radius of one or two miles, the English built up the nucleus of a colonial town not over a sprawling habitation but in a circumscribed area around the modern Chowranghee and Esplanade where the replica of their home city of London was sought to be created. The territory to the south of modern Circular Road was covered with jungles so that the native population could find their living space only to the north of the city itself. Between this nucleus of the forthcoming English town in Calcutta and the settlement of the natives in the north there was a short middle buffer where a mixed population of Muslims, Armenians, Hindus, and the Christian converts lived. Creation of this middle buffer was the greatest human shield against any attack of the *Nawab* from the north. A powerful stronghold of the *Nawab* was situated at Jessore where a *faujdar* was installed right from the beginning of the Mughal rule in eastern India. From Jessore the land-route to Calcutta ensured a straight and uninterrupted journey through Dumduma (modern Dumdum)] and this middle habitation acted as the most strategic human buffer against a prospective onslaught from the *Nawab*.

This is how the morphology of Calcutta in the early years of its foundation was patterned. Colonial town growth was essentially shaped only through responses to strategic challenges of the situation. The main concern of the company during the first six decades of the foundation of the city of Calcutta was to build their stamina and strength to retaliate in case of an attack by the country government. What seemed to be the greatest casualty in this situation was normalcy. It was only after the grant of *Diwani* in 1765 that political situations became stable in Bengal. A *de jure* Mughal *Subah* became a *de facto* protectorate of the English. The process of this transition was certainly not conducive to growth. Bengal had to wait for another two decades before the planners' dream to grow Calcutta as an imperial city could start realizing itself.

Notes

1. Calcutta, then a village called Kalikata, was selected with two other sites, Sutanuti and Govindapur, villages respectively to the north and south of this central location of the English settlement, which eventually absorbed the territory and configurations of habitations and market places of the two villages around to grow in later years as the greatest British metropolitan city in the east.
2. Geopolitics means the use of politics between two or more aspirants of power who aim at controlling territory, harbours, resources, and manpower for its or their own aggrandisement on specific calculations of geographical-economic inputs directed toward political ends. When eco-geo factors govern the politics for space we call it geopolitics. "The term was coined by Rudolf Kjellen, a Swedish political scientist, at the beginning of the 20th century. Kjellen was inspired by the German geographer Friedrich Ratzel, who published his book *Politische Geographie* (political geography) in 1897, popularized in English by American diplomat Robert Strausz-Hupe, a faculty member of the University of Pennsylvania. Halford Mackinder greatly pioneered the field also, though he did not coin the term of geopolitics." – Wikipedia, the Free Encyclopaedia.

3 It is strange that the urbanization of Calcutta did not rally around a pilgrim spot, Kalighat or Kalikshetra. Examples of urbanization around religious centres are not rare in India. But this did not happen in Calcutta. It is equally strange that Calcutta's station as the central administrative centre of the Company and as the capital of an empire did not give it any major incentive toward urbanization. The preoccupation of the Company's government with measures to promote natives as brown men with English tastes, their zeal for social and educational reforms, their continuous efforts to weed out elements of non-acceptance of British rule in the country manifested through innumerable revolts and mutinies, their concern for the health upkeep of their army, and finally their involvements in imperial wars did not provide them the necessary fiscal incentive and the tranquillity of a peace-time recess necessary for the promotion of the city as an effective urban centre. This was not only the fate of Calcutta, but almost all of the major colonial cities in India shared the same fate.

4 "In 1698 the English East India Company received the talukdari (zamindary by English version) of the three towns of Sutanuti, Govindapur and Calcutta. In 1699 these three places came to be considered by the English as 'a place where the Moors have nothing to do with all'. This sentiment was given a tangible expression in a more incautious phrase 'our dominion in Bengal'. In 1708–09 they called the Calcutta town as a 'settlement of Great Britain in Calcutta'. If the idea was ever worked out that behind the activities of a commercial Company there was the acknowledgement of a vast nation and a country, it lay here. In later years Clive only took this sentiment to its logical end when he wrote to the crumbling Nawab of Bengal that the King of England was in no way inferior to the Mughal Padshah. Even the Court of Directors asserted that the position of the Company with regard to the Calcutta towns was that of the 'Lord proprietors of the land'." – Ranjit Sen, *Metamorphosis of the Bengal Polity (1700–1739)*, Rabindra Bharati University, Calcutta, 1987, p. 40. In the first three chapters of this book, this point has been analyzed in detail. The titles of these chapters are "In Search of Territorial Roots and Military Power," "From Aspiration to Achievement," and "Supremacy Acquired: Sovereignty Anticipated." Also see C.R. Wilson, *Old Fort William in Bengal*, John Murray, London, 1906, Vol. I, p. 40. and M. Huq, *The East India Company's Land Policy and Commerce in Bengal 1698–1784*, Asiatic Society of Pakistan, Dacca, 1964, p. 26.

5 It is wrongly assumed in some quarters that the growth of the Calcutta towns (the three villages noted previously came to be collectively known as the Calcutta towns) was associated with the growth of the port itself. In 1690 when Job Charnock, the English agent of the East India Company, chose this spot, he had little idea of the potentialities of a small village to grow into a port in future. Calcutta as a village was situated 126 nautical miles away from the sea. It presented difficult navigational problems right from the beginning. There were some undetected sand bars and sharp bends in the river which ships had to negotiate. The Calcutta port really grew when the vast hinterland of the port comprising the present states of West Bengal, Bihar, Madhya Pradesh, Orissa, Uttar Pradesh, and the neighbouring countries of Nepal, Sikkim, and Bhutan – with their rich industrial, agricultural, and mineral resources – came directly under

British rule or under its sway in the nineteenth century. The transition of Calcutta into a modern port really began in the second half of the nineteenth century.

6. Calcutta is situated at 220 82' north latitude and 88020' east longitude, at an altitude 17 feet from sea level, 120 miles from the Bay of Bengal.
7. Chitpur is situated at 22034'11" north latitude and 88022'11" east longitude. Faujdari was a military district of the Nawabs.
8. Hugli is 35 km north of Calcutta. It is situated at 22053'44" north latitude and 88024'9" east longitude.
9. Murshidabad is about 60 miles north of Calcutta. It is situated at 24050'20" north latitude and 23043'30" south latitude and 88046'0" east longitude and 87049'17" west longitude. It is also situated at the southern bank of Bhagirathi, a tributary of the river Ganga. Its former name was Mukshusabad. From some time in the first quarter of the eighteenth century, when Murshid Quli Kahn shifted his capital from Dhaka to this place, it assumed the name of Murshidabad. Murshid Quli Khan became the Nawab of Bengal around the year 1716 or 1717 and the transfer of capital was effected perhaps after that. According to Ghulam Hussain, the author of *Riyaz-us-Salatin*, a merchant named Mukshus Khan was the first man to improve the present site of Murshidabad. In *Ain-i-Akbari* he has been referred to as a nobleman during the last decade of the sixteenth century.
10. Malda was situated at 42014'12" north latitude and 43047'49" east longitude. Its distance from Calcutta is 170.67 miles (274.65 km)
11. The *faujdars* of these places very often extracted huge money from the foreign companies, particularly from the English because they were doing a very brisk business in the country. Thus in 1723 the *faujdar* of Hugli demanded Rs. 40,000 from the English while the *faujdar* of Balasore demanded a handsome present for the Emperor. – Abdul Karim, *Murshid Quli Khan and His Times*, The Siatic Society of Pakistan, Dacca, 1963, p. 180. Balasore is situated at 21018' north latitude and 86054' east longitude. Its distance from Calcutta is 144.8 miles (233.1 km); by sea 125 nautical miles. Its elevation from the sea is 16 metres or 52 feet.
12. Rajmahal was situated at 2503'0" north latitude and 87050'0" east longitude. Its distance from Calcutta is 161 km.
13. This vigilance point has been discussed in detail in the following books : (i) S. Bhattacharya, *East India Company and the Economy of Bengal 1704–1740*, London, 1954, 2nd edn, Firma K.L.Mukhopadhyay, Calcutta, Calcutta, 1969; the major part of the book deals with this (ii) Sen, *Metamorphosis of the Bengal Polity*, Ch. II; (iii) Sen, *Calcutta in the Eighteenth Century*, Vol. I, Ch. I under the title "Did Calcutta Grow Territorially?"' (iv) Brijen K. Gupta, *Sirajuddaullah and the East India Company, 1756–1757: Background to the Foundation of the British Empire in India*, Photomechanical Reprint, Leiden, E.J. Brill, 1966, pp. 9, 35–40, 89; (v) Karim, *Murshid Quli Khan and His Times*.
14. "For about sixty years since 1698 when the taluqdari of Kalikata-Sutanuti-Govindapur was purchased by the Company the growth of Calcutta was almost at a standstill. The aim of the Company was to purchase taluqdari rights over the adjoining areas so that they could build up a substantially integrated mass of territorial possession around the nucleus of their power. Eventually they succeeded in obtaining the right to purchase 38 villages

around their seat of power in Calcutta but owing to the hostility of the Bengal nawabs that right could not be implemented in full. In later years when English assistance was invoked against Siraj-uddaullah, the price that was demanded of the members of the Bengal power-elite was the cession of these thirty-eight villages and if Hill is to be believed Scrafton wrote in elation: 'Omir Chand has a very good scheme to purchase as a full equivalent for the 38 villages'. The grant of the zamindari of the twenty-four Parganas was in the offing. In 1757 the Company's taluqdari of Kalikata-Sutanuti-Govindapur came to be merged with the Company's zamindari of the 24-parganasi. After about sixty years of standstill the Company's possession began to move" – Ranjit Sen, *A Stagnating City Calcutta in the Eighteenth Century*, Institute of Historical Studies, Calcutta, 2000, pp. 155–156. For further study on the point, see (i) "The Company becomes the Zamindar", in *Firminger's Introduction to the Fifth Report*, available in Indian Studies Past and Present, Ch. IV; (ii) J. Bruce, *Arnals of the Honourable East India Company etc*, Vol. III, p. 278; (iii) *Moreland: The Agrarian System of Moslem India*, 1929, pp. 19–20; (iv) A.K. Ray, *A Short History of Calcutta* (1912), pp. 47–48, 55–57, Rddhi Edition, Calcutta,1982.

15 The E.I. Company built two forts in Calcutta on the bank of the river Hugli. The old fort was started by Sir Charles Eyre and was finished by his successor John Beard. Sir Eyre built the South East Bastion of the fort, while the North East Bastion was built by his successor. The N.E. Bastion was completed in 1701. In 1702, the Company's factory was constructed inside it. The construction of the fort was completed in 1706. The building had two stories with projected wings. It also had a small guard room inside it. It is alleged that this room during the time of Sirajuddallah's raid of Calcutta in 1756 became the Black Hole. This fort was damaged by the Nawab's army when the English vacated it in 1756. This necessitated the construction of a new fort. Clive started this new fort in 1758 after the battle of Palasi. It was completed in 1781. Its estimated cost was approximately two million pounds. It had a green belt three km long and one km wide in front of it. This was where the army was drilled. The old fort was also repaired in time with a huge cost. From 1766 onwards, it began to be used as a customs house of the Company.

16 Quoted in Karim, *Murshid Quli Khan and His Times*, p. 176.

17 These reports from the English Consultations have been quoted by Karim, *Murshid Quli Khan and His Times*, p. 177.

18 Sukumar Bhattacharya and Abdul Karim narrates innumerable incidents which show the estrangement between the English Company and the government on account of English activities in Calcutta. On a little opportunity, the Company would arrogate to themselves what the Nawabs thought were the marks of sovereignty whereas, at the slightest pretext, the Nawabs would apply pressure tactics to fleece the English in Calcutta. Situations drifted so far that at one point of time – when the Company's broker was imprisoned, this being the normal practice at that time – the Calcutta Council, taking this to be "an insult that must be attended with the worst of consequences should we tamely bear it," ordered their vakil to "declare that if our broker was not speedily released we should seek our own satisfaction." The Nawab's reply to this was that "though he [the

vakil] was a servant to the English yet he was a subject and tenant of the kings." – Karim, *Murshid Quli Khan and His Times*, p. 178.
19 Karim, *Murshid Quli Khan and His Times*, p. 180.
20 The abuse of dastaki was reported and found valid as early as 1705. In March 1705, the Calcutta Council made elaborate rules to prevent the abuse of dastak. See Karim, *Murshid Quli Khan and His Times*, pp. 121–124.
21 Ibid. This happened on 3 June 1707, i.e. immediately after the death of Aurangzeb when everything was drifting in chaos.
22 Karim, *Murshid Quli Khan and His Times*, p. 125.
23 Sukumar Bhattacharya and Abdul Karim discuss this point in details in their books (*Murshid Quli Khan and His Times*). While Bhattacharya approaches the whole question of the English relations with the Nawabs from a dispassionate angle, Abdul Karim seems to be a little sympathetic towards the Nawabs.
24 Bhattacharya (*East India Company and the Economy of Bengal 1704–1740*, p. 29) writes: "The Calcutta Council accordingly empowered Edward Stephenson, chief of the Council at Kasimbazar, to offer the Nawab fifteen or twenty thousand rupees in consideration that the Nawab would be pleased to allow them 'to re-settle the factory at malda, build the house at Dacca and finish the house at Hughli'. The English were unwilling to spend money unless they had some benefit in return."
25 "The Council in Calcutta declared that instead of 'tamely and easily complying with every unjust and unreasonable demand' they would rather put a stop to their investment and all other business" – Ibid.
26 The farman of 1717 allowed the Company to purchase thirty-eight more villages from their respective owners, but the permission was subject to the approval of the Diwan of the Subah. This rider in the permission was cautiously camouflaged by the words "then permission given by the diwan of the subah." This, writes Abdul Karim, "made the privilege conditional upon the diwan's approval." – Karim, *Murshid Quli Khan and His Times*, p. 169.
27 Bhattacharya, *East India Company and the Economy of Bengal 1704–1740*, p. 18. The English urge for a consolidated farman had its own justification. Bhattacharya writes: "The fortified settlements at Bombay, Madras and Calcutta had already added to their physical strength. A consolidated farman issued by the Emperor ensuring their commercial privileges would clothe them with legal and moral justification to assert their rights, whenever they were violated by the provincial authorities." – Ibid.
28 Bhattacharya, *East India Company and the Economy of Bengal 1704–1740*, p. 18.
29 He wrote:

> "As we want the Phirmaund [farman] to be general, I must let you know how matters stand in Bengal and Suratt. In Bengal we have the King's Phirmaund and Prince's Nishan with several Nabob's Perwannas for being custom free in the Kingdom of Bengal, Behar and Orixa upon paying three thousand rupees per annum at Hugly into the King's treasury, and for our settlement at Calcutta, where we desire His Majesty would be pleased to grant us

SCANNING THE CONTEXT

leave to erect a Mint and to coin Rupees and Mores [mohors or gold coins] with Royal Stamp according to true matt and weight of those coined in his Royal Mint at Rajmall [Rajmahal] which conveniency would very much contribute to the increase of that trade." – Bhattacharya, *East India Company and the Economy of Bengal 1704–1740*, p. 18.

30 The English wanted to mint their coins at Murshidabad but their attempts were foiled by the Jagat Seths who controlled the royal mints during the reign of Murshid Quli Khan. For Jagat Seth's role in the banking system of the Nawabs, see J.H. Little [ed. by N.K. Sinha], *The House of the Jagat Seth*, Calcutta, 1967. It was previously published in the Bengal Past and Present, Vols. xx–xxii.

31 Salimullah in Tarikhi-Bangla (translated by Gladwin, 1788, p. 81) says that Murshid Quli Khan was "sensible that the prosperity of Bengal and the increase of the revenues depended upon its advantageous commerce, particularly that carried by the ships from Europe." But while as a Nawab he "showed great indulgence to merchants of every description, he was jealous of the growing power of the Europeans in Bengal."

32 Karim, *Murshid Quli Khan and His Times*, pp. 125–126.

33 Jadunath Sarkar wrote: "the English lost no time. Their land and sea forces moved up against Chandernagore. On 12th March, Clive encamped two miles from that town, and on the 14th attacked and drove in their outposts."

"Chandernagore was realy in no defensible condition, though its Director (chief) Mons. Reanult had done all that was in his power in his utter want of money, men, and trained officers. His garrison was hopelessly inadequate against a European enemy. He had only 247 soldiers (including 45 French prisoners and sick), 120 sailors, 70 half-castes, and private Europeans, 100 civilians, 167 sepoy, and 100 topasses or half-caste gunner – forming a total of 794 fighting men of all classes." – Jadunath Sarkar, ed., *History of Bengal*, Vol. II, Dacca University Publication, 1948, Second Impression, 1972, pp. 483–484.

34 Hugli was invaded as a part of a declared war. Brijen Gupta writes: "On December 30th [1756], Budge Budge was taken, and on January 2, 1757, Calcutta was recaptured. The next day Drake and his councillors were restored to authority at Fort William." On 3 January, a manifesto of war was drawn against the Mughal authority in Bengal. It read: "We do hereby on the behalf of the said East India Company and as their representatives in Bengal, in consideration of the several acts of hostility and violence already premised, declare open war against the aforesaid Sirajuddaulla ... and against the subjects of the said subah [Nawab], their cities, towns, shipping and effects, according to the maxims and rules of all nations, until ample restitution be made [to] the East India Company, their servants, tenants and inhabitants residing under their protection, for all damages and losses sustained by them ... and until full satisfaction be made the said East India Company for the charges by them incurred in equipping a large army and marine force to procure a reestablishment of their factories and towns." Gupta, *Sirajuddaullah and the East India Company, 1756–1757*, p. 92.

35 The rebellion of Sobha Singh in 1696, which rocked the whole of western Bengal, secured for the company the permission to fortify Calcutta. For details about the birth of a garrison Town see ch. 1, "The Birth of a Garrison Town" in Sen, *A Stagnating City Calcutta in the Eighteenth Century*, pp. 1–14.
36 A case in point was the conflict between the English and the Nawab at the beginning of 1727. Toward the end of 1726, the Nawab confined the English *vakil* [agent] in Murshidabad on a charge that Rs. 44,000.00 was due from the English on account of the Calcutta "towns." Immediately the Company retaliated. They stopped all Mughal vessels that were to pass by the fort and issued orders for the enlistment of additional forces from among the "Europeans, Portuguese and others as quickly as possible." Situations were so tense that the English refrained from sending their treasures to Kasimbazar and the Nawab thought whether it was wise on the part of the Jagat Seth to send his treasures to Hugli at a time "when the English were plundering boats and ships on the river." – Bhattacharya, *East India Company and the Economy of Bengal 1704–1740*, pp. 26–28.

Part II

EARLY FORMATIONS

5

WHO WAS THE REAL FOUNDER OF CALCUTTA?

Between two perspectives

Was Calcutta Pre-British?

Was Calcutta a Creation of the British?

Paradoxically enough the answer to both the questions is broadly "yes." Why "yes" we shall answer stage by stage taking the first question first and the second question second.

Calcutta was pre-British not in the sense that as a town it rose before the advent of the British or its ancestry can be traced to any urban from of pre-British origin. It was pre-British in the sense that it was a part of a region that was going through a metamorphic change since the sixteenth century and was evolving slowly with Hugli at it centre as the successor of the trade-complex of Satgaon. The axis of commerce in south Bengal was changing; trade settlements were taking a new shape and the habitation pattern was undergoing a vast change. Calcutta, Sutanuti, and Govindapur, along with all other stations in the neighbourhood of Hughli, were important points of deflection from Satgaon and they were gaining prominence. Patna, Balasore, Kasimbazar, Uluberia, Chinsura, and Hugli – a wide region in the eastern and south-eastern course of the Ganga was assuming a new importance with the change of time. The days of Tamralipti were over. Satgaon was on the decline and all trade directions were now moving toward lower Bengal centring in the region around Hugli.

The Portuguese who established their command over the Bay had a knowledge of this change. With their help, Maharaja Pratapaditya "during his transient struggles for independence"[1] built up some forts in this emerging region of south Bengal, mostly around Calcutta stretching over a vast territory from the river Matla at the Sundarbans to Chitpur in modern Calcutta.[2] Thus Calcutta was identified as a strategic place long before Job Charnock set his foot here. Before the English insisted that they should be allowed to build a fort for themselves, it was Maharaja Pratapaditya who had cordoned the area with a chain of forts. A.K. Ray writes the following:

> These small, mud forts, however useless and insignificant by modern standards, were greatly prized in those days for their strategic value, the river being navigable only by small sloops and boats. Being an island and surrounded by water and within an easy reach of the forts, and being moreover, covered with jungle except on the river bank, Calcutta was at that time a site not to be despised. Even at the dawn of the seventeenth century it had very considerable advantages over other neighbouring riparian towns and villages.[3]

Calcutta was thus slowly surfacing into the core of a trade area. It was not becoming prominent as a part of pilgrimage zone centring on Kalighat but was considered as a station noticeable on the trade route of sea-merchants. Bipradas Piplai's Manasha Mangal tells us that its hero in the course of his journey down the river saw south of Tribeni a series of settlements on both sides of the river starting from Kumarhatta, Halishar, Hughli, Betor, Rishra, Konnagar, Sukchar, Kamarhati, Ariadaha, Ghusuri, Chitpur, and Calcutta. Next to Chitpur Calcutta was prominent but not as prominent as Betor before it. This last named place was famous for being the site of an ancient temple of goddess "Betai Chandi" where merchants came to pay homage to the goddess and where they stopped as a temporary hault for their shopping and rest before they would set out on their onward journey. Two things we notice here. First, Betor derived as much prominence from being the site of the temple of "Betai Chandi" as from being a halt station and trade-centre itself. Calcutta's prominence up till then was not because of being adjacent to the temple of Kalighat but because of its position as a prospective station in an emerging trade zone. It is vital to note that in the whole region there were three temples noteworthy for being pilgrim spots – "Betaia Chandi" temple at Betor, "Sarvamangala Devi" temple at Chitpur, and "Kali temple" at Kalighat. Apart from these Halishahar was a holy place linked to Kalighat through a mud-road either running through Chitpur or adjacent to it.

Thus from Tribeni downwards a holy zone of goddess-ridden culture was growing up slowly from the sixteenth century, and the whole region was promoted by sea-faring merchants who, suffering always from the anxieties of an uncertain future, tended to propitiate goddesses by worship. It was in this goddess-ridden culture zone that Dakshineswar eventually grew up as a base for mother-worship in the second half of the nineteenth century with Ramakrishna Paramahansa at its centre. The ancient Kalikshetra was situated in the southern part of his holy worship zone of lower Bengal giving thus this holy zone a mythical ancestry which no pragmatic wisdom could contend.[4] This is one reason as to why Kalighat could not acquire the status which Betor had achieved before. Kalighat was at the southern end of an emerging trade zone whereas Betor was very much within the periphery of a trade-radiation centred at Satgaon. A.K. Ray says, "It was to Satgaon, what Jedda was to Mecca."[5] When Satgaon fell and it ceased to function as the nerve centre for all upcoming and sea-going traders of lower Bengal, Hugli emerged as a substitute entrepot for Satgaon. Opposite Hugli there was the pilgrim-line stretched from Kalighat to Halisahar via Chitpur. Calcutta was in the highest ground on the eastern part of the river that found itself comfortably positioned on this pilgrim-line of the east. When Job Charnock arrived at the Sutanuti-Kalikata territory of the river bank, he had a full knowledge of this. A shifting river trade and a promising pilgrim zone had a combined prospect for growth around south Bengal. Calcutta mirrored this growth and Charnock's screening eyes did not miss it.

The change of the river course had accounted to a great extent for the creation of a new trade zone in the south. From the sixteenth century "the great Ganges river system" in Bengal changed its course.[6] Abandoning its main course through western and southern Bengal, the bulk of the water of the river linked up with the Padma, the main channel of water in eastern Bengal, and flooded the subsidiary courses there. Long before this had happened, a more fundamental change began to take place on the formation of the delta itself. In its original course the Ganga had emptied itself to the sea at a place somewhere around Murshidabad. But the flow of the river was not powerful enough to flush the debris and the silt it carried into the sea. This whole mass thus remained deposited at its mouth, forming and enlarging the delta and pushing the confluence of the river with the sea further to the south.[7] This sedimentation not only caused the delta to rise but also changed the distribution of its watermass.[8] Eaton writes the following:

> When such sedimentation caused riverbeds to attain levels higher than the surrounding countryside, water spilled out of their former beds and moved into adjoining channels. In this way the main course of the Ganges, which had formerly flowed down what is now the Bhagirathi-Hooghly channel in

EARLY FORMATIONS

West Bengal, was replaced in turn by the Bhairab, the Mathabhanga, the Garai-Madhumati, the Arialkhan, and finally the present day Padma-Meghna system.[9]

Thus the change of the river course in Bengal and the formation of the Bengal delta were two concurrent phenomena which created the context of new changes for south and eastern Bengal in subsequent centuries. As the delta was forming steadily, the river courses changed correspondingly. The bulk of the water of the river Ganga changed its direction to the east.[10] Eaton writes the following:

> In 1574, Abu'l-Fazl remarked that the Ganges River had divided into two branches at the Afghan capital of Tanda: one branch flowing south to Satgaon and the other flowing east towards Sonargaon and Chittagong. In the seventeenth century the former branch continued to decay as progressively more of its water was captured by the Channels flowing to the east, to the point where by 1666 this branch had become altogether unnavigable.[11]

This un-navigability of the western course of the river eventually led to the fall of the Satgaon. Calcutta's rise was favoured by this. A.K. Ray has given us a real insight into the development:

> At this very moment, nature came to its [Calcutta's] help. The Nadia rivers began to sit up and a big 'char' formed at Halisahar opposite to Tribeni, near Satgaon.[12] This gradually reduced the Jamuna to a narrow nullah. The Saraswati, which was the channel of communication between Satgaon, the great emporium of trade, the chief seat of Government, and other parts, began also to shrink away. A largely increased volume of water came thus to be forced down the Bhagirathi, which deepened and widened it in its lower reaches. The Adiganga and all the khals, jhils and rivulets on the eastern bank of the Bhagirathi that were connected with the river shared the fate of the Jamuna, the Saraswati and the Nadia rivers. They gradually shrank away into tiny little nullahs. The result was the formation of a large amount of alluvial land fit for residence and cultivation.

Calcutta and its neighbourhood emerged out of the benefits of this new formation. The English in the seventeenth century oscillated between

WHO WAS THE REAL FOUNDER OF CALCUTTA?

Hughli and Chittagong. But none of these two stations was conducive for the English. Hugli was the headquarters of a Mughal *faujdar*. Chittagong was the playground of the Mags, the Arakans, and the Portuguese. With the transfer of capital from Dhaka to Murshidabad, the political and economic gravity shifted from its hinterland which, from the fifteenth and sixteenth centuries, was growing as a rice and cotton-producing area (called *Kapasia*) centred on Dhaka. The English were moving to Bengal from the west – from Orissa – and not from the east and their direction was toward Chittagong – the original station of their choice. From Chittagong they could move into south-east Asia where the Dutch were curving their zone of influence. At one point of time they even planned to capture Chittagong by force. Later the realization dawned on them that with Madras as the rear area a station in western part of Bengal would be a better position from where they could effectively maintain their control of the seaboard. Such a station would be effective if it was at the mouth of the river. Calcutta and its neighbouring areas adequately and admirably suited to these purposes of the geopolitics of the area.

The point to be noted is that the delta formation in southern Bengal, the changes in the courses of the river, and the closing of the animation of Western Bengal all became synchronizing phenomena in the centuries immediately preceding the emergence of Calcutta in the eighteenth century. Yet superseding decay new changes were coming up long before the eighteenth century was ushered in. Because of the drying up of the river system of Nadia, Bhagirathi became the main carrier of the water coming from the Ganga. A.K. Ray observes that this was a blessing for the lower region of the delta. Calcutta was situated in the bank of the Bhagirathi and it was benefited by whatever advantages the Bhagirathi offered it. Recognizing the navigability of the Bhagirathi, European adventurers thrust in from the sea. Marks of a new civilization opened up here. New settlements, clearance of jungles, migration of population, and brisk business activities were all crowding in the transitional moments of history of south Bengal. Calcutta and its neighbourhood were one compact area where the spirit of this new change seemed to have been thriving. It was not that the trading companies of the west did not have the knowledge of this. They made their settlements around Hugli prior to when the English settled themselves in Calcutta. The Portuguese were perhaps the first among the people of the west to scout the area and it was with their help that Pratapaditya cordoned the area with a series of small forts. Habitations grew and population migration became a regular phenomenon.

A.K. Ray writes the following:

> Migration of fishermen and cultivators from the upper riparian regions into these new formations, rapidly followed by that of higher castes, took place as a matter of course. The time was most opportune. Pratapaditya's independent little kingdom had just been dismembered. A large number of people that had been in his service were thrown out of employ. These included a number of Portuguese (and, it is also said, a few Armenians) who had settled down and built Christian churches in 1559 A.D. They all looked out for "fresh fields and pastures new."[13]

The neighbourhood of Calcutta was thus growing. Kalikata, Sutanuti, and Govindapur basked in the radiation of this growth and promoters and improving landlords were active in making the land inhabited by people of wealth, industry, and dignity.

"And we can imagine," A.K. Ray adds, "Lakshmikanta Majumder, whose influence with them [the migrating men] during Pratapaditya's rule must have been great, bringing them away and settling them in the new formations, all of which appertained to his jagir. A number of Brahmins from Halisahar, Neemta, Tribeni and Yasohara known to have come and settled down with their servants in and around Calcutta at this time."[14]

Immigration to a new habitat was in the logic of things particularly when trade seemed to be booming in the region. The trade boom was the result of an improved navigability of Bhagirathi. All water channels had been shut to trade because of their senility and Bhagirathi was the only course left to trade.

> The improved navigability of the Bhagirathi, and the increasing difficulty of carrying laden boats up and down the Saraswati for purposes of trade with Satgaon, diverted the entire trade of the 'famous port of Satgaon', as it was still called from the Saraswati into the Bhagirathi . . . it was here that the Portuguese *galiasses* used to lie at anchor between 1530 and 1569 A.D. It was to control its trade that Rodda, the Portuguese captain of Pratapaditya's fleet, had caused a fort to be built at Tanna, within sight of it. Since 1540, however, the Portuguese trade was being gradually transferred from Betor to Hooghly, where 59 years later they obtained permission of the Emperor, to build a fort and a Church.[15]

A region thus developed in course of three to four centuries prior to the emergence of Calcutta as a centre of trade and power in the eighteenth century. Long before the English eyes riveted on this tiny little ground on the bank of the Hugli, it had become a witness to the breakdown of the old-world commerce and the collapse of the river-network of trade that centred around Satgaon. In the vortex of change Calcutta became a noticeable locality which traders could spot and use as their station of temporary halt where they could replenish their resources. It was in this sense that Calcutta was pre-British. Its high ground, its strategic location, and its settlement prospects made it an upcoming neighbourhood around Hughli where an enterprising humanity could find its own nest. It was in this alluring milieu of a growing settlement that the English set their feet at the end of the seventeenth century.

Was Calcutta out and out colonial?

So long as this knowledge was not discovered we were attuned to the traditional belief that Calcutta was the creation of the English. It was founded by Job Charnock and the day of its foundation was 24 August 1690. The Honourable High Court of Calcutta, under the advice of a body of historians, passed an epoch-making judgement that Calcutta was pre-British. It has no founder and has no date of birth. Calcutta in the sixteenth century was referred to in Bipradas Piplai's *Manasamangal* and Abul Fazl's *Ain-i-Akbari*. But the Calcutta these texts refer was a village and not a town or a city. When the English purchased the villages of Sutanuti, Kalikata, and Govindapur, these three places were merely villages. Then how and when was Calcutta urbanized? One thing was certain that as an urban growth it was not a Mughal creation. Nor was it a creation of the indigenous people. Can we then surmise that it was the Armenians who laid the early foundation of Calcutta? We have no support of evidence to answer this question in the affirmative. Armenians were certainly there in Sutanuti and places surrounding it long before the English arrived here. The *Sutanuti Hat*, which in the eighteenth century was converted into Burra Bazaar, was a flourishing business centre which was under the control of the Setts, Basaks, and Malliks who, in course of the late seventeenth and early eighteenth centuries, lost their predominance in the *Burra Bazaar* to the Marwaris. As the rich Bengali traders – the Setts, Basaks, and Malliks – came from outside, their first effort was to build up their own settlement and their own habitation around the places near Sutanuti. Town-building was certainly not within the scheme of things in their new settlement. Traders founding a town was not in the Bengal tradition of urbanization. As a result, neither the Marwaris nor the rich Bengali merchants were credited with town-building. How was then Calcutta built? Was it manufactured just the way, as Fisher says, Prussia was manufactured? Or was it a creation of nature itself? There was indeed geopolitics behind the shaping of Calcutta as a city. But this geopolitics was not the same as the one which shaped the formation of Murshidabad. Dhaka was entirely a gift of nature; so was Chittagong. In this sense Calcutta was not an outcome of the sort of factors which shaped the formations of these two important cities of contemporary east Bengal. Calcutta was Mughal only outwardly. For a long time it was, in all practical sense masterless. That is why during the war between the English and the Mughals between 1686 and 1690 Charnock had the courage to land at Sutanuti. The rebellion of Sova Singh had adequately proved that the Mughal rule in Bengal that had its headquarters in Dakha was unable to control the western part of Bengal. The nearest *faujdari* in Bengal about that time was in Jessore and from Jessore it was difficult to impose a military control over the western part of Bengal. The result was that for a long time Calcutta and its surrounding region in southern Bengal was practically free of definite Mughal control. This control became possible only when the capital of Bengal was shifted to Murshidabad in central Bengal. By that time the English East India Company had found itself entrenched in Calcutta.

Given this, the question arises as to how Calcutta grew and under whose auspices? Here we shall try to answer this question. We shall compare the origin of Dhaka, Murshidabad, and Kolkata and will see as to how the process of Mughal town formation differed from that of the British. It should be noted that neither Murshidabad nor Dakha were sea-facing nor were they ports. None of these cities had a back-up rear area as Calcutta had in Madras. The Calcutta-Madras axis controlled the vast seaboard which even Chittagong could not do. In the contemporary geopolitics this axis had a great role to play. For example it was not possible for the Mughals to control Calcutta even from Murshidabad. Sirajuddaullah failed to do it. Whereas the English ships easily sailed over the seaboard and conquered Calcutta in the early months of 1757. One reason why Dhaka failed vis-à-vis Murshidabad was that with the shift of *diwani* to that city Dhaka became a capital-short city starved of bullion. The same thing happened when, after the grant of *diwani*, the gravity of the Bengal economics shifted to Calcutta. Money flowed where the office of the *diwan* was stationed. Thus after Murshid Quli Khan's detachment from the *Nawab* at Dhaka the latter city became financially lustreless. Calcutta captured the financial glow of Murshidabad when in 1772 and in subsequent years Warren Hastings transferred the entire finance department to Calcutta.

The dynamics of the foundation of the city of Calcutta lies here. It will be idle to battle on the question as to who were the real founders of Calcutta – the British, the Armenians, or the indigenous people of the land, the Seths and the Basaks. The founders of the city were impersonal forces – the economics of the situation. The English at the outset had no town planning. They wanted a fortified settlement from where they could conduct their Asiatic trade. Coming after a war with the Mughals (1686–1690) and also in the wake of a rebellion (Shova Singh's rebellion in 1696) the British possession of the three villages of Kalikata, Sutanuti, and Govindapur took the shape of a rough and ready settlement that would serve the dual purpose of a trade centre and a habitation of the English traders and sailors, the factors of the Company, and their white servants. The unrest of 1696–1697 convinced them that they needed a fort that would provide protection to their trade from zamindari onslaughts. Later on when they faced interference from the *Nawabi* administration from Murshidabad they wanted to reorganize their fortress as a defence against the aggressions of the Bengal *Nawabs*.

This is how the fort became the centre of the English settlement in south Bengal. This made Calcutta a fort-centric garrison town. When Murshid Quli Khan shifted his *diwani* headquarters to Murshidabad he did not have defence requirements to be installed in that city. The result was that it could not grow as a garrison town. Thus Calcutta and Murshidabad had a difference in their own status. Calcutta was a traders' city from the beginning which in later years was protected by a fort and a garrison. Murshidabad was simply an administrative city that housed the financial institutions of the government. The status Dhaka enjoyed was entirely different. It was the capital of the eastern part of the Mughal Empire right from the beginning. It was where the *Nawab* was stationed. It was the headquarters of the *nizamat* – the apex authority of the executive government and criminal administration of the country. When in 1765 *diwani* was granted to the English East India Company, the highest office of financial administration in the state came to be located in Calcutta. Nineteen years later when the Supreme Court was founded in Calcutta by the Act of 1773 the *nizamat* authority of Dhaka was appropriated by Calcutta. Calcutta was already centred around a fort so much so that all three institutions of the state – the ministry of finance, the apex court for criminal administration, and the army – came to be installed in Calcutta. Under the Mughal constitution the *Diwan* controlled finance and had no authority over army. The *Nazim* or the *Nawab* had control over the army and had no authority over finance. The result was that neither the *Nawab* nor the *Diwan* could revolt against Delhi. One maintained a check on the other. This was the Mughal system of checks and balance that was exercised on the provincial administration. After 1765 this system of checks was removed from provincial administration and with it a brake was lifted from Calcutta. The functions of the Company as the *Diwan* were now free from all restrictions. The Regulating Act of 1773 was important in the growth of Calcutta. "The Act created the new post of Governor General of Fort William in Bengal, and a council of four. The Governor General was given a superintending authority over the other two presidencies and thus Calcutta became the effective capital of British India."[16] Here was thus a lift in the status of Calcutta. Neither Murshidabad nor Dhaka could ever exercise any authority and claim any jurisdiction over any territory outside Bengal, Bihar, and Orissa – the territory which formed one administrative unit under the title *Subeh Bangla*. But now by the Regulating Act the jurisdiction of Calcutta was extended to the sea coast of both the west and the south. With the extension of the administrative jurisdiction also came the apex judicial authority of the city – another gift from the act of 1773. "In addition (by this Act) the Crown was empowered to set up a Supreme Court of Justice in Calcutta, consisting of a justice and three judges."[17] With the setting up of the Supreme Court, Calcutta acquired an exclusive existence for itself. It appropriated to itself the right to judge the offences of its own residents irrespective of the jurisdiction of the courts of the *nizamat*. Any resident of Calcutta who committed a crime in the territory of the *Nawab* outside the boundaries of Calcutta could claim exemption from the Mughal criminal procedures on the grounds that he or she resided in Calcutta.[18] This extra-territorial authority eventually gave Calcutta an exclusive jurisdictional supremacy which no other town in Bengal could claim. This was sustained by diplomatic battles and at the back by a superior military might.

Calcutta shared with Dakha the fame to be a sanctuary of men in distress. When Nadia fell before the advance of Muhammad Khalji, son of Bakhtiyar Khalji, in 1199 or 1202 the old Brahmanical prince Lakshmana Sena "retired to the neighbourhood of Dacca, where his descendants continued to rule as local chiefs for several generations."[19] In 1660 Prince Shuja, chased by Aurangzeb and his general Mir Jumla, fled to Dakha and from there eventually to Arakan where he was killed. Many years later Calcutta enacted the role of Dakha as a shelter for the fugitives. In the middle of the eighteenth century, Krishna Ballav, son of Raja Raj Ballav, *Diwan* of Dhaka, reversed the trend of men moving from the west to the east for shelter and himself moved as a fugitive from Dakha seeking asylum in Calcutta. Slightly more than a decade earlier, when Maratha invasions swept over western Bengal, a wave of panic-stricken populace around Calcutta rolled on into the city while a bulk of less fortunate men moved to eastern part of Bengal for protection and shelter. In acting as shelters for running away fugitives both Calcutta and Dakha became centres of political attention, which gave them added weights in contemporary politics. It is significant to note that with the coming of the Muslim rule in Bengal the trend toward eastward movement began. Islam Khan Chisti transferred the capital of *Subah Banglah* from Rajmahal to Dhaka in 1610. In 1717, when Murshid Quli Khan became the *Nawab* of Bengal, Murshidabad substituted Dhaka as the capital of the *Subah*. Thus, for slightly more than a century, Dhaka remained to be the capital of the Mughal province of Bengal. Murshidabad maintained its station as the capital till 1773 when Warren Hastings became the Governor General of the Fort William in Bengal. Thereafter began the transfer of all important official and administrative institutions of Murshidabad to Calcutta and the process was complete by the time Cornwallis dismissed Md. Reza Khan from the position of *naib nazim*, assumed to himself all powers and functions of the deputy *Nawab* and brought the *Sadar Nizamat Adalat* to Calcutta thus making the *nizamat* altogether defunct. The glory of Murshidabad as the capital of the province was in effect for slightly more than six decades. From the transfer of capital from Rajmahal in the early seventeenth century to the establishment of the capital in Calcutta in the late eighteenth century there was a period of less than 200 years when the capital of the province kept on changing from one place to another. Dakha and Murshidabad emerged as a result of a deliberate choice on the part of their rulers. Calcutta grew out of a process of evolution. Beneath the evolution there were exigencies which occasionally burst more as a result of the failure of the *Nawabi* administration in Bengal than as an outcome of a deliberate effort resembling the foundation of capital in Dhaka and Murshidabad. Somehow or other the geopolitics of Bengal was whirling and the Muslim rule was unsteady vis-à-vis the coming of the foreigners who had dominated the seaboard, established their mastery over trade and built up territorial enclaves in the country. Vis-à-vis Dhaka Murshidabad had no pretension to become sovereign and independent, but vis-à-vis Murshidabad Calcutta had pretensions lofty and vast which were sustained by all means available at the disposal of traders – representation, reconciliation, and the use of force. Therefore, the emergence of Calcutta enshrined a process of fulfilling pretensions hatched not in moods of indifference but in moods justified by traders' spirit of defending at one point and aggrandizing at other their own interests vis-à-vis the impingement of the *Nawabi* rule in Bengal.

From the time of the foundation of capital in Calcutta the inner organic units of administration were geared up to take responsibility of bigger administrative functions. The judicial departments were separated from the executive government and modern administrative machineries were brought into force. This helped the process of substitution and eventual subversion of the administrative entity of the old capital. This was done very quickly and very effectively so that in no time Calcutta became the substitute rallying point of an emerging territorial power. The Company was functioning as the *diwan* of the Mughal Empire in Calcutta just the way Murshid Quli Khan had functioned as the *diwan* of the Bengal *Subah* in Murshidabad prior to the founding of the city as a capital. It was principally because of the efforts of the *diwan* that the two cities of Murshidabad and Calcutta became capital cities in the east. Dhaka was different. It became a capital city because of the deliberate decision of the Sultan to transfer capital from Rajmahal to Dakha. Jadunath Sarkar, who charted the course of events of the period, wrote the following:

> The transfer of the capital was not the outcome of a preconceived plan on the part of Islam Khan, but rather the result of exigencies of circumstances. Dacca grew into political and military importance owing mainly to its strategic position. As a result of the prolonged stay of the Bengal viceroy Man Singh (1602–1604) here, a town sprang up round the old imperial outpost of Dacca, serving as the nucleus of the future capital. Man Singh seems to have strengthened the fortifications of Dacca, so that it soon came to be regarded as one of the four fortresses of the Bengal *Subah*. The same military and political exigencies attracted Islam Khan as well to Dacca, and his continued residence there finally determined its status. From a military settlement, Dacca became the seat of the civil government, and ultimately emerged as the official capital of the Bengal *Subah*, and it also became a busy centre of trade and industries.[20]

Here in the earlier description we find the seventeenth-century model of urban growth in Bengal. "From a military settlement" to a "seat of a civil government" – this process of transformation was as much marked in the case of Dhaka as it was in Calcutta. Dhaka grew in the seventeenth century and Calcutta in the eighteenth, but their experiences of growth had a shared model in which Dhaka anticipated Calcutta. Dhaka satisfied the entire needs of the empire-builders when the Mughal Empire was spreading to the east. Calcutta satisfied the needs of empire-builders when the territorial empire of the British was bent on an expanding to the west. Murshidabad's growth did not properly follow the Dhaka-Calcutta growth model. There the civil government had no need of a fort which was so strongly felt in Dhaka and Calcutta. From 1698 when the three villages were purchased by the East India Company in south Bengal till the 1760s when the present Fort William was erected, the main urge of the Company's administration in Calcutta was to build a fort so as to protect their commerce. About a hundred years ago in the beginning of the seventeenth century, Islam Khan was moved by the same urge to protect his new base of an east-moving power and undertook the construction of a fort. This fort-centricity of urban growth was one heritage of town-building in Bengal which Dhaka handed over to Calcutta.

J.N. Sarkar writes the following:

> Islam Khan himself, contributed much to the development of Dacca. A new fort was built, inside which a new palace was constructed, no vestige of which now exists, and new roads were laid down, all skirting the river which is at present known as the Buriganga. The defences of the city were improved by means of two forts made on either side of the point where the river Dulai bifurcated (one branch joining the Lakhiya at Demra and the other at Khizrpur) described by the author of the *Baharistan* as the forts of Beg Murad Khan, and also by means of artificial canals the course of some of which may still be traced.[21]

Thus, as in Dhaka so in Calcutta, the fort-centricity of the city was urged by the defence requirements of the town. The English in Calcutta did not consciously adopt the Dhaka model. They had their own model available in the castle-centric growth of European towns. In the west castles were built on hilltops whereas in Bengal forts were constructed by the side of a river with canals surrounding them.[22] When the English built their settlement on the bank of the river, there was a creek running adjacent to the site of the old fort moving towards east.[23] Calcutta was thus as much a product of the fort as Dhaka was and its port grew under the shadow of the fort so much so that in later years the fort and the port together built up the supremacy of Calcutta. The fort and its army presented as the force behind the territory-hunting imperial mind of the English. Since the Empire was the achievement and acquisition of a mercantile company, its merchant mentality was satisfied by the aggressive proclivity of the port that cast its commercial and utilitarian charm on a vast hinterland outside. Calcutta grew out of the momentum derived from a fort-port complex which itself was enormously self-propelling so that the urban growth in Calcutta went of its own heedless to conscious planning or its absence till such time as Wellesley's coming to Calcutta. After 1757 the English were certainly the masters of the city, but they were not the ones who put their conscious mind in the development of the city. They were not the creators of the city. They were its makers putting forth much effort to make it an eastern replica of their own city – London.

Armenian Calcutta turns British

Calcutta was thus not a creation of the English. But as a city it certainly was manufactured by them.[24] It was simply a small village when Job Charnock set his foot here, and it was as a village only that it got mention in all earlier references.[25] When the English came here, Calcutta, the hamlet which lay between Govindapur and Sutanuti[26] was as ordinary as any other nearby village – Sutanuti, Govindapur, Salkia, Chitpur etc. Since the beginning of the sixteenth century with the coming of the Portuguese in the Hughli river, the importance of the eastern bank steadily gained momentum. Some Basaks and Seth families came and settled at Govindapur.[27] The Govindapur-Sutanuti area ever since gained importance as trading centres.

In 1698 when the English East India Company purchased the three villages of Sutanuti, Dihi, Calcutta, and Govindapur, these places were termed as maujas in Mughal land records.[28] In 1596 it got entry in the *Ain-i-Akbari* as a small rent-paying village.[29] Thus, prior to the coming of the English, Calcutta had no importance.

The real importance of Calcutta began when the English consolidated their rule in the three villages of Sutanuti, Kalikata, and Govindapur. From the beginning the English had made a conscious effort to organize Calcutta as an area which might flourish in contrast to both Hugli and Murshidabad and might bear the stamp of the estate which was essentially English. To this end Calcutta was made to grow over nearly six decades, i.e. from 1698 to 1757. At first Calcutta was organized as a garrison town and the principal centre of trade for the

WHO WAS THE REAL FOUNDER OF CALCUTTA?

English in eastern India; then it was developed as a centre of administration; and finally it was developed as a seat of power. Thus there were three aspects of the growth of Calcutta the first two of which were coextensive and coincident to each other. The effort to build Calcutta as a seat of power only came to take shape after 1772.

It is this part of British achievement in building urban sites which prompted and eventually promoted the colonial belief that Calcutta was founded by the British. To say that Job Charnock was the father of the city of Calcutta is to deny the imperial dynamics which eventually led to the growth of Calcutta. Charnock's arrival here opened the dynamics of Calcutta's growth that had remained pent up for so long. The excerpt quoted here shows how irresistibly the dynamics of colonialism was at work behind the promotion of Calcutta as a city:

> The history of modern Calcutta began on the day Job Charnock stepped down from his boat at a landing place on the river Hooghly. With the English factory in Calcutta as the nucleus, trade and commerce began to expand fast and population multiplied. To facilitate trade and commerce and to serve a growing population the need for a city administration came to be acutely felt for the construction and maintenance of roads and drains, for building houses conforming to recognized standards of public health and hygiene, for supply water, etc. With the British victory at Palassey the importance of Calcutta was further enhanced, and the people of Calcutta came under more and more tax burdens. Setting up of a municipal machinery for tax collection became an imperative. It was felt that without the active association of the native population with the municipal machinery, raising of the taxes might not be a success. In order, therefore, to reap a higher revenue the British rulers set about the task of democratizing the municipal machinery. In the beginning native response was lukewarm in as much as the local people were as yet unfamiliar with and unused to the methods and modes of self-government. Some years later, however, the situation was radically transformed and the native population became vociferously claimant for greater participation in municipal affairs. The attitude of the British rulers, too underwent a corresponding change, and from the time of Calcutta's Chief Magistrate David M. Farlan's initial experiment in 1833 till the passing of the Calcutta Municipal Act of 1863, the policy of the British over the question of democratization was one of alternate advances and retreats.[30]

From this observation it is clear that the English did not consciously promote the growth of the city. The inexorable logic of imperialism was operating behind the growth of the town. In this one may say that the English were the unconscious tools of history in exercising themselves for the promotion of this place. There is also another point in this. When we speak of the role of the English in the uplift of Calcutta, we forget that the English could not have exercised it at all if the Armenians had not helped them.[31] Professor C.R. Wilson wrote in 1895 that, during the previous year, he discovered the earliest Christian tomb in Calcutta available in the Calcutta Armenian Churchyard. Dated 1630, this tomb gave him some basic enlightenment about the origin of the city of Calcutta. He writes:

> It is gratifying to learn that the efforts which have recently been made by various enquiries and in various ways to push back the history of Calcutta to the remoter part, before the formation of the English settlement under Job Charnock, have not been altogether without fruit. By slow degrees evidences are being accumulated which tend to connect Calcutta with earlier traders and prove that even before the building of Fort William the place was not without importance. Among such evidences one of the most striking is the discovery which has recently been made by Mr. M. J. Seth, an enthusiastic Armenian scholar, who at the instance of Government has translated a larger number of the classical Armenian inscriptions in the churchyard of St. Nazareth, Calcutta. The earliest inscription runs as follows:
>
>> This is the tomb of Rezebeebeh, the wife of the late charitable Sookias, who departed from this world to life eternal on the 21st day of Nakha in the year 15 i.e. on the 21st July, 1630.
>
> What a world of questions is suggested by this newly-found record? Why was this source of information never utilized before, who was the 'Charitable Sookias' and how did his family come to be living in Calcutta sixty years before the advent of the English? Was there already an Armenian Settlement here? *Are the Armenians after all the Founders of the City?*
>
> Upon these considerations our early records do not cast much light, but they supply other equally important

information about the Armenians in Calcutta. If they do not enable us to decide whether there was an Armenian colony settled here before 1630, they show that it was through the Armenians that the English colony secured a footing in the country. *If Job Charnock be the founder of Calcutta, the author of its privileges and early security is the great Armenian merchant, Khojah Isreal Sarhad.*[32] [Italics mine]

The enlightenment coming from the pen of such a great historian as Wilson seems to be significant. It at least settles the point that there was a very flourishing Armenian community living in Calcutta long before Job Charnock set his foot on the soil of this city. The Armenians were important as traders and in the politics of Bengal over many years since the time of the revolt of Sobha Singh they played the role of political brokers. But in spite of all their importance in politics and trade they could not promote a village into a city. Under them Calcutta was never made a rallying point of politics or a centre of trade as large as Calcutta turned out to be under the English. Calcutta's real take-off in politics and trade was ushered in during the time of the English.

Yet the role of the Armenians in installing the English in Calcutta cannot be minimized. It was the Armenian, Khojah Sarhad – "Cojah Surhand" of the English records – who had mediated between the English and Mughals during the years of crisis at the closing of the seventeenth century when Shova Singh unfurled the banner of revolt. It was the same Sarhad who played the role of go-between between the English and the Mughals during the period of expectation when the Surman Embassy met the Emperor at Delhi. Of this Khojah Sarhad Wilson writes: "He was apparently more successful as a Political Agent than as a merchant."[33] Between 1696, when the revolt of Shova Singh took place, and 1698, when Calcutta, Sutanuti, and Govindapur were acquired by the English, the Khojah was the principal door through which the English could maintain their contact with the Mughal authority. An official English record of 5 June 1714 said this: "It is absolutely necessary that some person who is perfect master of the Persian language and understands our affairs very well, and that may be useful for us, be sent to Delhi along so qualified in both these respects as Cojah Surhand. He is therefore, the fittest man to send."[34]

Given the political acumen of Sarhad the question that arises is this: why did the English feel the necessity of utilizing the diplomatic

EARLY FORMATIONS

talent of Sarhad? The answer to this question may be given in the following lines:

> after Job Charnock had settled in Calcutta in 1690 it was deemed necessary to build a Factory with its usual adjunct a Fort for the protection of their emporium and the valuable goods to be stored therein, and for such extensive building, large tracts of lands were necessary, but how were they to acquire the lands without the permission of the hostile Moghul Government which viewed the growth and the expansion of the Company's trade with suspicion. It may be mentioned that the Armenians were the most favoured subjects of the Delhi government at that time and had been held in high esteem by the Mughal Emperors from the days of Akbar downwards for their loyalty and integrity. The English were not slow in recognizing the worth of the Armenian in Bengal, whose valued friendship they eagerly sought for the furtherance of their cause in the country. There resided at that time an eminent Armenian merchant at Hooghly, Khojah Isreal Sarhad by name, a nephew of the illustrious Khojah Phanoos Kalandar of Surat with whom he had been to England in 1688.
>
> The English being aware of the abilities of the Armenian merchant, approached Khojah Isreal Sarhad and requested him to proceed to the Camp of the Mogul Emperor, Azim-ush-Shan, the grandson of the Emperor Aurangzeb, who had come down from Delhi to quell the rebellion of Subha Singh of Bengal towards the end of the year 1697.[35]

Therefore, it was the Anglo-Armenian partnership which led to the making of Calcutta in the early years of the eighteenth century. The real security and promotion of Calcutta began only after 1715 when the Surman Embassy went to Delhi to meet the Emperor and more correctly after 1717 when the Embassy derived a rich crop of privileges for the English in Bengal from the Mughal Government in Delhi. Stewart in his *History of Bengal* clearly wrote that "the inhabitants of Calcutta enjoyed, after the return of the Embassy, a degree of freedom and security unknown to other subjects of the Mugul Empire, and that city increased yearly in wealth, beauty and riches." From 1698 to 1715 was a period when Calcutta was really founded. The entire foundation was made possible by the collaboration of the Armenians.

WHO WAS THE REAL FOUNDER OF CALCUTTA?

The role of the English in Calcutta clearly shows that from the beginning they had a definite stake in organizing the security of the city. Truly speaking, the security which the English provided to Calcutta was one very important factor in the transformation of Calcutta from a village into a city. From Shova Singh's rebellion in 1696 to the invasion of Siraj-ud-daullah in 1756, through the years of the Maratha invasion between 1742 to 1748, Calcutta owed its protection, recovery from chaos and reinstatement to order to the English might. At the time of Shova Singh's rebellion the English were not in possession of Sutanuti, Govindapur, and Calcutta. Yet the English used their arms to protect Calcutta vis-à-vis the rebels. "The part played by the English at Calcutta in those events," say Wilson and Carey, "was subordinate, but not unimportant." The role of the English have been detailed out by these historians:

> On the 23rd December 1696, finding that the rebels, who occupied the opposite bank of the river, were growing "abusive," they ordered the Diamond to ride at anchor off Sutanuti Point and keep them from crossing the stream. They also sent the *Thomas* to the governor of the Thana fort to lie off it as a guardship. On receiving full instructions round their factory, and in January 1697, reported that they were employed in fortifying themselves, but wanted proper guns for the points, and desired the people at Madras to send at least ten guns for the present use. At the beginning of April a neighbouring rajah secretly deposited the gun of forty-eight thousand rupees with the agent for safe custody, and a week or two afterwards the late governor of Hughli honoured Calcutta with a visit. In May, learning that the rebels were all dispersed, they got rid of the band of fifty native gunners which they had raised, but continued building their fort, and substituted a structure of brick and mud for the old thatched house which used to contain Company's stores and provisions.[36]

From this observation it is clear that the English had given status to Calcutta. The "governor of Hugli honoured Calcutta with a visit" only when the English had showed to the Mughals that Calcutta was worthy of recognition by the Mughal rulers. Immediately after this, the English, accompanied by Khojah Sarhad, met Prince Azim-us-Shan, and, after a little negotiation in July 1698,

> for the sum of sixteen thousand rupees, the English procured letters patent from the Prince allowing them to purchase from the

existing holders the right of renting the three villages of Calcutta, Sutanuti and Govindapur. The grant, after some delay in order that it might be counter signed by the Treasurer, was carried into execution, and the security of Calcutta which began with the permission to build a fort, was now completely assured.[37]

This, one may say, was the real beginning of Calcutta.

When the English first arrived in Calcutta it was almost an area of wilderness. Everything was unsettled and unorganized. Out of a general situation of chaos they brought order in and around the area. When one says that Calcutta was founded by the English one does not mean that it was set up by the English just the way ancient rulers used to set up cities to perpetuate their names. For the English founding the city meant that it was made habitable by them and its status was raised before the eyes of the Mughals rulers. Calcutta certainly had no dignity of its own when the English first arrived here. Its dignity was achieved. The English struggled very hard to achieve this dignity and all their later struggles were certainly not for the sake of the area but for the people who lived there. This was all for their settlement. The English wanted an area that would be insulated from the influence of the Mughals. All their struggles were for an insulated settlement, and fortunately for Calcutta it fitted in the English map of insulated settlement here in Bengal.

What the condition of Calcutta and its neighbourhood were like at the time of the arrival of the English may be recounted from the annals of historians:

> when the English first came to Calcutta their position was precarious and ill-defined. The land in the neighbourhood being to a large extent wild and uncultivated, there was little or nothing to prevent any body of men that chose from seizing a piece of unoccupied ground and squatting on it. In this way the Setts and Bysacks had, more than a hundred years before, founded Govindapur, and the English, coming to Calcutta with the good-will and probably, at the suggestion of these very Setts and By sacks, had nothing more to do than to take as much waste land they needed, clear it, and build houses and offices. They trusted that the natural strength of the position would protect them, and that the acquiescence of the government leave them undisturbed in their new home.[38]

WHO WAS THE REAL FOUNDER OF CALCUTTA?

From this condition Calcutta grew, and it grew under the auspices of the English. The grant of the letters patent by the Mughal Prince gave the English a station in the Mughal body politic. Truly speaking Calcutta owes its origin and growth to this change in the status of the English and historians write the following:

> The letters patent granted by Prince 'Azimu-sh-Shan in 1698 changed all this. The English Company gained a definite status in the eyes of the Indian Governors. It became the Collector of the three towns, Sutanuti, Calcutta, and Govindapur. As such it was empowered to levy internal duties and customs on articles of trade passing through its districts and impose petty taxes and cesses on the cultivators, as such it managed the lands and exercised jurisdiction over the inhabitants. The exact relations of a Collector to the supreme government are a matter of dispute. Ordinarily, we are told, the collector realized the public revenue arising from the land under him, and, after deducting a commission of ten per cent and various other small charges, transmitted the sum to the Imperial Treasury. In the case of the Company this sum was fixed. In short, the Council at Calcutta paid the Mogul an annual rent of twelve hundred rupees, more or less, and was free to tax and govern the place almost as it pleased.[39]

Thus, for the first time in history Calcutta got a ruler for its own. Formerly it did not occur prominently in the priority considerations of the *Nawabs*. The result was that Calcutta did not rise above the status of a very prominent village on the bank of the river Hugli. In the revenue parlance of the time, Calcutta was not more than a *mouja*. For the first time the English appointed an officer whose explicit function was to collect the revenue of the village[40] and the Calcutta Council acted as its government, thus presiding over the phase which saw the transition of a village to a town. This town was not to be what the Mughals used to call a *qasba*. Its orientation was different. It has within its midst the seat of a government and for many years the legal jurisdiction of the government did not extend beyond the boundaries of this town. Many years later it was observed "The legal jurisdiction . . . which the Company derive from the charter and acts of parliament, as they now stand, extends or is allowed to extend, only to the town or settlement of Calcutta, and some subordinate factories."⁴¹ It is true that, at the beginning, the English in Calcutta held power "in subordinate to the Mohgals, or Nabobs."⁴² But as time went on this power became absolute and was thought of as independent of any other power separate from the Company and superior to it. The Company's Government in Calcutta became all powerful. Bolts wrote: "No warrant or subpoena from the Mayor's court is permitted to be served on persons, even at the subordinate factories, except with the express leave of the Governor, and in such case this permission is looked upon as a favour."⁴³

The power and jurisdiction of the Governor and his government superseded in practice that of the *Nawab*, and, when Bolts wrote his book in 1772, he had no hesitation to write about the supremacy of the Company. "But the jurisdiction now assumed and exercised by the Company and their substitutes is, in fact, entirely unlimited, and without check or control throughout all the provinces called the NABOB'S, of which they collect the revenues."⁴⁴

The importance of Calcutta under the English was this. It gave the English the base from where their majesty was practically built. It was the base of the new government parallel to the *Nawab*'s. Under the *Nawab*, Calcutta was a village, a trade-centre, or at best an emerging spot of flourishing community of which the Setts and the Basaks were a part. But now Calcutta was a base of power. Calcutta was urbanized because it was a base of a political and mercantile power. This position of Calcutta was essentially a gift of the English. The English were aware of this and hence their concern for the defence of the city, which on all occasions was unique. Bolts wrote:

> The gallant behavior of the inhabitants, free merchants and free mariners, when Calcutta was lost in 1756, and retaken in 1757, may be mentioned as a proof of what we advance. But still a stranger instance of the same kind was given in the year 1759, against the Dutch, when it has not been for the spirited and active behavior of the inhabitants, the Company's military force would not have been able to cope with their enemies. Again upon the rupture with Cossim Ally Khawn, in the year 1763, the European inhabitants of Calcutta were formed into four companies of militia, and properly disciplined for the defense of the settlement, while all the regular troops were sent to a distance against the enemy.⁴⁵

WHO WAS THE REAL FOUNDER OF CALCUTTA?

Apart from defence the English gave Calcutta one more thing. This was religious toleration:

> In Calcutta all religions are freely tolerated but the Presbyterian, and that they brow-beat. The pagans carry their idols in procession through the town, the Roman Catholics have their church to lodge their idols in, and the Mohammedan is not discountenanced, but there are no polemics, except what are between our high Churchmen and our low, or between the Governor's party and other private merchants on points of trade.[46]

Thus the cosmopolitan outlook necessary for the growth of a town was first propounded by the English. This outlook helped assembly of people in Calcutta and contributed towards stimulating the internal unity and cohesion of the population-mix that had not yet taken the shape of a well-defined community here in Calcutta.

From the protection the English offered to the town of Calcutta grew the concept that Calcutta was a creation of the English. Even the Muslim rulers believed that prior to the coming the English Calcutta was nothing but a village and its revenue went to the service of the Kali temple which stood there.[47] In the Middle Ages, Calcutta existed as a village, but its importance either as a city or as a pilgrim-centre was not properly felt. At least during the time of Sri Chaitanya Calcutta was not very significant. Even those who are very enthusiastic to prove that Calcutta was a place of ancient reputation have to beat retreat here:

> It is contended by some learned Vaishnavas, that in the Chitayana Charitamirita (Life of Chaitayana), no mention is made of the great Reformer of Bengal having visited Kalighata. Born in 1485 A.D. he flourished in the early part of a sixteenth century. During his peregrination he came as far as Varahanagara, but he never thought of seeing the Kali of Kalighata. As the founder of Vaishnavism, his religious instincts might have repelled the idea of Sakta worship, but it is not unnatural to suppose that if Kalighata for the sake of his beloved mother Sachi, who belonged to the sect of Saktas and worshipped Kali. But this fact cannot be adduced as an argument against the existence of Kalighata at the time. Chaitanya's travels being spiritual tours for conversion, he was led to go to places

where he expected to gain his object, and not merely as a random pilgrim, to place reputed for their holiness only. There may be thousand other reasons to account for his not visiting Kali, or for the non-mention of the goddess in the Chaitanya Charitamrita.[48]

Even if we accept the view that Calcutta was an important centre of pilgrimage it does not mean that Calcutta's urbanization was in any way connected with its being a holy place. Seven miles south-east of Calcutta there is a place called Behala. It was the place where Devi Behula was worshipped.[49] This place was under the Savarna Chaudhuri family, and, in point of importance as a *pitha* [pilgrim-centre], it is compared to Nalhati or the place where Devi *Yasaresvari* was placed, i.e. Jessore. But this place did not grow as an important area where a town could flourish. The point to be noted here is this that for a long time Calcutta was under the sway of a very remarkable *zamindar* of eighteenth-century Bengal, namely Maharaja Krishna Chandra of Nadia. As late as the end of the nineteenth century he was referred to as "the Zamindar of Pargana Calcutta & c."[50] What did he do to stimulate the growth of Calcutta? Almost nothing:

> It is stated in the Life of Krishna Chandra that he was the constant companion of Aliverdi Khan (Muhabat Jang), and that during his trips on the river he used to read and explain the Mahabharata to him. It is also said that he succeeded in obtaining from the *Nawab* a remission of arrears of revenue due from him to the amount of fifty-two lakhs or so, by cleverly taking, on one of these river trips, the *Nawab*'s party on shore on the northern side of Calcutta, where there were settlements, and leading the *Nawab* on towards the south, where, in the distant thickets and woods, the roar of the tiger was heard, and wild elephants were seen, pointing to him the nature of his Zamindary, and the obvious reasons of his having been a defaulter. Such a favourite of the *Nawab* could not but have obtained from his concessions in favour of the Kali shrine.[51]

From this observation it is clear that Calcutta under the native *zamindars* did not grow very much. Nor did it grow effectively as a religious place. Some believe that the importance of Kalighat grew only in the eighteenth century when the English had set Calcutta on the orbit of urbanization. Thus the urbanization of Calcutta helped Kalighat grow.

WHO WAS THE REAL FOUNDER OF CALCUTTA?

This meant that the growth of Kalighat as a pilgrim centre was a later phenomenon and cannot be adduced as a factor helping the growth of Calcutta as an urban centre.[52] Tradition says that the image of Kali as worshipped in Kalighat was first worshipped by

> "A Sevayet Sannyasi, one of the Dasanamis, who had become a follower of the tenets of Yogi Chaurangi and Jangal Gur [Giri] by name. . . ."[53] The reason why Jangal Gur Chaurangi selected this site on the confines of Govindapur for the establishment of his Tirtha is apparent. Although situated in a belt of jungle, infested as it was at the time, with all kinds of wild beast, he saw that he and his goddess would be within the search of human aid. He looked to the then few inhabitants of Govindapur for his maintenance and that of this goddess.[54]

This meant that the prospect of habitation in Calcutta-Govindapur area prior to the coming of the English was extremely bleak. The temple of Kali, a pilgrim centre, from very ancient times, did not succeed in organizing habitation around it. Its pull factors were weak and the population did not veer around it. In this condition the possibility of Calcutta taking to urbanization with Kalighat as its rallying point does not seem to be a reasonable proposition. The true urbanization of Calcutta began in the late eighteenth and early nineteenth century and the credit of commissioning the three villages to urbanization goes really to the rule of the English East India Company in Bengal.[55]

Notes

1 A.K. Ray, *A Short History of Calcutta*, Rddhi Edition, Calcutta, 1982, p. 29.
2 Relying on Harprasad Sastri's Pratapaditya, A.K. Ray identifies the places where the forts were built to be as follows: the first fort at Mutlah (banks of the river Matla in modern Canning), the second at Raigarh (Garden Reach), the third at Behala, the fourth at Tanna (Thana slightly away from Garden Reach), the fifth at Sulkea (Salkia in modern Howrah district), the sixth at Chitpur (in modern Kolkata), and the seventh at Atpur (near Mulajor) – ibid.
3 Ray, *A Short History of Calcutta*, pp. 29–30.
4 "Kalikshetra, the land of the legend, 'extending from Dakshineswar on the north to Bahula on the south' was according to Hindu tradition, valuable enough in the time of King Vallala of Gaur to have constituted a royal gift to a Brhamin family." – Ray, *A Short History of Calcutta*, p. 17.
5 Ray, *A Short History of Calcutta*, p. 18.
6 This was a subject of discussion in the first four decades of the twentieth century and has been ably analyzed in the following works: R.K.

Mukherjee, *The Changing Face of Bengal: A Study of Riverine Economy*, University of Calcutta, Calcutta, 1938, pp. 3–10 and S.C. Majumdar, *Rivers of the Bengal Delta*, University of Calcutta, Calcutta, 1942, pp. 65–72.

7   For detail, see Richard M. Eaton, *The Rise of Islam and the Bengal Frontier 1204–1760*, Oxford University Press, New Delhi, 1997, Ch. 8, pp. 194–198.

8   This point has been discussed in W.H. Arden Wood, "Rivers and Man in the Indus-Ganges Alluvial Plain", *Scottish Geographical Magazine*, 40, No. 1, 1924, pp. 9–10 and C. Strickland, *Deltaic Formation, with Special Reference to the Hydrographic Processes of the Ganges and the Brahmaputra*, Calcutta Longmans, Green, 1940, p. 104.

9   Eaton, *The Rise of Islam and the Bengal Frontier 1204–1760*, pp. 194–195.

10 While detailing out the changes in the courses of the river, Kanangopal Bagchi writes: "When the distributaries in the west were active, those in the east were perhaps in their infancy, and as the rivers to the east were adolescing, those in the west became senile. The active stage of delta formation thus migrated south-eastwards in time and space, leaving the rivers in the old delta, now represented by Murshidabad, Nadia and Jessore with the Goalundo Sub-Division of Faridpur, to languish or decay." – K. Bagchi, *Ganges Delta*, University of Calcutta, Calcutta, 1944, p. 58. For further information read N.D. Bhattacharya, "Changing Course of the Padma and Human Settlements", *National Geographic Journal of India*, No. 1 and 2, March–June 1978, pp. 63–65.

11 Eaton, *The Rise of Islam and the Bengal Frontier 1204–1760*, p. 198.

12 Ray, *A Short History of Calcutta*, p. 30

13 Ray, *A Short History of Calcutta*, p. 30.

14 Ibid.

15 Ibid, pp. 30–31.

16 Percival Spear, ed., *The Oxford History of India by the Late Vincent A.Smith*, 3rd edn. Part III, Oxford at the Clarendon Press, 1958, Reprint 1961, p. 504.

17 Ibid.

18 The conflict between the Nawabi government and the English in Calcutta on jurisdiction over criminals began during the rule of Murshid Quli Khan and it reached its climax at the time of Sirajuddaullah when Krisnaballav (alias Krishnadas, son of Raja Raybalav of Dhaka) escaped from Dhaka with a huge treasure to Calcutta and the English refused to hand him over to the Nawab.

19 J.B. Harrison in Spear, *The Oxford History of India by the Late Vincent A.Smith*, p. 236.

20 J.N.Sarkar, *History of Bengal*, Vol. II, Dacca University Publication, 1948, Second Impression, 1972, Vol. II, Dacca, 1948, Second Impression, 1972, p. 283.

21 Sarkar, *History of Bengal*, pp. 283–284.

22 The fort-centricity of Calcutta has been discussed in Pradip Sinha, *Calcutta in Urban History*, Firma KLM Private Ltd., Calcutta, 1978, Ch. 1 & 2.

23 The Creek Row, a long lane in central Calcutta, still carries the old memory of the creek.

WHO WAS THE REAL FOUNDER OF CALCUTTA?

24　It is said that Charnock landed here on 24 August 1690. Some suggest that it was the famous Baithak-Khana tree "whose shade captivated the venerable Charnock" and he landed here for rest. His contemporaries frequently assumed that a more unsuitable site for landing and for a great city could not have been found. Subsequent developments and modern opinion vindicated the judgement.

25　"literary references to Calcutta and Kalighat is found as early as 1495 A.D., in a poem written by the Bengali, Bipradas." – W.W. Goode, *Municipal Calcutta Its Institutions in Their Origin and Growth*, Edinburgh, 1916, p. 3.

26　Ibid.

27　"With the advent of the Portuguese at the beginning of the sixteenth century, the light of history falls across the Hughli. At Betor, by the site of the modern Sibpur, the foreigners carried on a brisk trade, while five Bengali families [four Byzacks and one family of Setts] broke, as their family archives show, new ground on the east bank of the Hughli, with the settlement of Govindpur, South of the modern Chowringhee." – Ibid.

28　"The territory over which the Company assumed control was about 5077 bighas, or 1692 acres in area, comprising roughly the land between the river and the Salt Lakes, from Govindpur to Sutanuti. These limits of course included a much larger area than 5077 bighas." – Goode, *Municipal Calcutta Its Institutions in Their Origin and Growth*, p. 4.

29　The entry was under the title "Kalikata."

30　Keshab Chaudhuri, *Calcutta: Story of Its Government*, 1973, p. 3.

31　Professor C.R. Wilson published in the *Englishman*, dated 31 January 1895, an article under the title "Armenian Founders of Calcutta." This article is the pioneer in proving that Calcutta was not built by the English. What they did to promote the well-being of the city was done not without the help of the Armenians. This article of Prof. Wilson is not available now because the *Englishman*, which was published from Calcutta, has long become defunct. Reference to and excerpts from Wilson's article are available in Mesrovb Jacob Seth, *Armenians in India: From the Earliest Times to the Present Day, a Work of Original Research* (first published 1937), Reprint, Calcutta, 1983, Ch. XXXII, p. 419.

32　Quoted in Jacob Seth, *Armenians in India: From the Earliest Times to the Present Day, a Work of Original Research*, pp. 419–420.

33　Ibid, p. 420.

34　Quoted Ibid.

35　Jacob Seth, *Armenians in India: From the Earliest Times to the Present Day, a Work of Original Research*, pp. 422–423. William Bolts in his Consideration on India Affairs, published in London, in 1772, wrote (p. 61): "Being sensible likewise of the precarious tenures of their establishments in Bengal and elsewhere, in the year 1715 the Company sent a deputation of two gentlemen, named John Surman and the other a very considerable Armenian merchant, named Coge[Khojah] Serhaud to solicit redress for past and security against future oppressions; for an extension of their old, and for many new privileges, and particularly for a small spot of ground to be allowed them wherever they settled a Factory."

36　C.R. Wilson and W.H. Carey, *Glimpses of the Olden Times: India Under East India Company*, Calcutta, 1968, pp. 110–111.

37 Ibid, p. 111.
38 Ibid, p. 112.
39 Ibid, p. 113.
40 "In consequence of this change [acquisition of Calcutta by the E.I. Company] in the position of the Company, a new member was added to the council to represent it in its new capacity. Henceforth a special officer, known as the Collector, was appointed to gather in the revenue of the three towns and to keep them in order. In 1700 Relph Sheldon became the first Collector of Calcutta, and from him through many inheritor . . . the line of the Calcutta Collectors run in unbroken succession down to the present day." Ibid.
41 William Bolts, *Consideration on India Affairs Particularly Respecting the Present State of Bengal and Its Dependences*, 2nd edn, London, MDCCLXXII, p. 89.
42 Ibid.
43 Ibid.
44 Ibid.
45 Bolts, *Consideration on India Affairs Particularly Respecting the Present State of Bengal and Its Dependences*, p. 145.
46 This is the statement of Captain Hamilton and quoted by Wilson & Carey, *Glimpses of the Olden Times: India Under East India Company*, p. 125. Captain Hamilton's account was published around 1727.
47 Nawab Muhabbat Khan, who is said to have authored Akhbar-i-muhabbat "A General History of India from the Time of the Ghaznivides to the Accession of Muhammad Akbar, at the close of the year 1806," gave the history of the foundation of Calcutta by Mr. Charnock and, in that connection, he said: "Calcutta formerly was only a village, the revenue of which was assigned for the expenses of the temple of Kali Devi, which stands there." – Elliot's History of India, & c, Vol. VIII, p. 378.
48 "Kalighat and Calcutta" by Gourdas Basak in Calcutta Review No. CLXXXIV, Vol. XCII, January, 1891, p. 309 note.
49 Ibid, p. 309.
50 Ibid, p. 310.
51 Ibid, note.
52 "Bharat Chandra, the famous Bengali poet of the last century, who wrote his Annada Mangala, & c, in Saka 1674 (A.D. 1752), of course, mentions in his Pitha-Mala, Kalighata, as originating from the fall there of the four toes of Sati's right foot, and speaks of the presiding goddess as Kali, and of Nakulesa, as Bhairava. This proves that in the days of the Sakta Maharaja Krishna Chandra of Nadiya [Nuddea of English records], who was the Zamindar of 'Pargana Calcutta, & c', and whose poet laureate Bharat Chandra was, the current Kalighat legend had acquired a maturity, and that under some of the tolerant Nawabs of Bengal, but chiefly under British protection, even in the early days of the English period, Kalighata had reached the climax of its celebrity." [Italics mine] – Ibid, p. 310. "Mythically, Kalighat, may of course, claim priority over Calcutta, but historically their comparative antiquity in uncertain." – Ibid, p. 311.
53 Ibid, p. 311.

54 Ibid, p. 312. In later years when the Chaurangi temple of Kali was demolished because Govindpur was taken for the building of a new fort there the image of the goddess was shifted to Kalighata. "It is said that in 1809, the Savarna Chaudhuris of Behala erected for her the present temple." – Ibid, p. 312 note.
55 Dr. Pratap Chandra Chunder, "Calcutta the Controversial City", *The Quarterly Review of Historical Studies*, XXXVII, Nos. 1 & 2, April–September, 1997, pp. 44–53. This is the Professor Nisith Ranjan Roy Memorial Lecture, 1997–1998 delivered at the Institute of Historical Studies on 10 January 1998.

6
HOW CALCUTTA SUPERSEDED INTERIOR TOWNS

There was no dearth of towns in *Subeh Bangla*. Dakha, Murshidabad, Chittagong, Hugli, Chandernagore, Malda, Burdwan, and many other small and medium towns made up the galaxy of urban settlements in the province. In spite of this, Calcutta was the only city that was properly urbanized and no other town could share the fortune of Calcutta. No city of Bengal in the colonial period matched the growth of the urban settlement of Calcutta. Was it because of colonial indifference to interior settlements or because of the compulsive logic of certain economic forces that did not allow habitations to take the shape of urbanized centres of growth? To this question we address ourselves in this chapter.

A challenged interior

A general cause of the slow growth of the interior was that, like deindustrialization, the country went through a process of de-urbanization in the colonial age. Under the general impact of the process almost all the towns of Bengal – Dakha, Murshidabad, Chittagong, Burdwan, Hugli, Malda, and Chandernagore – suffered.[1] The character of urbanization is normally determined by the strength of population living in towns. It is well known that between 1800 and 1872 the urban population of the traditional cities in India did not increase. The urban settlements of Bengal were parts of this shrinking demographic landscape. Only Calcutta, Bombay, and Madras and some smaller towns of the interior had shown signs of the increase of population. Among the towns which suffered in terms of population, the important ones were Dhaka, Murshidabad, Burdwan, Lucknow, Tanjore, and some other traditional settlements. Some small towns grew up about this time. Notable among them were Ara, Bhagalpur, Chhapra, Munghyr, Srirampur, Cuttack, and some other towns of the same status.

HOW CALCUTTA SUPERSEDED INTERIOR TOWNS

Calcutta rose but Dakha and Murshidabad fell. With their fall the growth of Burdwan, Malda, Hugli, and Chittagong was arrested. The hinterland of Chittagong centred around Dakha. As business was directed toward Calcutta Chittagong was turned into a peripheral port. Dakha had long passed under the shadow of Murshidabad. With losing animation, it was no longer able to feed the growth of Chittagong. Malda was an adjunct of Dakha and Hugli was a satellite of Murshidabad and therefore with Dakha and Murshidabad they collapsed. Burdwan, a river-fed deltaic area, grew as a perennial centre of agriculture and showed little potential to fix itself up as a permanent centre in the bigger trade-network of the country. According to Walter Hamilton the total population of Dhaka in 1815 was 1,50,000. In fifteen years' time it suffered a catastrophic fall, so that in 1830 the Magistrate of Dhaka could barely fix it at 66,989. In 1872, the year of the first census, it was stated to be 68,595,[2] which meant that in four decades the increase of the population of Dakha was marginal. Between 1830 and 1872 Dakha thus stagnated. About the same time or a little earlier, Burdwan and some other towns of Bengal were in the grip of stagnation. W.H. Bayley listed them as Burdwan (54,000), Chandernagore (41,000), Chinsura (19,000), Chandrakona (18,000), and Serampur (11,000).[3] Commenting on this S. Bhattacharya observes : "The first two in order of size experienced a population decline of the order of about 40 per cent by 1872 Census; the smaller towns, excepting Khirpai, increased in size."[4]

It is thus clear that from the beginning Burdwan and some other towns in Bengal lagged behind in the race for urbanization. This lagging behind started in the middle of the eighteenth century when the rule of the Bengal *Nawabs* was slowly giving way to the coming of the British protectorate in Bengal. About half a century before that, in 1696–1697, the *Radh* region of Bengal, i.e. the wide area consisting of Midnapur, Burdwan, Birbhum, and Bankura, was devastated by the rebellion of Shova Singh. The rebels defeated and killed the Raja of Burdwan in a pitched battle and massacred all members of his family. Only Jagatram, the son of the Raja fled to Dakha and saved his life. The English at Sutanuty, the Dutch at Chinsura, and the French at Chandernagore applied to the *Nawab* for the permission to build their own fortress for protection and the *Nawab* acceded to it.

This is the only instance in the annals of Mughal Bengal where the foreigners were given separate right to build their own system of protection outside the security provided by the *Nawab*. It was this privilege on which the English had based all their subsequent efforts to build a fort in Calcutta. All *Nawabs* resisted these efforts, for in this was implied that a body of merchants had appropriated for themselves the authority to create an exclusive military defence for themselves. Ultimately, however, all efforts at resistance were in vain. The English proved themselves irresistible and it was in this irresistibility of a body of merchants taking the postures of a band of armed soldiers that Calcutta eventually owed its prominence as a place secured for habitation. Neither the French nor the Dutch could do this. None was as determined as the English to hold on persistently to their privilege of protecting their own trade with their own might. This sent to every corner of the interior the message of the invincibility of the English might. None of the country lords could dare build up this charisma of a defiant authority based on the invincibility of one's own arms. When Calcutta was thus defining its position in terms of an individuality marked with arrogance, other cities of Bengal remained steeped in subservience unaware of their own potentialities to shape their own destinies.

Journey from a garrison town

This was how Calcutta began its journey as a garrison town in the eighteenth century. Its other attributes, namely those of a trading city, a port town, and an administrative centre, were real and functional marks of which gradually clustered around its principal character namely that of a garrison town. No other city in the interior had the potentiality of this. Calcutta was really in an extraordinary situation. It was then an administrative town for a mercantile settlement. It was a budding port for an all India business world bursting into shape. It had in its rear a sprawling hinterland over the vast Indo-Ganga basin that had powerful trade links with the north-west and Afghanistan. In no time it would become the capital of an emerging empire in south Asia. A trade settlement, a garrison town, a port, an administrative centre and finally a capital – the phases of Calcutta's urbanization were marked and they were exactly this. No other town in the interior could go through this process of evolution. As a port Chittagong could have been the rival of Calcutta; Murshidabad could have been Calcutta's contestant as an administrative centre; Dhaka and Murshidabad both could be the challenger as a capital. But none could be a unit with a quadruple character, namely those of a trade settlement, a garrison town, a port, and finally an administrative centre cum capital. Some of the interior towns of the *Subah* – Burdwan, Malda, Hugli, Rajmahal, Munghyr – did not have these promises. Calcutta grew not only as a triumph of a site over situations,[5] but also as a beneficiary of multiple other developments that made its ecological shortcomings a matter of indifference.

The English were comfortably settled in Calcutta when in 1760 Midnapur, Burdwan, and Chittagong were handed over to them. They did not need these districts to expand the territorial limits of Calcutta because even in later years Calcutta did not grow by absorbing any part of these territories. Calcutta's hunger for territory was satiated immediately after the battle of Palasi when, because of a promise inherent in the pre-Palasi conspiracy, the English Company got expansive territory adjacent to Calcutta running as far as Kulpi near the sea. Moreover the whole of the twenty-four Parganas, the district in which this territory was situated, was granted as a zamindari to the Company. The Company needed these territories because Midnapur and Burdwan were granaries of Bengal. Chittagong was an outlet to the sea alternative to Calcutta that could act as an English watchtower over the flourishing overseas trade in south-east Asia. The English knew that the Portuguese could build up their mastery over the Bay of Bengal because they had their base in Chittagong. The English had never considered Midnapur or Burdwan as a part of their base territory, so the glow of Calcutta did not penetrate into the interior of these districts. Chittagong was a far-flung territory and when in later years Burma was annexed the English attention came to be riveted on Rangoon. Chittagong then, sandwiched between Rangoon and Calcutta, lost much of its glamour. The revolt of the Raja of Burdwan in the beginning of the 1760s and the uprisings of the small *zamindars* of Midnapur, particularly those of the Jungle Mahal at the advent of the Company's rule in Bengal, had created great anxieties for the English in Calcutta and as such they had no mind to build the interior as a supportive extension of the urbanized centre of Calcutta. Up till the enunciation of the Permanent Settlement in 1793 the countryside and the district towns of Bengal were treated as revenue-yielding territories from where rice, timber, *chunam* [lime], salt, saltpetre, and indigo could be procured. District towns and their adjacent areas were centres for textile productions housed in vast and sprawling rural and semi-urban cottage industries. In the eighteenth century their market network in almost all cases led not to Chittagong for an outlet and not even to Dhaka and Murshidabad for effective distribution but to Calcutta where the port and the *burrabazar* had created a powerful market pull for commodities of the interior. The English from the beginning had a jaundiced eye for Burdwan. In the 1760s they wanted to dispossess the Raja of Burdwan because the latter had joined hands with the Raja of Birbhum and had staged a revolt against the English.

He drew his fighting manpower from a mass of robbers and mercenary "peons" who were basically the rural toughs whose basic station was in agriculture. This mobilization of robbers had introduced a new element into the body-politic of the country. Robbers in Calcutta and in the districts in the second half of the eighteenth century had become the greatest force of notoriety that did not allow the Company's rule to become stable. At one point they were plunderers and at other they were the most formidable form of social resistance to the economic and political changeover from the Mughal to the Company's rule in Bengal. They built up a very effective response to the tyranny the Company's government had introduced in the countryside. One may say that through them one may find the point where the terror of the state met the response of the people.[6]

Banditry and reduced urbanization

The bandit aspect of the story has to be detailed out a little further in order to understand why some of the important centres of the interior like Midnapur or Burdwan did not become urbanized as was desired. From the middle of the eighteenth century to the middle of the nineteenth, banditry in Calcutta and its immediate neighbourhood districts had increased beyond control. The roads that connected Calcutta with its interior towns and suburbs were infested with dacoits so much to that business with Calcutta had become difficult. For example the entire area between Midnapur and Calcutta had become unsafe for travellers who were not protected with arms. There were inter-district rings of bandits who functioned with interchangeable groups and in changing positions often functioning on cross-district arrangements. In lower Bengal there were three major centres from where dacoits conducted their operations – Calcutta, Midnapur, and Burdwan. When the Raja of Burdwan rose against the Company's administration in the 1760s in conjunction with the Raja of Birbhum[7] he had recruited a vast number of dacoits from his zamindari and almost an equal number of "peons" from the floating cultivators and rural vagabonds who formed the unstable population of the countryside. J.C.K. Peterson informs us that in the district of Burdwan there were in the second half of the eighteenth century at least 200 dacoits functioning under the local Raj.[8] Suranjan Das, in a recent study of dacoits, has shown how an inter-district ring of dacoits operating in Calcutta and its neighbourhood in the middle of the nineteenth century performed astounding events of dacoity around. On one occasion dacoits of Calcutta clubbed with dacoits from nearby districts and travelled as far as

Kanthi (Contai) in Midnapur and plundered the house of the zamindar of the same place. Before doing this one dacoit moving in the guise of a *sanniyasi* was entertained in good faith in the hospitality of the Raja and it was he who scouted the loopholes of the entire defence system of the Raja's palace and his household and passed all information to his colleagues in Calcutta and elsewhere.[9] These acts of daring robbery had unsettled the basic ambience necessary for urbanization in Bengal.

Burdwan was a typical case of reduced urbanization that contrasted the glamour of efflorescent Calcutta in the first half of the nineteenth century. On the one hand there was the Raja's uprising in conjunction with the Raja of Birbhum, and on the other there was the prevalence of dacoity as one of the most disturbing elements in the social life of the province. There was a third factor that baffled prospects of urbanization in the district in the eighteenth century. It was insolvency which was a marked feature of the zamindari in the middle of the eighteenth century. The Maratha invasions in the 1740s had devastated the western flank of Bengal – Midnapur, Bankura, Birbhum, and Burdwan – the entire *Radh* region of the Bengal *suba*. Throughout the course of the second half of the eighteenth century the Burdwan zamindari was a defaulting zamindari and the Company's government had very strained relations with the zamindar of the estate. Sick of insolvency he always pleaded his inability to pay of the revenue demand of the Company. This insolvency was the functional state of affairs in Burdwan throughout the course of the second half of the eighteenth century. The recovery of the district began in the early years of the nineteenth century. The *Fifth Report* of 1812 spoke of "the enlarged compact and fertile zamindary of Burdwan, which is like a garden in wilderness." This was a sign of recovery which did not pass unnoticed with the Company's authorities in England. But it also showed that as late as 1812 Burdwan was shaping more as a traditional, rural, agricultural suburb than as a prospering urbanizing centre of development in the neighbourhood of Calcutta. This happened when from the end of the eighteenth century Calcutta was gathering momentum for urbanization. Under the auspices of the Lottery Committee money was being churned up for the urbanizing welfare of the city. There was no conscious process of urbanization in the interior where pockets of habitation clustered around rural handicrafts and where markets manifested their trade networks in their tradition-bound functional set-ups. Coming out of the disasters of the eighteenth century it was necessary for Burdwan, Malda, Murshidabad, Hugli, Dakha, Chittagong, or any other town in Bengal to be more economically vibrant so that out of their own momentum they could shape themselves as centres of urbanization. This was not possible because of two reasons. Firstly, the *Nawabi* regime was gone; the old order had collapsed; the silk and cotton textile industry had showed signs of contraction; the indigenous banking led by the *sharafs* which had so long provided fiscal lubrication to the agricultural economy of the countryside was disbanded; the office of the *qanungos* that had for centuries functioned as the most effective record-keeping office of the provincial administration of the Mughals had dwindled into insignificance; the Company's government had monopolized trade on some important items of life like salt, betel-nuts etc., and they had allowed private British merchants and Company's officials alike to lay hands on rice trade, money-lending, land-speculation, and other available means of investment; the inevitable result of all these was that the interior trade was bottle-necked. When the economy of the interior thus showed trends of regressive transformation the second process of catastrophe set in. There was a unilateral flow of capital from the countryside to the growing metropolis of Calcutta. From the middle of the eighteenth century all leading *zamindars* of Bengal began to dispatch their wealth to Calcutta and save money there. The process started when Krishnaballav, the son of Raja Raj Ballav, the finance minister of Siraj-ud-daullah's government, fled to Calcutta with a huge treasure secretly screened from the revenue of the government. As Calcutta began to grow as the capital of an emerging empire the moneyed men of Calcutta and interior began to purchase land-property in the city. In the nineteenth century there was a real estate boom in Calcutta so that financiers were allured to promote bazaars, gunges, habitation, settlements, and buildings which housed a swelling population in the city. Nowhere in the interior was there any incentive for town growth and the entire growth initiative appropriated by the government became applied as a functional trend unique for the city alone. In this situation no city in the districts could acquire the necessary input for town growth and the interior became a lustreless expanse of territory with an economy of no outlet. This shutdown of the interior was the basis on which Calcutta rose as a metropolis.

Growth momentum occasional

Some towns in Bengal enjoyed occasional and rare moments of growth. Thus, Dakha and Chittagong enjoyed an artificially created moment for their growth when Bengal was partitioned in 1905. Dhaka then became the capital of a new province of East Bengal, and Assam and Chittagong sprang into a new life as a port providing an outlet for the whole trade of Assam and East Bengal to the sea. This was, however, a transitory event. In 1911 the partition was annulled and the corpus of enterprise, business, capital, and employment that had flared up in the direction to Dhaka and Chittagong collapsed. The effort to promote Calcutta as a port and trade centre had begun in the seventeenth century. It was in that century that the Bengali merchants lost their lead in the riverine and coastal trade to the Marwaris and up-country businessmen who eventually wrested the control of the *Burrabazar* on the eastern bank of the river from the Seths, Basaks, and Malliks and established their sway on trade-networks of Sutanuti-Kalkata complex of the south Bengal trade zone. In later years, when the English founded their settlement in Calcutta, the port became the sheet anchor of its growth with the fort and its garrison acting as the rear base of support of its entire networks on the river and the sea. In later years all governors general from Warren Hastings to William Bentinck acted for the promotion of both the port and the town of Calcutta. The rulers never wanted that Calcutta should be dwarfed by the rivalry of any district town and hence the state patronage for the promotion of town was never bestowed on any urban settlement in the districts. At some moments, some settlements in the districts derived opportunities from their own economic momentum to grow as a town. Hitherto the government patronage was not adequate to allow them to fulfil their promises of growth. Such opportunities came for Burdwan when coal and iron ores were discovered in the district in the nineteenth century. The railways had connected Burdwan with other trade centres and also with the metropolis of Calcutta. Flickers of urbanization were visible in Raniganj and Asansole and it was expected that Burdwan would grow. But neither Burdwan nor any of these two settlements assumed the shape of a developed township that could serve as models of urbanization outside the periphery of Calcutta. With the coming of Calcutta into prominence in the eighteenth century, Chittagong went into an eclipse. In later years, with the annexation of Upper Burma, a new blow was inflicted on Chittagong. Rangoon was developed as the port from where rice and teak could be exported outside to places where the British Empire required them. The process was similar to that by which Karachi was promoted as the export-outlet for wheat from the regions of north and north-west of India. This passage of resources of the interior through sea outlets was not possible from Rajmahal, Malda, Burdwan, Dhaka, Rajshahi, or from any other place in Bengal. Chittagong and Hugli had the potentials to act as such outlets. But Hugli was dwarfed by Calcutta, and Chittagong was sandwiched between Rangoon on the one hand and Calcutta on the other. With the fall of Dhaka, Chittagong lost its glamour and the shift of the gravity of trade, culture, and administration to the west deprived the eastern part of Bengal of its chances to present itself as an effective hinterland of any outlet integral to its own trade zone. Throughout the second half of the seventeenth and the early years of the eighteenth century, the English in south Asia showed deep concern for Chittagong, and, on occasions when their foothold in Calcutta territories was not acquired, they had a plan to capture Chittagong by force. This interest dimmed slowly as they consolidated their position in Calcutta. For about a hundred years from the middle of the eighteenth century, the Bengal towns fell into utter neglect. The result was that Malda, like Patna, paled as a closed and falling city without any chance of recovery. It lost its control over the Ganga as its trade artery. Burdwan was essentially an agricultural territory with remote chances for urbanization. Its fate was sealed as the agricultural hinterland for the town and port of Calcutta. Toward the end of the nineteenth century, Amritsar became a centre of carpet industry and trade. Although that was a temporary phenomenon, it gave this pilgrim centre a new boost toward building up its own economic momentum. Burdwan was not like Patna, a place situated on the bank of a navigable river that had flowed as one of the major trade routes of India from the ancient times. It had never been what Lucknow was – a seat of a regional ruling power that had a strong heritage drawn from the Mughal Empire. It could not be likened to Allahabad as well, which became a centre of later administration.[10] It had never been a pilgrim centre as Amritsar, Benaras, Mathura, and Gaya happened to be. Most of the Bengal towns were like Burdwan: devoid through neglect of the basic animation for urbanization. All these towns noted previously sank in the colonial period although they had the requisite potentiality and heritage for town growth. There was a massive spate of de-urbanization in colonial India and many traditional cities of India, small but important, suffered. Almost all the Bengal towns shared with them the same fate. Bombay, Madras, Calcutta, and a few small towns like Ahmedabad absorbed all initiatives of town growth. Some Bengal towns, Hugli, Burdwan, Midnapur, Chandernagore etc. were within the immediate orbit of Calcutta so that they were overshadowed by the pretensions of an imperial city. It was not that they did not have the potentialities for growth. But the growth model available in the rise of Ahmedabad, Madurai, and Kanpur did not suit the Bengal towns. Ahmedabad was the centre of trade for cotton and cotton textile goods. But most of the people there were engaged in employment in industry. Thus, Ahmedabad became a centre of growth based on the admixture of trade and industry. None of the Bengal towns outside the complex of Calcutta and its periphery could blend trade and industry into a live source of economic momentum. Kanpur became the centre of the leather, wool, and cotton textile industry. A city in the south, Madurai, flourished because it functioned as the centre of oilseeds, cotton, and crops. Originating from local roots, the trade and industries of these regions helped each other in their own flowering. In Bengal the tyranny of the East India Company's administration in the eighteenth century destroyed the general conditions of the economy[11] in which an urban settlement could flourish. Dakha was a cotton-producing area and was known as *Kapasia* (from *Karpas* which means cotton). It had an industrial base which was destroyed in course of the first hundred years of the British rule in Bengal. This loss was irreparable.

Population a factor of urbanization

The growth of urban settlements very often depends upon the influx of population from outside, mostly from the countryside. This happens when there is a famine and the rural population has no supportive entitlement with which they can stave off disasters. In Bengal no famine of great magnitude took place between 1770 and 1943.[12] As a result migrations of population from countrysides did not take place in the routine course of things. In 1868, because of a famine in Rajasthan, the population in Agra and Delhi increased. The granaries of western Bengal were sufficient enough to feed the people of the area. From the national statistics we learn that during the last two decades of the nineteenth century – during 1872–1881 and 1891–1901 – population migration from villages to towns was at its height. These two decades were marked by great famines of the century. Calcutta experienced a population surge in the middle of the eighteenth century when the Maratha menace drove the population of the countrysides into the fold of Calcutta. In the nineteenth century the swell of the Calcutta population was caused by the influx of a huge labour force from the west which thronged around the jute factories along the river belt. Calcutta had little experience of the rise of population due to famine in the countrysides. One point was, however, sure of Calcutta. The city had its own attraction but that attraction had never been such as to enable it to poach Bengal's interior population. There was a fear in the countrysides that health-wise Calcutta was not a very congenial a place to live in. Coming to Calcutta was an adventure for the rural folk and they had very little desire to detach themselves from their homes and hearths in their native villages. Land transports being weak and roads being undeveloped, there was little incentive for rural population to move into towns for more secure and comfortable settlements. Roads were infested with dacoits and as such the journey was an organized effort rarely indulged in by people of the interior. In this situation towns of the districts in Bengal were deprived of a steady and perennial supply of population from the countryside. This explains why many of the district towns in Bengal, after having suffered a population loss because of the various vicissitudes of life, failed to recover their demographic position by drawing a supply from nearby villages. Population deficit was one major factor as to why small urban settlements of Bengal, which had otherwise traditions of town growth, failed to develop themselves as self-promoting cities in the colonial period.

Winds of change in global trade had rarely fanned Bengal towns. In the 1860s when the Lancashire cotton famine struck the world, the demand of Indian cotton rose high in foreign markets. The entire cotton from north and central India was drawn for export. This export passed through Mirzapur down the Ganga[13] and Mirzapur began to grow. But this growth was transitory. Very soon railway lines were built along the Ganga and the river traffic began to suffer. With this Mirzapur began to decay.

The story of the rise and decay of Indian towns described here presents us with a pattern. The Bengal towns resembled them only in their decay. The basic incentive behind Calcutta's rise came from its port and the benefits this port yielded to the city. No city of Bengal was equal to Calcutta as the site of a port. None had the command Calcutta had over domestic and overseas business. Calcutta had connections with the north Indian business world through the river. Its access to the trade universe outside was through the sea. The river gave it a vast hinterland. The sea gave it its necessary aperture for export. The entire western part of Bengal known as the *Radhbhumi* contained some of the agricultural surplus districts of Bengal[14] and provided Calcutta with a hinterland. Malda which was situated far away from the sea could not be an outlet for the export trade of the north. Chittagong was at an enormous distance from the cash crop zone of north-central India and had no river link with that vast hinterland. Thus sheer geographical incompatibility between the hinterland and these two river and sea bases of interior Bengal did not allow them to come into any rivalry with Calcutta. In later years, when Burma was annexed to the Empire, Rangoon sprang into life as a port through which·timber and rice exports from Burma were channelized. As Rangoon came up, Chittagong was sandwiched between Rangoon and Calcutta and its prospects became bleak. That port gradually passed into neglect.

The British Empire had created a kind of metropolitan economy in and around Calcutta that functioned as an appendage to the yet bigger economy of England and the world at large. No Bengal town in the nineteenth and the twentieth centuries had the competence to provide the necessary bridge between these two economies of the world. The inner world of Bengal was basically agricultural and the ambience of agriculture hung like a settled mist even in the nineteenth century on the *Radh* region[15] of western Bengal, on the Surma-Barak[16] valley of north-eastern Bengal and on the regions washed by the water of Meghna-Padma-Buriganga in eastern Bengal. The production and trade systems of these regions did not move much beyond the stage available in the pre-Palashi days. Before the advent of coal, iron, and jute industries in Bengal, there was no catalyst in Bengal's economy which could change the stable core of Bengal's agricultural districts. No revolutionary impulse had ever touched the inner complacence of agriculture so that urbanization did not come in the natural way of things. So long as indigo was the main crop for cultivation, a vast interior territory of Bengal – Nadia, Jessore, Khulna, Pabna, and twenty-four Parganas – remained to be the supply zone of the metropolitan economy of Calcutta. Thus a wide region functioned as the satellite of Calcutta under the canopy of a governing economy of the Empire.

Individually Calcutta and the interior towns in a group acted as complementary to each other. Calcutta had no economic sovereignty, so had not the district towns. Calcutta was a satellite to the bigger metropolitan economy of the Empire. The district towns were satellites to Calcutta's economy. When coal was found in Burdwan the entire district became the supplier of coal to the needs of the Empire. On the top of this Burdwan coal was inferior in nature so that the availability of coal did not raise the status of the entire district.

Was there any propelling force for South Bengal cities?

History had given many north Indian cities a propelling force. They shared the heritage of a specific model termed by the Cambridge economic historian as the *"administrative-court cities of the eighteenth century type."*[17] In Bengal, truly speaking, only Dhaka and Murshidabad could claim the status of a court-city. For a little while Mir Kashim shifted his capital to Monghyr. But he did not make Malda, Burdwan, Rajmahal etc. his station. This was because he wanted to stay at a distance from the English in Calcutta. In the 1760s Burdwan was anti-English on the one hand, and on the other was very weak in revenue collection. The Company's government operating from Calcutta wanted to dispossess the zamindar there. Mir Kashim was opposed to this and the zamindar was retained in his position.[18] In the second half of the eighteenth century Burdwan, living on the mercy of the *Nawab*, failed to build up its own effective entity as an able and competent site for development. Even in situations of emergency, which arose during Mir Kashim's war with the English, Burdwan could not present itself as an alternative to Murshidabad. Mir Kashim knew that the trade axis of the English had moved through Burdwan, Malda, Rangpur, and Dinajpur. Therefore, his pragmatic wisdom took him further west – to Monghyr. The result was that when the *Nawabi* rule began to wane no city in the interior inclusive of Burdwan could build up its stamina to become a competitor of Calcutta. The major stations of production and habitation in the districts in the eighteenth century were parts of the old world existence not very much touched by the rays of a transforming era. In the 1760s, Burdwan was a revenue-deficit area and its zamindar was locked in a relation of conflict with the Company. The Company's administration wanted to dispossess the Raja but could not do so because of Mir Kasim's opposition. Burdwan in the second half of the eighteenth century was then this – a capital-short economy ineffectual because of being weak as a zamindari, unable from all considerations to become an alternative to Murshidabad even in a situation of emergency during war. The result was that when the *Nawabi* administration was on the wane neither Burdwan nor any other district town of Bengal could present itself as equal in power to Calcutta. There were a good number of towns in Bengal which were situated on the river bank. But none had a command over trade as much as Calcutta had and none enjoyed a protection of arms similar to what the Calcutta garrisons could provide. Hugli, Malda, Dhaka, Khulna, Rajshahi, Chittagong – all had commanding trade positions because of their situations on the river and the sea but none had a thriving hinterland which could be comparable to that of Calcutta which consisted of the whole of the Gangetic basin of north India. Even in the first quarter of the eighteenth century, Malda, Rajmahal, and Hugli proved to be quite effective centres of *Nawabi* administration. During the reign of Murshid Quli Khan the English tried to develop their factory in Malda into a fortress. Murshid Quli Khan opposed it and under his advice the faujdars of Hugli, Malda, and Rajmahal became active against the English. This had stopped the English efforts to build some kind of an enclave within the territory of the *Nawab*. The strength which Malda and Hugli could demonstrate was not to be found in Burdwan. Situated between Hugli and Malda, the two effective *faujdaries* of the *Nizamat*, Burdwan could not build up its own military glamour. Hugli, Burdwan, Nadia, and twenty-four Parganas were in the immediate neighbourhood of Calcutta and were thus very much in the zone of interference of the Company's administration. The glory of Calcutta radiated and eventually dwarfed the importance of the interior towns of these four districts.

While Murshidabad fell, Berhampore[19] emerged. But this new city was a satellite of Calcutta. After the battle of Palasi the English felt a necessity to keep a watch on the activities of the *Nawabs* at Murshidabad. In 1767 a cantonment was established at Berhampore. "The cantonment," a commentator observes, "was established to serve two-fold purpose. Firstly to safeguard British commercial interest at Kasimbazar, then a thriving commercial centre, and secondly, to keep a strict vigil over the *Nawab* Nazims at Murshidabad. The city of Berhampore developed around this cantonment."[20]

The cantonment provided security to Berhampore and in no time its population increased. Gorabazar, a market, was set up to provide essential commodities to the cantonment. A belmetal industry had come into existence at Khagra in the eighteenth century. Now the population increase gave it a boost. Country *zamindars* now came to reside there. In an age of absentee landlordism this was natural. The *zamindars* brought with them a vast retinue of attendants – clerks, doctors, *pundits*, *purohits*, cooks. Berhampore took the shape of a growing town. A middle class came up and lawyers were predominant in it. In spite of all these Berhampore lived in the shadow of Murshidabad. A great part of its population came from Kasimbazar. In the early nineteenth century, around 1813, the river Bhagirathi changed its course. Disease became rampant in Kasimbazar and some of the diseases became epidemic. People fled the place and found new shelters in the Barrack area of Berhampore.[21] In the fleeting population the Murshidabad culture found a new vehicle to travel in this newly growing settlement. The affinity of Berhampore with the dying city of Murshidabad was greater[22] than its affinity with the globalized cosmopolitanism of Calcutta. The city suffered in its orientations in the long run. The city lacked a predominant section of merchants and in their absence trade had no incentive to grow. Merchants are very often flag-bearers of urbanism and trade provides the real stimulus for urbanization. In the culture of the city in Berhampore, lawyers were predominant and they introduced a middle-class motivation for rootedness in traditional aspects of life. The shadow of the Kasimbazar Raj did not allow the feudal aspects of life to die down. The result was that, in spite of the new wind of change from Calcutta, Berhampore turned its face to Murshidabad[23] and eventually could not get rid of the feudal rusticity which precluded its becoming as urban as Calcutta was.

The metropolitan Calcutta had no competitor

The neighbouring towns of Calcutta suffered vis-à-vis the metropolitan city. Burdwan, Midnapur or the towns of Nadia and the twenty-four Parganas were very much within the radiation zone of Calcutta and its influence overshadowed their aspirations. So long as the *Nawabi* administration was powerful the English in Calcutta were under a perpetual apprehension of interference from Murshidabad. Likewise when the rule of the *Nawabs* fell after the battle of Palasi, every town in the immediate neighbourhood of Calcutta was under a similar apprehension of interference from Calcutta. In 1769 *Supervisors* were appointed to act as administrators over zamindaris and through them the influence of Calcutta was clamped on the centres of growth in the districts. Their aim was to excavate all sources of revenue, hidden or apparent, so that their appointment was justified by an increasing trend of revenue maximization. This drive for the last dreg of social surplus had destroyed the potentiality of interior towns and *gunges* and the surplus that was raised from the countryside was syphoned to Calcutta without any equivalent return to the villages. After the enunciation of the Permanent Settlement the *zamindars* of interior Bengal were maintaining themselves in a precarious condition. They stood with a burden on their shoulders – a sky-high revenue demand from the state – and their existence was clouded with the apprehension that their zamindaries in part or whole would be sold if they failed to meet the demand of the state. Their attention, therefore, was to keep agriculture buoyant in a revenue-yielding position so that the inner spirit of the agrarian life remained bereft of any desire to get rid of the rusticity of a peasant world. The internal marks of urbanity was absent there so that when the rule of the *Nawabs* collapsed there was no town in Bengal that could function as a successor of Murshidabad just the way Lucknow and Hyderabad became the successors of the Mughal culture of Delhi within the general ambience of imperial decadence. Lucknow was the biggest city of north India and even after the fall of Delhi it could maintain itself as the most vibrant centre of Islamic culture in south Asia. Later on it became the capital of a regional state, which in many ways was the miniature replica of the Mughal Empire. There was only one town in Bengal that could grow as a successor of both Dhaka and Murshidabad to function as a centre of Muslim culture. It was Hugli, a Shia colony for a long time which was particularly favoured by Murshid Quli Khan.[24] But unfortunately while recapturing Calcutta in the beginning of 1757, Clive bombarded Hugli and Chandernagore and destroyed the two cities so that in future they could not raise their heads again. Long before this Surat was sacked and eventually was pushed to destruction by the marauding hordes of Shivaji. The destruction of Hugli and Chandernagore offered an indirect blow to Burdwan. The *faujdari* of Hugli and the French base at Chandernagore acted as a buffer between Burdwan and Calcutta. This buffer was removed and Burdwan was exposed to the full blast of the English power in Calcutta. The *Nawab* allowed the Raja of Burdwan to maintain in his zamindari a large number of *Najdean* force which maintained the security of the Raja and helped the *faujdar* of Hugli in time of distress. If necessary in collaboration with the *faujdar* of Hugli he could build up Burdwan into a garrison town. But unfortunately the English after coming to power in the second half of the eighteenth century disbanded this *Najdean* force. Calcutta thus disarmed a rival town and Burdwan lost the potential of urban growth. Slowly after this almost all the Rajas of the interior were disarmed in the same way so that the military potentials of the districts were stifled and the supremacy of the English in Calcutta was ensured. The police functions of the *zamindars* in the days of the Mughals allowed them to retain paramilitary forces – *paiks, barkandages*, and *lathials* – and these men cordoned both the cultivators and their fields of cultivation so that no one could escape from the vigilance of the *zamindars* and flee their fields. The base of rack-renting remained secured for the *zamindars*, and the countryside remained perpetually steeped in an agrarian economy. This had robbed the entire countryside of any initiative to grow in the line of urbanization. When Calcutta emerged as the most predominant town in south Bengal, the English saw to it that its suburbs and the hinterland did not proceed beyond the margin of an agricultural economy set by tradition.

The smaller towns of Bengal were mostly scattered and their dispersed condition did not allow them to enjoy the benefits of a hinterland favoured by an organized, long-distance-trade – such as was enjoyed by Amritsar. This city reaped the benefits of a twin trade zone – the Kashmir-Afghanistan trade zone that served both as a hinterland and an outlet for Amritsar and the vibrant trade zone of the Ganga and its basin that linked Amritsar with Calcutta. Amritsar was a pilgrim city and its strategic trade location helped it to remain buoyant even in moments of crisis. No Bengal town had the benefits of such strategic locations. The trade and economic parameters necessary for urbanization were never allowed to blossom in Bengal after the emergence of the English in Calcutta. Nor did any of the Bengal towns in the eighteenth and nineteenth centuries experienced rejuvenation because of the rise of a new kingdom such as Lahore and Lucknow did in the course of their concurrent rise with Calcutta as parts of two new kingdoms. Lucknow emerged into a new life with the rise of Awadh as a separate kingdom and Lahore emerged when Ranjit Singh established his Sikh kingdom in the north-west. Lahore at that time was called the London of the east. She suffered a temporary eclipse with the fall of the Mughal Empire. With the rise of the Sikh Empire under Ranjit Singh, the city temporarily recovered its lost glory. The city was at its peak later. Burdwan could have enjoyed the same experience if in 1696 Shova Singh's revolt had led to the formation of a new state in the western part of Bengal. Shova Singh's rise contained within itself the force of a change that could have stalled the rise of Calcutta and made Midnapur and Burdwan the most prime cities in Bengal. But this rebel and his associate Rahim Khan unfortunately led their adventure not toward making a new kingdom but toward securing wealth through loot and plunder. This robbed the *Radhbhumi* – the western part of Bengal consisting of Midnapur, Burdwan, and Birbhum – the chance of evolving into a new state. In the sixteenth and seventeenth centuries, the *Radh* area of Bengal had its distinct characteristics. Burdwan gave it an agrarian solvency; Midnapur gave it a contact with the sea; and Birbhum gave it a rich reserve of forests. Then there was no *faujdar* in western Bengal. It was not possible for the *faujdars* of Malda, Jessore, and Rajmahal to keep a watch on this vast expanse of territory in which coastal trade, agrarian wealth and treasures of forest made the economy vibrant. In 1760 when Mir Kashim, the *Nawab* of Bengal, handed over Midnapur, Burdwan, and Chittagong to the English East India Company, he parted with the most prosperous districts of Bengal. The entire *Radh* area thus passed under the control of a corporate body of merchants who operating from Calcutta kept its hinterland a subdued adjunct of the seat of a rising empire.

All these happened in the aftermath of a grave event, namely the rise of the Marathas in the Deccan and their raids into Bengal. Emerging from Nagpur and commanding fast-moving cavalry hordes, the Marathas swept over a vast territory spreading from the borders of Maharashtra to the western and central part of Bengal. What emerged from the Maratha expansion in Bengal were loot, plunder, and battles. The western part of Bengal, the *radhbhumi* – Midnapur, Birbhum, Burdwan, and part of Murshidabad – were devastated. This was the neighbourhood surrounding Calcutta which collapsed. Calcutta benefited out of it. There was a massive influx of population into Calcutta and the worth of the city as an effective shelter for men in crisis was proved. The city received the admiration of the population; from this time onward, the population gave respect to the English might and reposed their trust on their system of defence. From the collapse, the western part of Bengal did not recover in the rest of the eighteenth century. In a three decades' time a major famine – the famine of 1770 – visited the area and made recovery absolutely difficult for the entire region. Some of the Deccan towns which suffered because of the rise of the Marathas limped back into recovery by 1830 and 1840. But none of the towns in Western Bengal that suffered colossally from Maratha raids could recover even by the middle of the nineteenth century. In some ways the towns of Rajputana were stable about this time. This was because they did not suffer from political instability on the one hand and on the other from the vagaries of rivers which affected many important towns of Bengal. Where the river was, the main artery of trade towns grew in association with both the river and its trade. Changes in the course of rivers affected the fortunes of such towns very much. Some of the Bengal towns decayed because of changes in the course of rivers. Modern researches show that the towns in Nadia and Murshidabad declined because of the silting of the river Hughly.[25] It shows that the rise of Calcutta was facilitated by the natural decline of the cities of its hinterland.[26]

Interior towns had potentialities but no incentives

From the earlier observation one should not come to the conclusion that the interior towns of Bengal had no potentiality for growth. The immediate neighbourhood of Calcutta which, comprises of western part of Bengal, were the emporium of cotton, textiles, and silk. It was the tyranny of the Company's servants that led to the ruin of the textile and the silk industry of Nadia, Burdwan, and Birbhum. Aditee Nagchowdhury-Zilly who researched on rural vagrancy during the early years of the Company's rule said that Burdwan and its surrounding areas were the biggest cotton textile centres of western Bengal – in Zilly's own words: "the most important centre for cotton manufacture in West Bengal."[27] Within the context of a developed agriculture, the entire *Radhbhumi* had the potentiality for urbanization but bereft of state protection it could not fulfil its destiny. From the middle of the nineteenth century, Burdwan took a lead in mineral industry. In 1858 when the Sepoy mutiny and the great revolt were going on, Burdwan had forty-nine coal mines. With the help of twenty-seven steam engines 2,16,580 tonnes of coal were lifted from the mines. In 1859 the amount of coal raised from the mines there was 3,27,590 tonnes. In 1860 it was 3,13,300 tonnes.[28] In the fields adjacent to coal, iron ores were discovered. Hunter wrote: "There can be little doubt that, were the manufacture of iron successfully introduced, Ranigaanj would become one of the richest and most important Districts in Bengal."[29]

In the thirties and forties of the nineteenth century, the money world of Calcutta was essentially a tormented zone. The Agency Houses collapsed and the Union Bank was closed in 1847. The Calcutta capitalists were shattered and the Bengali business community withdrew from collaboration with the English. The cultivation of the indigo – the "remittance good" of Bengal – was coming to a standstill. New avenues for investment were not opened. A capital-short economy prevailed over Calcutta and a vast part of its neighbourhood.[30] In this situation all development schemes centred around Calcutta and efforts were made to rejuvenate the money market of the city. Concerns for the districts were well-nigh absent.

From this it should not be deduced that industry and urbanization in the neighbourhood of Calcutta did not grow because of a lack of capital. Throughout the course of the nineteenth century, no heavy industry developed in India. It was not that capital shortage was at the root of this. Foreign capital began to come into India from the middle of the nineteenth century. It was this capital from outside which financed the jute industry and the railways in India. Historians say that two factors were responsible for obstructing heavy industries in the country. They were, Amales Tripathi says, "lack of high grade iron ore" and "inadequate production of coal."[31] in 1839 Jessop and Co. began iron works in Barakar. Mackay and Co. and Bengal Iron and Co. did the same, respectively, in Raniganj in 1855 and in Asansol in 1875. But none of these projects were successful. The result was that domestic demands for iron had to be satisfied by importing iron from outside. The requirements for the railways, the textile mills, agriculture, and the establishment of the planters were met by iron and steel brought from outside. Till the beginning of the World War I the total import of foreign iron was 8,08,000 tonnes worth Rupees 12½ crores. This event retarded the growth of industries in India. In England industrialization came under the lead of steel and iron industry. In India industrialization started with the application of steam in jute and textile industries.[32]

This explains why the towns of interior Bengal, particularly those of the *Radh* area, could not grow into big cities equal to the premier city of Calcutta. Throughout the colonial period no great industry developed in the interior of Bengal which could give Bengal towns a fillip to grow. The British administration in India did not allow the necessity for industry to grow into an effective demand so much so that the vast interior of Bengal being bereft of commerce remained steeped in agriculture. It was not in the interest of England and its Indian Empire to permit the blooming of an industrial civilization in Bengal, which would rival the industrial revolution at home. This uncharitable attitude of the Empire was the real barrier for urbanization in Bengal. In England industrialization started with an initial advantage. It had enough coal which ensured an abundance of fuel for industry. In Bengal the situation was different. Vis-à-vis British coal, the Bengal coal had two deficiencies – its quantity as available to industry was small and, quality-wise, it was inferior. Its deficiency in quantity was made up in the nineties of the nineteenth century when more and more coal was lifted from the mines. Between 1896 and 1900 the total coal lifted from the Bengal mines was 40½ lakh tonnes. Did this increased supply of coal anyway help to promote the industry of the districts? The answer will certainly be in the negative. It was used for the interest of three other industries – Jute, textile, and the railways. The growth of jute industry eventually benefited Calcutta and helped it to emerge as an industrial city in south Bengal.

No internal stimulation for Bengal districts

It is thus clear that the Bengal districts vis-à-vis Calcutta lacked sources of internal stimulation. Trade and industry – the providers of stimulus for urbanization – had little chance to grow in a situation where deindustrialization had become the order of the day. In later years industry came along the axis where jute was the central commodity for agriculture and trade.[33] Jute factories developed not in the far-off districts, not even in the *Radh* region, but in the immediate neighbourhood of Calcutta – along the course of the river Ganga. This gave Calcutta a tremendous boost in all its processes of urbanization and deprived the interior towns of chances to promote their own selves. The first jute spinning mill was set up in Rishra in 1855. The first power-driven looms were set up at Barahanagar in 1859. These were followed by the establishment of a series of jute mills in Calcutta regions – the city and its immediate suburbs. Industry helps urbanization, and naturally Calcutta saw its own uplift because of the surrounding jute industries appearing along the axis of the river. An industrial society grew up in the region between Barahanagar and Budge Budge and its influence was never felt in the districts to the west and north of Calcutta. This was how Calcutta grew toward the nineteenth and the early twentieth centuries but the district towns remained dwarfed under the shadow of this growing metropolis.

Calcutta was urbanized because of being the seat of power of a vast empire where a port and commerce, fort and a garrison, industry and administration merged to develop one unit of power. It should be remembered that, throughout the course of the nineteenth century, India offered hospitality to a vast and inchoate alien business community who invested their wealth in this country and created the field of India's industrialization. Tomlinson notes: "Throughout the nineteenth century India was host to a large and diverse expatriate business community that created the modern industrial sector of Bengal."[34] The aim of this expatriate community was profit and not the promotion of welfare of a country which was not theirs. Urbanization of a territory was always a part of a conscious scheme and expatriate capital would not have been invested in such schemes deliberately if it had other options of investment in their own world. In Burdwan foreign capital was invested in coal and iron industry but this did not lead to the growth of urbanization there. In Calcutta the river axis provided a very effective trade artery and backed by this Calcutta encompassing water-land communication and administration created a big zone of influence in which Hughly-Howrah-twenty-four Parganas-Nadia-Midnapur-Burdwan operated as a clustered hinterland for the Calcutta port. The river provided Calcutta a passage to the sea and a traditionally rich link with the sprawling Ganga basin of north India as its hinterland. This advantage very few cities in India enjoyed. In later years when railway lines were set up along the river routes a very powerful system of conveyance emerged in which the cost of communication and time of transportation were slashed down. The newly set-up railway tracks connected Calcutta with the vast sectors of the economy – the interior areas of production, storehouses and emporia, markets, fields of agriculture, habitations, and diverse centres of distributions. The metropolitan economy of Calcutta burst into a dimension not known to any city in contemporary India. Calcutta could thus build up its network, which was necessary for its own modernization. The other towns of Bengal were mostly static habitations fenced by agriculture absorbed in a sleepy culture of a non-industrial world. From this sleepiness, Calcutta did wake up in the early eighteenth century. That was the time when the Agency Houses of Calcutta were financing commercial agriculture of the interior – particularly indigo. But they too did not mess up their existence with the whirlpool of agriculture. They used their own agents – their *banians* and sub-contractors – as links with the agrarian world and the relation of these parent fiscal bodies with their subordinates were determined by sub-contracts.[35] Thus between the fields of agriculture and the city capitalists there were different layers of small and intermediate capitalists and contractors who spared their Calcutta promoters of the clumsy attachment with the world of agriculture. The world of sub-agents was vast and varied and they helped to maintain the flow of commerce and the necessary and periodical replenishment of the stock. This was how the basic parameters of the economy – capital, enterprise, management, and communication – were conducted through impersonal and objective channels of give and take. Thriving on these impersonal bonds the money world of Calcutta assumed a character necessarily governed by the motivations of a growing urban culture. Calcutta was actuated by this – the impersonal force of business give-and-take which was completely absent in the interior because the interior was wholly structured by zamindari imperatives shaped under the requirements of the British rule.

Burdwan: a case-study

Given the previous text, we can take Burdwan as a case in point and carry our discussion a little further. From the beginning of the colonial period till the end of the first five decades of the nineteenth century, Burdwan had witnessed the growth of four towns – Burdwan, Kalna,[36] Katwa,[37] and Dainhat.[38] No other traditional towns could grow there. Meanwhile coal and iron mines were discovered in the district and ores were begun to be lifted from the mines there. As a result two new towns grew up around coal and iron fields – Raniganj in 1869[39] and Asansol in 1896.[40] The first four cities of Burdwan were situated in alluvial river basins where their orientation was naturally toward agriculture. From time immemorial, their whole communication and business transactions were based entirely on the river transport. In the colonial period the condition of the rivers deteriorated and the systems of communication lost their functional efficiency. The incentive for town growth was thus lost. This led to the benefit of Calcutta. In matters of urbanization, Calcutta did not receive any challenge from any of the urban and semi-urban settlements of the district of Burdwan and as a matter of fact from any district around. Meanwhile new growth was registered in the colonial economy. Roads were constructed and new railway tracts linked the interior with the metropolis. As importance of rivers functioning as arteries of communication dwindled the settlements which flourished along the banks of rivers also began to fade.[41] Because of the spread of railways big cities like Mirzapur[42] lost their glamour. This city was an entrepot for the riverine traffic that catered the business of the entire Gangetic plain of the north. With the coming of the railways, a system of fast transport with lesser costs was explored and the river traffic was automatically bypassed. As the railways superseded rivers as arteries for business many of the prospective semi-urban settlements of Burdwan and other districts of Bengal lost their charm. The rivers of Burdwan – Bhagirathi, Damodar, Barakar, Khadi, Banka, Ajay, Dwarakeswar, and Mundeswari – which once served as the life-lines of the district were now relegated to the background. In the past these rivers ensured a civilization based on plentiful agriculture and incentives for town-growth were, therefore, largely absent. The growth of towns in Burdwan was mostly a post-independence phenomenon. At the time of Indian independence there were altogether fourteen towns in the district. With the coming of the five-year plans and the Damodar Valley Corporation the number of towns increased and at the end of the twentieth century the total number of towns in Burdwan was forty-nine.[43]

From this it is clear that throughout the colonial period Burdwan could not grow its potentiality for urbanization. She had water resources, strength of population, capacity for sound agriculture, and a vast sprawling territory. None of these resources were properly taken care of under the British rule. The entire district remained steeped in the sleepy atmosphere of agriculture. Buchanon Hamilton informs us that in the beginning of the third decade of the nineteenth century – in 1822 – Burdwan was number one district in agricultural production in India. Next to Burdwan was Tanjore in the province of Madras. From the same source we learn that in 1811 the population of Lancashire was 476 per square mile. About the same time the population in Burdwan in every square mile was 600.[44] Thus, with a manpower potential greater than that of industrial Lancashire, Burdwan could not become the base of any industry. And devoid of industry it could not become urbanized. The misery of the Bengal situation lay here. The case of Burdwan was indeed tragic. There was no attempt to promote some of the settlements which in the past acted on their own efficiency as inland ports. These places were Burdwan, Katwa, Dainhat, Kalna, Nadanghat, and Nutanhat. It is true that the colonial government had planned road and railway networks and foreign capital was inducted in priority sectors. But the emphasis ultimately was on overland growth because of which the traditional networks of water communication suffered. It is vital to note that internal ports and water communications grew in association of agricultural economy and when road and railway networks developed the utility of the old systems dimmed slowly into insignificance. Calcutta triumphed over its internal rivals because it controlled an outlet to the sea and its river networks linked it to the vast up-country hinterland which was as sprawling as the water-fed Ganga basin. Burdwan and the other neighbouring districts of Calcutta had enough supply of water from rivers which washed their shores and provided the alluvial soil necessary for agriculture. But agriculture also needed better technology for growth. But improved technology and modern farming techniques were never applied in the fertile lands on the banks of the rivers. As time went on, the silting of rivers became a common phenomenon. The courses of rivers changed and their navigability began to be diminished.[45] In this situation there was no scope for interior towns to grow. Meanwhile coalfields were discovered and quickly they were linked with the metropolis by railways. In the changed economy, Calcutta occupied the central stage. In the meantime, jute industry flourished and jute factories lined up along the axis of the river around Calcutta. Calcutta now became an industrial town. Its urbanization thus became an irresistible necessity of the time.

Notes

1 See S. Bhattacharya's study of urbanization in Dharma Kumar, ed., *The Cambridge Economic History of India*, Vol. 2, c.1757–c.1970, Orient Longman in association with Cambridge University Press, pp. 270–332.
2 Kumar, *The Cambridge Economic History of India*, pp. 277–278. Read, for further study, D.R. Gadgil, *The Industrial Evolution of India in Recent Times*, 4th edn, Oxford University Press, 7th impression, Ch. X.
3 Cited by S. Bhattacharya in Kumar, *The Cambridge Economic History of India*, p. 278.
4 Ibid.
5 In an article entitled "The Victory of Site Over Situation: Exploring Ecological Dynamics Behind Calcutta's Selection as the Seat of Colonial Capital", [*The Quarterly Review of Historical Studies*, XLIX, Nos. 3 & 4, October 2009, March, 2010 (Published by Institute of Historical Studies, Kolkata)]. Jenia Mukherjee argued that the foundation of Calcutta was really a triumph of a geographical site over ecological situation. In its origin Calcutta was really this but this alone cannot explain the whole of it.
6 This point has been properly analyzed in Ranjit Sen, *Social Banditry in Bengal: A Study in Primary Resistance 1757–1793*, Ratna Prakashani, Calcutta, 1988.
7 The *zamindar* of Birbhum was the only Muslim *zamindar* in Bengal who had the title of "Raja."
8 He wrote this in his *Bengal District Gazetteers: Burdwan*. There are good references to the Burdwan dacoits and their involvement with the Raja in the book in the section where the history of the zamindari has been discussed.

9. Suranjan Das, "Behind the Blackened Faces: The Nineteenth Century Bengali Dacoits", in Keka Dutta Roy and Chittaranjan Mishra, eds., *Reflections in history Essays in Honour of Professor Amalendu De*, Raktakarbi, Calcutta, 2009.
10. In 1868 Allahabad became the capital of the newly formed province called the North Western Provinces.
11. Writing in 1772 William Bolts shows how the tyranny of the East India Company's government destroyed the economy of Bengal. He writes: "All branches of the interior Indian commerce, are, without exception, entirely monopolies of the most cruel and ruinous natures; and so totally corrupted, from every species of abuse, as to be in the last stages towards annihilation. Civil justice is eradicated, and millions are thereby left entirely at the mercy of a few men, who divide the spoils of the public among themselves; while, under such despotism, supported by military violence, the whole interior country, where neither the laws of England reach, [n]or the laws or customs of those countries are permitted to have their course, is no better than in a state of nature. In this situation, while the poor industrious natives are oppressed beyond conception, population is decreasing, the manufactories and revenues are decaying, and Bengal, which used not many years ago to send annually a tribute of several millions in hard specie to Delhy, is now reduced to so extreme a want of circulation, that it is not improbable the Company (whose servants in Calcutta have already been necessitated, in one season, to draw above million sterling on the Directors, for the exigencies of their trade and government) will soon be in want of specie in Bengal to pay their troops, and in England eenpleading incapacity to pay the very annual four hundred thousand pounds which is now received from them by Government." – *Considerations on India Affairs; Particularly Respecting the Present State of Bengal and Its Dependencies*, 2nd edn, London, MDCCLXXII, [1772] Preface, p. vii.
12. These two years were the two major famine years in the colonial history of Bengal.
13. Gadgil, *The Industrial Evolution of India in Recent Times*, p. 139.
14. Because of being agriculturally surplus districts, the English East India Company at the first opportunity seized Midnapur and Burdwan from the Bengal Nawab in 1760.
15. The Radh region consists of Midnapur, Burdwan, Bankura, and Birbhum
16. The southern part of the Indian state of Assam is known as Barak valley. The main city of the valley is Silchar. The place has acquired its name from the river Barak. The Barak valley mainly consists of three districts namely Cachar, Karimganj, and Hailakandi. Karimganj is the cultural centre of the region.
17. *Cambridge Economic History*, Vol. II, p. 266.
18. "If anyone was indispensable in the Mughal system it was the zamindar whom Ramsbotham is his Studies in the Land Revenue History of Bengal (1769–87) described as 'practically impossible to dispossess by constitutional methods,' if he performed his customary duties attached to a zamindari." – Ranjit Sen, *Metamorphosis of the Bengal Polity (1700–1793)*, Rabindra Bharati University, Calcutta, 1987, p. 182.
19. Berhampore is the sixth largest city in West Bengal after Kolkata, Howrah, Asansol, Siliguri and Malda. It is situated 200 kilometres from Kolkata.

20 Rajarshi Chakrabarty, "Murshidabad City & Berhampore Town: Two Urban Centres Representing Two Ages", a paper read at the 17th Biennaial Conference of Bangladesh History Association held at Khulna on 22 November 2012. About the origin of Berhampore Jadunath Sarkar observes: "Its origin and importance were solely due to the cantonment built by the British here. For a time it was the most important military station between Calcutta and Dinapur." – Ibid.
21 Ibid.
22 The shadow of Murshidabad culture loomed large in the city of Berhampore. Rajarshi Chakrabarty thus gives an example of this: "From the end of the 18th century 'Baijibilash' became an integral part of the various pujas and ceremonies performed by the zamindars residing in Berhampore. Many well known baijis came from Murshidabad Durbar and performed among the 'babus' at Berhampore. Along with 'Baijibilash', 'Khamta' also became popular among the 'babus' of Berhampore." – Ibid.
23 "Thus we see that Berhampore looked towards Calcutta which was now the capital of British Raj but couldn't forget the old capital of Subha Bangla which was fast sinking into oblivion." – Ibid.
24 Jadunath Sarkar, ed., *History of Bengal*, Vol. II, Dhaka University, 1948, Ch. on Murshid Quli Khan.
25 "In western Bengal," the Cambridge economic historian observes, "the Bhagirathi river system declined; the Bhagirathi was not navigable throughout the year according to Rennell (1781) and Colebrooke (1794). The Hugly was the artery of trade. In central Bengal the silting-up of rivers and oscillation in river courses was observed in Murshidabad and Nadia; the decline of Murshidabad town was partly for this reason. Such changes in the course and the volume of effluent discharge of rivers affected, among other things, navigability and the location of entrepots and urban settlements. The river was the highroad in eastern India, and in some parts of eastern Bengal it was the only channel of communication and bulk transport of commercial goods." – *Cambridge Economic History of India*, Vol. II, p. 271.
26 The relation between river and urbanization in Bengal has not been studied at length. Scholars have concentrated much on the changes in the course of rivers but how these changes impacted upon urbanization is yet to be studied. For changes in the course of rivers see James Renell, *Account of the Ganges and Burrampooter at the Royal Soceity, 25 January, 1780*, London, 1781; and *Memoirs of Map of Hindoostan*, London, 1793; M.M. Martin, ed., *The History, Antiquities Topography and Statistics of Eastern India*, London, 1838; H. Blochmann, "Geographical and Historical Notes on the Burdwan and Presidency Divisions", in W.W. Hunter, ed., *Statistical Account of Bengal*, Vol. I, 1975.
27 Aditee Nagchowdhury-Zilly, *The Vagrant Peasant Agrarian Distress and Desertion in Bengal 1770–1830*, Fraz Steiner Verlag, Wiesbadan, 1982, p. 80. Zilly wrote (p. 84): "Midnapur, Burdwan and Birbhum were important centres for the cultivation of silk, where the desertion of silk weavers was due to the oppressive measures of the EIC (East India Company)."
28 W.W. Hunter, *Statistical Accounts of Bengal*, Vol. IV, p. 116.
29 Ibid, p. 125.

EARLY FORMATIONS

30 For details see N.K. Sinha, *The Economic History of Bengal 1793–1818*, Vol III, Firma K.L. Mukhopadhyay, 1970, pp. 70–72.
31 R.C. Majumdar, ed., *British Paramountcy and Indian Renaissance Part-I (Bharatiya Vidya Bhavan's History and Culture of the Indian People, Vol. IX)*, Bharatiya Vidya Bhavan, Bombay, 1963, p. 1106.
32 "While the Industrial Revolution in Britain was ushered in by the growth of iron and steel industries it began in India with the application of steam to jute and cotton textiles: The latter lacked Britain's solid basis of domestic production of iron and steel, and even the ancillary engineering industries (like Jessop's workshop) were dependent on foreign trade for development." – Ibid.
33 "Jute was in many ways the central commodity in the agricultural and industrial economy of Bengal in the second half of the nineteenth century, and became the focus of the manufacturing activity of most of the larger colonial firms in Calcutta between 1880 and 1929." – B.R. Tomlinson, *The New Cambridge History of India, III. 3: The Economy of Modern India, 1860–1970*, Cambridge University Press, 1998, p. 119.
34 Tomlinson, *The New Cambridge History of India, III. 3: The Economy of Modern India, 1860–1970*, p. 92.
35 "On the whole, the Calcutta agency houses did not develop direct business connections with the agricultural economy of the interior, preferring to sub-contract such dealings to Indian agents, or banias, who often contributed independently to the trading mechanisms by making capital advances for trade and stocks." – Tomlinson, *The New Cambridge History of India, III. 3: The Economy of Modern India, 1860–1970*, p. 119.
36 The original name of Kalna is Ambika Kalna. At present this town is a municipality and the headquarters of Kalna subdivision in the district of Burdwan. It is situated on the western bank of the river Bhagirathi. Kalna is sixty kilometres from the city of Burdwan.
37 At present Katwa is the headquarters of the Katwan subdivision in the district of Burdwan. It is situated between the Ajay river and the Hugli river. It is at a distance of 150 kilometres from Kolkata and 56 kilometres from Burdwan. In ancient time it was variously known as Kantak Nagari and Indrani Pargana. It was devastated by the Maratha invasions in the eighteenth century.
38 Dainhat is situated on the Kalna-Katwa Road. Its present area is 10.36 square kilometres.
39 Raniganj is situated between two rivers Damodar and Ajay. In the past it was a forest-ridden area and was industrialized only after the discovery of a coalfield. The coalfields directly led to the introduction of the railways from Howrah to Raniganj then known as the East Indian Railways. This railway line was opened to traffic in early 1855.
40 Asansol is the second largest city in West Bengal after Calcutta. It is the thirty-ninth largest urban agglomeration in India. The name Asansol is derived from Asan tree, a species of tree found around the river Damodar in the district of Burdwan.
41 Yogneswar Chaudhuri, *Bardhaman: Itihas O Sanskriti*, Vol. I, (1990), 2nd edn, 1995, Calcutta, p. 2.

42 Mirzapur was a city on the Ganga and was equidistant – around 650 km – from both Delhi and Calcutta. It was brought into life by the officers of the British government and the merchants of the East India Company.
43 Chaudhuri, *Bardhaman: Itihas O Sanskriti*, Vol. I, p. 60.
44 Buchanon Hamilton, *Geographical, Statistical & Historical Description of Hindusthan*, Vol. I, pp. 155 & 157.
45 "In the lower reaches of the rivers, increase of population leads to the construction of embankments, roads, and railways, which facilitate the silting up of river beds and the change of water courses, leaving a legacy of soil exhaustion, water-logging, and fever for the next generation." – Radha Kamal Mukherjee, *The Changing Face of Bengal*, University of Calcutta, Calcutta, 1938, p. 15.

7

THE LOGIC OF URBANIZATION

How Calcutta staged a breakthrough

Calcutta which in the beginning of the eighteenth century grew as a garrison town was eventually converted into a port town and then finally into a seat of administration. It grew under the pressure of geopolitics unleashed first by the fall of the Mughal Empire and then by the global trade working under the stress of the formative stages of Western imperialism. The vigilance of the *Nawabi* administration was a permanent brake on its potentialities of urbanization. The Mughal watch at Hugli kept Calcutta within constraints because Calcutta with its potentialities of trade, security, and global network had made itself a formidable competitor of Murshidabad. Madras was its rear area and the entire seaboard of the Bay of Bengal gave Calcutta a sea-route link with Madras. The removal of the Portuguese from the seas left the English almost the masters of the waves. Equipped with a powerful navy the English East India Company acquired the functional superiority of military manoeuvre which the *Nawabi* army never had. In the face of aggression they had an escape route through the seas. From the sea came the necessary reinforcement with which they overpowered their competitors and defeated their enemies on land. This was a kind of strategic flexibility with which they built up a kind of insulation around the city. Since they purchased the three villages of Kalikata, Sutanuti, and Govindapur they misconstrued the *sanads* which permitted them to purchase the land from a local zamindar. What they purchased was a *taluqdari* right which in all pragmatic sense they converted into a property right. Hence their urge was to keep their Calcutta lands as their property. They used to refer to their Calcutta lands as their estates and this was at variance with the constitution of the Mughals. They tried to build up an exclusive judicial jurisdiction in Calcutta so much so that a resident of Calcutta was considered to be their citizen who was thus made immune from the application of the rules of Mughal justice. A territorial enclave thus grew up on the soil of Bengal. The nucleus of a territorial possession was created. The components of a city came later. In the second half of the eighteenth century, the territorial revenue of the Bengal *Subah* came under their possession. The sinking of the *Nawabi* rule brought power within their sight. Calcutta was now free to acquire the parameters which made a city a tangible unit of growth.

The first major breakthrough toward making the city a unit of stable and functioning urbanity came in 1757. That year by the secret treaty with Mir Jafar the English Company got an extension of territory up to Kulpi a territory in the south of the twenty-four Parganas, a place that was near the sea. For nearly sixty years since the purchase of the three villages of Sutanuti, Govindapur, and Kalikata, Calcutta did not experience any territorial dynamism. The Bengal *Nawabs* did not allow them to purchase any one of the thirty-eight villages which the Emperor had sanctioned them. A very powerful *Nawabi* vigilance had cordoned the activities of the English in Bengal. This vigilance was maintained first from Hugli, then from Murshidabad and finally from Dakha. From this cordon Calcutta suddenly got release in 1757 just immediately after the Battle of Palasi. Two things happened simultaneously. One was the destruction of Hugli and Chandernagore by Clive on the eve of the retaking of Calcutta in the beginning of 1757. The second one was the military conquest of Calcutta by the English about the same time. These two events had great implications in history. Firstly, they destroyed two settlements which had very big potentialities of urban growth. They stifled their potentialities either as competitors of Calcutta or their capacity to act as a break upon the aspiration of the new city for growth. Secondly, the English now held Calcutta as their conquered territory although their right to conquest they never exercised. Yet they extracted their pound of flesh. They made the *Nawab* to surrender many of his sovereign rights to them and this was done through innumerable concessions which the *Nawab* was forced to make over. The Company's territory was now free from *Nawabi* vigilance and *Nawabi* interference. This was freedom that was necessary for getting into a start for a territorial sovereignty. With the capture of Calcutta one thing became certain. There was no power in eastern India which could overpower the English. Thus the whole of the eastern flank of Mughal Empire lay at the mercy of the English. This position was brightened by the British victory at the Battle of Buxar in 1764. In this battle the combined force of the Emperor Shah Alam of Delhi, Shujauddaullah of Awadh and Mir Qasim of Bengal accepted a defeat in the hands in the hands of the English. Save the Rohillas there was no power in the whole of the Gangetic basin that could stop the march of the English to Delhi. But Clive did not do that. He knew where to stop. Instead he kept the territory of the English confined to Bengal, Bihar, and Orissa. This was a masterly decision. In 1757 the territory of Calcutta was extended up to the sea. Now the influence of Calcutta extended over the whole Gangetic basin.

The strategic importance of the seaboard

In the meantime a new thing was explored. The English discovered the strategic importance of the seaboard that lay open from Madras to Calcutta. Madras had done its job in functioning as the military supply base for Calcutta in a time of crisis in 1756–1757. Now it became free of its obligation to act as the feeder base for Calcutta. Henceforth Calcutta became the English base to supervise the Company's influence over the Gangetic trade routes and their hinterlands in the upper Gangetic valley and Madras acted as its centre in promoting English interests in the south. Thus two power bases were created, one in upper India and the other in south India where from the English could encircle the rest of the country in time to come. Meanwhile Bombay emerged as the western power base of the English and the English became anchored in positions from where they could fence around the whole of central India with the advance of time. Thus between the Battle of Palasi and the Battle of Buxar, Calcutta emerged as one of the most strategically located centres in India from where power radiations could effectively take place. With this assumption by Calcutta of the status of an all-India power base, it easily superseded Murshidabad and all other Mughal towns in eastern and central India. In the west, Bombay was gradually overpowering Surat which became a victim of Maratha depredations. Shivaji sacked Surat more than once and its potentiality to contain the rise of Bombay was destroyed. With Hugli in Bengal and Surat in Gujarat having gone down, the power equation between Calcutta and Bombay assumed a linear axis. Calcutta now stood in a position to turn its face effectively from any of the Mughal power bases in the east to further radiations in the west.

In this situation the English made two things. First they made Calcutta the centre for a centripetal attraction for Bengal politics. This was done through an introduction of a new practice. The previous practice was that the English Governor of Calcutta or any of his agents, particularly the Resident at the Durbar, met the *Nawab* at Murshidabad when situations demanded. Now the process was reversed. The

THE LOGIC OF URBANIZATION

Nawab or any of his agents had to come down to Calcutta to supplicate the favour of the English. This meant that the political gravity in Bengal shifted from the seat of the Mughal administration to the seat of the English administration in Calcutta. The second thing was even deeper than this. They reared a class of rich people called the *banians* who controlled the money world of Bengal. These men supplied the Company, its officers and all its agents with cash. As a result a new class of capitalists grew in the city which could challenge the positions of the old magnates of the money-world, the *shroffs* (*sarrafs*) whose supreme leader and representative was the Jagat Sett. As the eighteenth century progressed the house of the Jagat Setts became an institution of the past. A process of supersession of old institutions began. In the rural world the institutions of the *qanungos* were withering away. The institutions of the sarrafs decayed. As Murshidabad sank as the capital of the *Subah* the house of the Jagat Setts also collapsed because the Mughal state in Bengal and the institution of the Setts were intrinsically linked in a closed mutually support system. As the state and its fiscal support institution collapsed a community of new men emerged as the business partners of the East India Company and its employees. They were not a homogeneous people. They emerged from both towns and villages and consisted of a medley of people shattered into splinters of a community undergoing change. They were small *dewans* and *amlas* of broken zamindaris, *dalals* and *gomastas* of small indigenous business houses and factories of various East India Companies of the Europeans, *munshis* and *mutsuddies* of local courts, *do-bhashi* (i.e. interpreters and agents of interior magnates and the various foreign companies), disjointed Mughal officers like *sazawals* and *wadedars*, clerks and accountants of various orders who supplied the intellectual know-how, and the writers' skill to whoever required their service and many other such men. The emergence of such men helped to create the man-power support and the social base of collaboration with which the city could get on to its own foundation. All these had created in the second half of the eighteenth century the socio-economic and political ambience in which the imperial city of Calcutta could see its own start.

Calcutta assumes power

From Hastings to Bentinck there was a conscious drive on the part of the British rulers to make Calcutta the seat of an imperial rule. It was here that Calcutta had aspects of power that influenced its evolving shape as a metropolis. Clive had initiated the city's installation in power when after the Battle of Palasi he allowed the new fort to come up under his auspices. Hastings gave a boost to the process when he transferred the major offices of the administration of the *subha* from Murshidabad to Calcutta. Along with the foundation of the executive authority the Supreme Court of Justice was set up in Calcutta. The sovereign status of Calcutta was thus fixed and the early beginning was thus made toward what later came to be called paramountcy. The functional supremacy of tile *Nizamat* gradually went down and the *Nawab*, the head of the *Nizamat*, stationed at Murshidabad, lost his glamour as the apex authority of the Mughal rule in the *subha*. Since the time of the Battle of Palasi a new process of give and take began between the Company's administration in Calcutta and the *Nawab*'s administration at Murshidabad. The administrative etiquette and the power protocol changed. Previously the English Governor of Calcutta or his agents visited the *Nawab* at Murshidabad. Now the rule of the game changed. The *Nawab* came down to Calcutta to see the Governor who was harboured in the pretension of a new-found power. There was no need from the English side to reciprocate the gesture. The gravity of power shifted from Murshidabad to Calcutta. A new culture of power based on Calcutta began to evolve. With the change in the equation of power the dynamics of the country's economy changed. Revenue was extracted from the interior of the districts and they were syphoned to Calcutta without any equivalent return to the countryside. Capital dried up in the rural world which thus went under the shadow of a money-short economy. The interior Rajas began to transfer their capital to Calcutta and began to purchase landed property there. Every one needed a foothold in Calcutta. This is how the districts began to rally around Calcutta, the newly emerging centre of power. The need for Calcutta to reach the interior was less than the need of the latter to build its nexus with this city which had substituted Murshidabad as the centre of power. With this the tendency began to grow a new legion of service elites both in the interior and also at the capital. The introduction of new principles of revenue extractions aimed at squeezing the last dreg of social surplus from the interior. New revenue managers called Supervisors were inducted in 1769 and their in-depth penetration into the finances of the *zamindars* shook up the stability of the interior revenue structures of the country. Everywhere there was a hunt for the hidden treasures of the land. The whole countryside, already under the stress of a capital-short economy, collapsed like a house of cards. There was tremendous breakdown of zamindaries and *amins, shiqdars, sazawals, munshis, gomastas* – the old Mughal revenue personnel – were now formed into a class of revenue undertakers to provide the supportive platform to these ramshackle zamindaries. As the countryside collapsed, the majesty of Calcutta grew. In the midst of surrounding destitution the glamour of Calcutta increased. This happened when the three towns of *Subah Bangla* – Dakha, Murshidabad, and Hugli – had gone into eclipse. Employment and business now converged in Calcutta. With this Calcutta appropriated the functions of three important centres of activity, namely those of a garrison town which Calcutta originally was, those of a port which were growing then in leaps and bounds, and finally those of a seat of administration which the city had become since the administration of Warren Hastings. Thus the functions of the three rolled into one and Calcutta was thrust into the role of a beamed majesty. It was in this situation that the colonial masters contemplated that Calcutta would replicate London as the eastern centre for the east-moving Britons. As an appendage to this a power elite grew up in the city. This is how Calcutta became a model of power not only in south Asia but also in the whole of the east.

In the earlier observation, we find the eighteenth-century scene of Calcutta's rise to prominence. How did Calcutta then contrast with the other colonial towns in India? Here is an observation on the point:

> Portuguese Goa was a museum of sixteenth-century imperialism, more plentifully supplied with churches than trade and with monks than soldiers. Bombay was a British possession but as yet the heir-apparent rather than actual successor to the wealth of Surat. The British settlement of Madras and Calcutta were prosperous and populous but centres of trade rather than of political power. French Pondicherry fulfilled the same function to a lesser degree. Other European stations, such as French Chandernagar, Dutch Chinsura and Negapatam, and Danish Tranquebar, were trading posts without political significance.[1]

Calcutta's political take-off

This was the condition of the colonial towns in the middle of the eighteenth century. Calcutta's political take off started after that. In the beginning of 1757 when Clive recovered the city from the control of the *Nawab* the status of the city changed. It was now a conquered city where the English might could be stationed permanently as its base. Understanding this the new *Nawab* Mir Jafar Khan granted the whole of the twenty-four Parganas, the district where the city was geographically located, to the Company as its *jagir*. Immediately with this the status of the city changed once again. It was now a gift in perpetuity in all practical terms. From a pragmatic standpoint the status of Calcutta and Bombay now became akin to each other. Bombay was a dowry gift and Calcutta was a gift in the form of a prize for enthroning a *Nawab*. With a puppet *Nawab*, at Murshidabad that city lost its old supremacy and became an appendage to the power that was growing from Calcutta.

A power-packed take-off of the city started thus. In course of the next hundred years the internal character of the city changed. The first major example of the display of power of the city was an attempt to apply English justice in the case of Maharaja Nanda Kumar, the Brahman minister of the Muhammadan *Nawab* of Bengal, Mir Jafar.[2] It is widely believed by historians that Nanda Kumar was implicated in a false case and, as Percival Spear says, that "there was a miscarriage of justice for which the blame cannot be fastened on any one man."[3] Sir Elijah Impey,[4] the first Chief Justice of the Supreme Court of Judicature at Fort William, Calcutta, which was established under the Regulating Act of 1773, was a friend of Hastings and it is alleged that he acted as the instrument of the Governor General to quash the case so stoutly put up by Nanda Kumar. Spear comments:

> Historically the incident is the supreme example of the absurdity and injustice of attempting to apply English legal methods to Indian conditions. The Supreme Court wished to impress on the Indian mind the seriousness of the crime of forgery;[5] it actually very successfully convinced men that it was dangerous to attack the governor general.[6]

The Nanda Kumar case proved beyond doubt that the Governor General was supreme in Calcutta and the English laws practised in Calcutta had already superseded the Muslim law practised under the *Nawabi* rule. The Regulating Act of 1773 – which had created power as an institution – had set up two organs of supremacy: firstly, the office of the Governor General who was given supervisory authority over two other presidencies and was thus made the supreme authority of a unitary control over all the British possessions in India; secondly, the Supreme Court which declared a *de facto* primacy of English law over the laws of the Mughal Government. The directional instructions given to the first Governor General of the British possessions of India contained large discretions. Hastings was efficient enough to make a full use of that. The Directors wrote to him:

> "We now arm You with full powers to make a complete reformation".[7]

THE LOGIC OF URBANIZATION

The power to implement reformation was given to a man who was stationed in Calcutta. This, in terms of power, made Bombay and Madras satellites of Calcutta. For the east-looking Britons, Calcutta was now the most coveted place to move, a place of pride where the British might have restored British possessions through conquest and forced the *Nawab*, the viceroy of the Mughal Government at Delhi, to formalize it through a legal grant in terms of the Mughal law. There was none to challenge the position of Calcutta now. In the south, Madras was still shaky vis-à-vis Haider Ali of Mysore, and, in the west, the position of Bombay was not completely secure vis-à-vis the Marathas. Only in Calcutta the English were unchallenged since the time when the united force of the Emperor Shah Alam II, Shuja-ud-daula of Awadh, and Mir Qasim of Bengal fell in the Battle of Buxar in 1764. The army that had so long guarded the eastern flank of the Mughal empire now collapsed and the might of the English in Calcutta became supreme. This might was located in the garrison town of Calcutta and gave Calcutta a boost in the power balance of the country. The victory at the Battle of Buxar, the new fort at Govindapur Calcutta, the Supreme Court of judicature and the office of the Governor General made Calcutta's position paramount. Stationed in Calcutta the British power became both an instrument for coercion and an agency for persuasion. Operating from power, Hastings defined Calcutta's role anew in the power structure of the country. Calcutta now became the seat of an overlord that could claim tribute from any subordinate authority that was suspected to have money stored in secret. The field where this claim was experimented was Benares and the hapless zamindar on whom the coercion was applied was Raja Chait Singh. The Company was in need of money. To the expenses of the Company's external wars and internal consolidation was added the lust of the masters of the Company manifesting both in individual greed and collective desire for tribute. From Calcutta Hastings did what formerly the Bengal *Nawabs* used to do from Murshidabad – fleecing money from the local *Rajas*. All *Nawabs* from Murshid Quli Khan to Siraj-ud-daullah squeezed the European Companies whenever they got a chance to do it. Now Hastings was in the mood of revenge and retribution. The *Raja* of Benares was the first victim. *The Oxford History*[8] says that Hastings was "well assured" that the *Raja* of Benares "had plenty of both men and money." This was one assurance that came mainly from power. Seated in Calcutta,

> He was so assured by his own representatives, whom he had thrust out into every key position, so that the administration was becoming one vast extension of his own masterful will.

Their opinions were his own and their conclusions jumped eagerly with his, even if they sometimes slightly anticipated those which suited his policy.[9]

A huge money was fleeced from the *Raja* and it was alleged that Hastings himself accepted a bribe from him. The Select Committee of 1783 remarked: "With £23,000 of the Raja's money in his pocket, he persecutes him to destruction."[10] We do not go into the ethics and legality of Hastings's dealings with Raja Chait Singh of Benares. The point we stress is that, through his dealings, in the cases of Maharaja Nanda Kumar as well as Chait Singh Hastings, he was demonstrating a show of power which scared the native people in Calcutta and around, and this fear and its memory provided a barrier to the unity between the ruler and the ruled in years to come. Historians say that Hastings was "lifted up with an egoism and complacency worse than those of Clive at his worst."[11]

The "egoism" of the Governor General of the East India Company's possessions in India made Calcutta a dreaded seat of a new power which appeared to be ruthless in imposing its own will and unfailing in aggrandizing its own jurisdiction. Hastings admitted this in open mind and flattered himself for what he had achieved for the Company and its city. His confidence in the Benares affair he expressed thus:

> "I feel an uncommon degree of anxiety to receive the sentiments of my friends upon it. I have flattered myself that they will see nothing done which ought not to have been done, nor anything left undone which ought to have been done."[12] At the source of his self-compliment there lay his confidence of power. He wrote: "Every power in India dreads a connexion with us."[13]

From a native town to an imperial city

This was the legitimate boast that came at a time when a native town was being given the boost for its conversion into an imperial city.[14] The power-packed character of the city was thus created. It surely was the creation of Hastings and his own times.

In the 1770s, Calcutta had become the invincible centre from where the Company's government tried to stretch out to neighbouring Indian rulers. Hastings was the masterful mind here and would become the will of the city. The command of the city emerged from Hastings's position in relation to the total Indian administration of the Company.

> Hastings governed the three Presidencies for eleven years after Lord North's Regulating Act, but he was Governor of Bengal for two years before it, and it is in the civil administration set up during those two years that the foundation of our system in India were laid. Hastings brought twenty-three years of Indian experience to the work: for those two years his hands were free; he planned, organized, and executed his own policy unhindered; it is by the action he then took that he must stand or fall. Whether the object of study be his character or the justice of our rule in India the years that follow can best be understood in the light of his original aims, for much of the legislation of the three succeeding decades was designed either to carry out those aims or to prevent their fulfilment.[15]

With the power of an absolute ruler, Hastings fleeced the Begums of Awadh. In removing Nanda Kumar from the political scene in Calcutta Hastings successfully negated the most formidable leader of the power elite of the old order. Nanda Kumar represented the last vestige of the power of Murshidabad and his fall only ensured Calcutta's triumph over that Mughal city in the east. Benares was the nearest city and its Raja was the most wealthy ruler in the immediate neighbourhood of Calcutta. Once they were crushed there remained no power in the vicinity of Calcutta that could stand as a barrier to the rise of the new city. Power has a tendency to radiate and Hastings made Calcutta the seat from where this radiation could direct itself to various ends in the immediate surroundings. We do not know whether Hastings wilfully did it. He was operating under financial stringency and the desperation born out of stringency propelled power to manifest itself in the most awkward political ambience of the time. In the process the Company's power crushed the primacy of men and cities that represented traditional sources of authority and affluence. It was this necessity that motivated Hastings's impingement on Awadh. The financial need of the Company was the most pertinent pretext that concealed the Company's megalomaniac and hegemonic demonstration of power. The *Nawab* of Awadh could not pay his subsidy arrears to the Company. Hastings put "relentless pressure to keep the *Nawab* up to the mark, exercised both on the *Nawab* himself and on two successive British residents" (Middleton, his own nominee, and Bristow a French man).[16] Percival Spear observes,

> In February 1782 Middleton wrote "no further rigour than that which I exerted could have been used against females in this country," and in June Bristow added the opinion of the officer commanding the troops, "all that force could do has been done." By these means 100 lakhs (£1 million sterling) were eventually secured, the *Nawab*'s debt paid and the Company's finances restored.[17]

One may argue that Hastings could do this because the power of the Mughals had sunk. From a deeper understanding it may be said that the English could do it because they had consolidated their base of power in Calcutta. The whole series of the traditional cities, bases of Indo-Islamic power, had gone down. Dakha, Murshidabad, Hugli, Malda (where during the time of Murshid Quli Khan the *zamindars* were mobilized to move against the English), Benares, Patna, and Monghyr (a temporary escape resort of Mir Qasim in his conflict with the English), which could cordon the supremacy of Calcutta, had become degraded centres of native power, almost satellites to the rule of a city that had suddenly raised its head. From this situation, a power was assumed whereby the ambition of a city was blown into a majesty cloaked under an overlord's right to intervene. The self-assumed power to swoop down upon the interior of the household of a native prince marked an impropriety of action unparalleled in the whole annals of the British rule in India.[18] It was deliberately demonstrated as a manifestation of a boast of power that was housed in the Fort William in Calcutta, a city now invested with pretension and pride to mark its supremacy as a centre of an upcoming empire in India. Hastings believed that the Indian institutions were still valid to be the basis for a British Empire,[19] but all institutions, he thought, should be subordinate to the will of Calcutta the city that housed the Fort William and its Council – the citadel of English power in India. He was impeached, three years after his retirement in 1785, on twenty charges arising from his activities in office – but one thing was sure about the way he functioned. He grasped very quickly while others of his community could not, the implications of assuming a hegemonic power that was to rest in a city. He gave lead in contemplating the idea that the British possessions in India could not be ruled from a merchant's emporium but from a majestic city – a feeling that eventually manifested in full bloom in Lord Wellesley's declarations of 1803. It should not be thought that Hastings's achievement in transforming Calcutta into a seat of power was a feat of individual prowess. Rather it was a part of a process that began with the hatching of the conspiracy against Sirajuddaullah, the *Nawab* of Bengal which set the Bengal revolution in 1756–1757. It was this conspiracy that led to two things – firstly, a series of revolutions beginning with the Battle of Palasi in 1757 and ending with an assumption of power by the Company in 1772 – a natural follow-up of the grant of the *diwani* in 1765. The second one was the eclipse of the *nizamat* and the emergence of the Calcutta Council as the superintending authority in the governance in the east. Clive was its master because it was his masterly intervention in Bengal politics,[20] which had dwarfed the *Nawab*, the Mughal ruling icon at Murshidabad who lent charm to this seat of power in the eastern flank of the Mughal Empire. What is significant to note is that Clive was not the first European to intervene in Bengal politics. The Portuguese had done it before him. But they had not earned a position for themselves by which they could participate in power. Calcutta owed her emergence to this situation of transforming Bengal politics where participation in power by the Company was made possible by Clive. A mercantile body situated in Calcutta suddenly became a partner in power not because it had a command in commerce but because it had a command over military might. Clive was invested with the title, *Sabat Jung* – "the tried in battle" – a title which Mir Jafar himself procured for him from the Emperor.[21] The district of twenty-four Parganas where the Company was made the zamindar was assigned to Clive as his *jagir*. *Sabat Jang*, the wielder of sword, was now the supreme master of the district in which Calcutta was situated. A *jagir* denoted both revenue and rank and Calcutta now became the seat of a defined position in which Mughal rank and revenue combined to highlight the dignity of a mercantile Company. The construction of a fort that was envisaged long ago was made possible in this context of transfer of power from Murshidabad to Calcutta. The territorial dynamism of the city, which was arrested so long, was now released and the city expanded up to Kulpi at the fringe of the sea. Calcutta suddenly seemed to have been lifted into glamour which it lacked earlier. This glamour was not so much an outcome of a growing port that Calcutta seemed to be but of a conquered city where the *de facto* authority of a Company had overshadowed the *de jure* sovereignty of the *Nawab*. All *Nawabs* from Mir Jafar onwards lived in Murshidabad by mortgaging their fortunes to the Company in Calcutta. A huge drain of wealth flowed from Murshidabad to Calcutta so much so that the officers of the Company here acquired and exercised a new power based on their new-found wealth. Calcutta flourished at the cost of Murshidabad.

Calcutta-Madras partnership

The process that led to this destiny of Calcutta was ushered in 1756. When Calcutta was captured by the *Nawab* that year, the Madras Council decided to temporarily withdraw from their involvements in the Deccan politics and concentrate their efforts in Bengal. "Had we been finally committed to the Deccan expedition when Calcutta was lost," writes Henry Dodwell, "Clive could not have sailed for its recovery and the course of events in Bengal might have been widely different."[22] Dodwell adds: "The Deccan could never have afforded the resources which, derived from Bengal, permitted to the capture of Pondicherry in 1761."[23] Calcutta thus became the resource-providing centre from where conquests could be planned. In this it was not Bombay but Calcutta which became the associate of Madras in working out the strategies of an emerging empire. This was long before Hastings took over the reins of administration as Governor General over the British possessions in India. Calcutta became the source of a new military strength for the English fighting their battles against the French over the Carnatic in the south. Dodwell was the first historian to understand Calcutta's position in the geopolitics of the time. He wrote: "Clive dispatched an expedition from Calcutta under Colonel Forde, who defeated the French in the field, captured Masulipatam, held it under great difficulties, and obtained from the deserted Salabat Jang, without any obligation of service in return, the cession of the provinces which the French formerly had held."[24] Calcutta had thus been commissioned into its all India career as a stronghold of the English might that could step into safeguard the ramshackle position which Madras was presenting at the time. This position Calcutta gained not through the renovation of the old fort or through the mending of the garrison there. This resulted from the removal of the watchful eye of the *Nawab* on Calcutta and the disappearance of the *Nawabi* cordon around Calcutta that was effected through the *Nawabi* station at Hugli, Malda, Chitpur, and Dumdum. A part of it was due to the collapse of Chandernagore from where the French maintained their watchful eye on Calcutta. The extraction of huge money from the *Nawab* Mir Jafar added to the self-confidence of the English. Calcutta in the immediate aftermath of the Palasi did not cease to be an old world city but its spirit had undergone a change. Clive's arrival in the city had always been a source of confidence not only for the English but also for the natives as well. His arrival at Calcutta for the second time on 3 May 1765 was hailed by all with exuberance.[25] The confidence necessary to consolidate an achievement

THE LOGIC OF URBANIZATION

had gone with the departure of Clive after the Battle of Palasi. This confidence returned now. Calcutta was now confident of a good governance and good governance was the real source of its power. Historians have seldom taken into account the fact that Clive's administrative and political achievement had gone a long way toward the consolidation of Calcutta's status as an over-mighty city that could defy frowning of the superior. Clive had given Calcutta the confidence to do this. Dodwell thus defines Clive's role in this as the following:

> His [Clive's] mission had a double purpose. He was to establish with the country powers such relations as should not in themselves offer occasion for ceaseless revolutions: he was further to put an end to that insubordination which had recently pervaded all branches of the Company's government, refusing obedience to orders from home, or resolutions of the Council whenever these seemed to threaten pecuniary loss, and almost establishing private interests as the criterion of public policy.[26]

This courage to sustain the worth of his political and administrative settlement against opposition from superior authorities gave Calcutta the political glamour it needed to become in future the seat of an empire. At the head of this courage came the decision that the Fort William would be relocated on a more convenient site. This was a remarkable decision taken in 1766[27] which eventually buttressed Calcutta's position as a city rallying around a fort not only for its own defence but also for the defence of the whole protectorate of which it had become the core. This was the protectorate of Bengal, Bihar, and Orissa, the eastern *Subahs* of the Mughal Empire, which served as the perennial source of revenue to the Mughals. In true sense of the term, Calcutta now became a garrisoned town and its strength was now equivalent to that of Madras. The removal of the *Nawabi* vigilance and the new fortification of the town ushered in a new age of hope and aspiration for Calcutta. The southern stations of the English were more or less free from the intervention of the subahdar[28] there.[29] Vis-à-vis these, Calcutta suffered from *Nawabi* stringency. In the past Calcutta did not compare with Madras in terms of wealth and power.[30] Now because of the Plassey Plunder[31] a huge wealth was extracted from the *Nawab* of Murshidabad and in various ways that city had drained its wealth to Calcutta. Calcutta had become rich by the time Clive ended his second term of office in that city. It had been a developing city for many years but the Fort William was in a wretched state. Dodwell says that when the *Nawab* invaded Calcutta in 1756

"Fort William was in a wretched a state as was Madras in 1746."[32] From the position of a conquered and a defeated stronghold in 1756 Calcutta in ten years' time had become a centre of strength from where military reinforcements could be sent to the south to vindicate the British position there. On the basis of this military might a political status was conjured up. Clive while instituting his first government invited the *Nawab* to Calcutta. It was almost a conqueror's advice to the conquered and in doing this Clive was in effect creating a new balance of power not only between the *Nawab* and the President of the Council at Fort William, but also between Murshidabad as the capital of a *Subah* and Calcutta as the seat of power of an emerging empire. Clive wrote to Watts: "I need not hint to you how many good purposes the nabob's presence will answer."[33] He was thus initiating a process whereby the centrality of Murshidabad as the seat of Mughal power in Bengal was being surrendered to the rising authority of another city which had of late burst out of its fetters created and imposed so long by the vigilance of the *Nawabi* rule. The radiance of Mughal glory had dimmed after the Battle of Palasi and Clive was now undertaking an effort to regularize a process in which the dimming of the legitimacy of the *Nawabi* rule would seem to be a part of the consciously driven project of the English.

Calcutta's emergence an eighteenth-century phenomenon

Calcutta emerged under these conditions over which the Company presided. Looked from this standpoint the emergence of Calcutta under the English was essentially an eighteenth-century phenomenon. Till the end of the seventeenth century, the English eyes were riveted on Chittagong. It was only under Clive and Hastings that Calcutta replaced Chittagong from the early English dream to build up their settlement in the east. The Mughal attack on the English factory at Hugli in October 1686[34] was mostly responsible for this. It convinced the English authorities at home and their men at Madras that two things had to be done at the earliest opportunity. Firstly, they had to capture Chittagong,[35] a station far away from the Mughal base at Hugli, and, secondly, their settlement wherever it was should be fortified in order to give protection to the English trade in Bengal. As a matter of fact the settlement of the English at Sutanuti came after two broad failures of the English in their fight against the Mughals between 1686 and 1690. They planned to blockade the entire western coast of the Mughal Empire with the help of the coastal settlements there and capture Chittagong as a base for future settlement. Both the strategies failed and the English withdrew to Hijli at the mouth of the river from where they swooped down upon Balasore, sacked the city, and burnt the town. It was a desperate act of revenge against the Mughal authority for the damage it had caused to English trading in Bengal.[36] There they were attacked once again by the Mughal forces while fever destroyed a sizeable part of their small army.[37] These experiences were never lost with the English and when they returned to Sutanuti in the autumn of 1687 their first task was to build up a fortified settlement in Bengal. This was not only a local urge but a sentiment which the home authorities very powerfully drove into the minds of their local agents.[38]

It is, therefore, clear that the English settlement in Calcutta emerged only in the background of this failure of the English to capture Chittagong and establish there a strong English base of naval power outside the orbit of Mughal interference.[39] In 1760 when Mir Qasim granted Midnapur, Burdwan, and Chittagong to the Company, the English were already firmly settled in Calcutta and there was no need for them to revive their old dream to settle at Chittagong. Since the last English attempt to capture Chittagong by force in 1688 down till the time of Hastings's assumption of power Calcutta had absorbed in its growth three major experiences of crisis that taught them the need of fortification. These were the rebellion of Shova Singh that shook the western part of the *Subah* in 1696–1697, the Maratha invasions of 1740s, which helped the English to demonstrate their defence capabilities, and the loss of Calcutta in 1756 and its subsequent recapture from the *Nawab* in early 1757. All these events taught them that the English town had to be properly garrisoned. It was out of the logic of this that Calcutta was built primarily as a garrison town. At the time of the Maratha invasions, Calcutta was a sanctuary for men in flight although its innate capacity to protect men was really very weak.[40] Both the rebellion of 1696–1697 and the Maratha invasions in the middle of the 1740s showed how unprotected the western part of the Mughal *Subah* of Bengal was, whereas the invasion of Calcutta by the *Nawab* in 1756 showed how unprotected the English were vis-à-vis the outrageous Mughal rulers in the state. All these drove home with the English the fact that the Company's government must have a strong military force at its command and for this a fort had to be built which would house a strong garrison in the city. This was all the more a necessity because the population of the city had increased by leaps and bounds during the time of the Maratha invasions.[41] Despite the influx of native population the domestic development of Calcutta took

EARLY FORMATIONS

the shape of a Christian town in the western lines.[42] The heritage of the town had also to be protected. Out of this need an imperial city was conceived. From the beginning it was clear that the city was not to go the way of a Mughal city. A Mughal city had no racial compartments. But, in the new city, the settlement of the whites was developed in contradistinction to the settlement of the brown people. From Govindapur and Calcutta, natives were gradually driven to the north to Sutanuti and its beyond. The fort and its immediate neighbourhood became the nucleus of a white city. A port and a garrison town were now to be merged and on the basis of this merger the seat of a new power was to be erected. There was no declared aim in the eighteenth century toward which the city would direct its growth. But imperceptibly all orientations were taking shape. After the Palasi, the office of the *Nawab* had sunk. After 1765 the office of the *Diwan* passed under the English custody. The Port, the fort, and the office of the Governor now assumed importance. A new urbanity was ring-fenced. Beyond this the old *Burra Bazaar* remained to be the central hub where native business enterprise remained to be a brisk phenomenon of the old world. The new city assumed its orientations outside the bustles of the old world.

Notes

1 Percival Spear in Percival Spear, ed., *The Oxford History of India by the Late Vincent A. Smith C.I.E.*, 3rd edn, At The Clarendon Press, Oxford, 1958, reprinted 1961, Part III, pp. 452–453.
2 "In March 1775 Nanda Kumar accused Hastings of accepting a large bribe from Munni Begum in return for her appointment as guardian of the young Nawab Mubarak-ud-daula. The charge was welcomed by the majority, who immediately resolved 'that there is no species of speculation from which the governor-general has thought it reasonable to abstain'. Hastings refused to meet his accuser in council and dissolved the meeting, whereupon the majority ordered him to repay the amount into the Company's treasury, Hastings now brought a charge of conspiracy against Nanda Kumar. While this was pending Nanda Kumar was arrested at the instance of a Calcutta merchant on a charge of forgery unconnected with the previous controversy. He was tried before the new Supreme Court, found guilty and executed. Thereafter the charges against Hastings were dropped and never revived." – Spear, *The Oxford History of India by the Late Vincent A. Smith C.I.E.*, pp. 505–506.
3 Spear, *The Oxford History of India by the Late Vincent A. Smith C.I.E.*, p. 506. Elijah Impey, it should be noted, was a class-friend of Warren Hastings at Westminster and at Calcutta their relationship got more cordial.
4 For Sir Elijah Impey read Elijah Barwell Impey (1780–1849), *Memoirs of Sir Elijah Impey, knt: First Chief Justice of the Supreme Court of Judicature, at Fort William, Bengal*, Batten, Simpkin-Marshall, London, 1857.

5 "Forgery was not a crime punishable by death in the current criminal law of Bengal derived from the Muslim code, and the application of English penalties in Indian cases was opposed to a well-established Indian legal tradition." – Spear, *The Oxford History of India by the Late Vincent A. Smith C.I.E.*, p. 506.
6 Ibid.
7 Cited in Spear, *The Oxford History of India by the Late Vincent A. Smith C.I.E.*, p. 502.
8 Spear, *The Oxford History of India by the Late Vincent A. Smith C.I.E.*, p. 537. This old book of Vincent Smith was one of the four major standard British interpretations of Indian history of the time, the three others being the old several-volume *Cambridge History of India*, Mr. P.E. Roberts's, *History of British India*, Professor H.H. Dodwell's British India.
9 Edward Thompson and G.T. Garratt, *Rise and Fulfilment of British Rule in India*, Central Book Depot, Allahabad, 1962, p. 159.
10 The Select Committee said: "The complication of cruelty and fraud in the transaction admits of few parallels. Mr. Hastings . . . displays himself as a zealous servant of the Company, bountifully giving from his own fortune . . . from the gift of a man whom he treats with the utmost severity." Most of the British historians write in defence of Hastings and try to exonerate him from the charges which were levelled against him. Spear, *The Oxford History of India by the Late Vincent A. Smith C.I.E.*, pp. 515–516 and Thompson and Garratt, *Rise and Fulfilment of British Rule in India*, pp. 159–160.
11 Thompson and Garratt, *Rise and Fulfilment of British Rule in India*, pp. 161.
12 Cited in Thomson and Garratt, *Rise and Fulfilment of British Rule in India*, p. 162.
13 Ibid, p. 161.
14 The real beginning of Calcutta's becoming an imperial city started only in the 1770s when the Company decided to stand forth as a Dewan.
15 M.E. Moncton Jones, *Warren Hastings in Bengal 1772–1774*, Oxford University Press, Preface.
16 Spear, *The Oxford History of India by the Late Vincent A. Smith C.I.E.*, p. 516. British troops were sent to the house of the Nawab and the eunuch stewards of the Begums of the interior household were tortured, imprisoned, and "subjected to fetters, starvation, and the treat of the lash." – Ibid.
17 Ibid.
18 "The begums were not left penniless, or even uncomfortable. Nor was their title to their riches quite certain. But there is no doubt that faith was broken, that the Company's government interfered in what was essentially a domestic and intimate situation in the nawab's own household, that the begums were severely treated and their dependants bullied and ill-used. There also seem no doubt that Hastings's was the moving spirit egging on reluctant British resident and officers. When due allowance has been made for the dire necessities of Hastings's position at the time and the strains to which he was subjected, the fact remains that in both these cases (Benares and Awadh) Hastings sank below not only modern codes of conduct but *the accepted Indian standards of the time*." (Italics mine) – Spear, *The Oxford History of India by the Late Vincent A. Smith C.I.E.*, p. 516.

19 "The first governor-general, Warren Hastings, appointed under the first Parliamentary Regulating Act for India of 1773, took up his position with the view that the historical institutions already developed in India provided the best basis for British rule." – Burton Stein, *A History of India*, Oxford University Press, New Delhi, 1998, p. 212.
20 Clive's intervention did not immediately change the old order. Spear writes: "Legally and to most outward appearance the old order continued. There had been revolutions before and the assistance of foreigners was well understood. The English were not even the first Europeans to interfere in Bengal politics, for the Portuguese had done it long before them." – Spear, *The Oxford History of India by the Late Vincent A. Smith C.I.E.*, p. 468.
21 Spear, *The Oxford History of India by the Late Vincent A. Smith C.I.E.*, p. 469 note.
22 Henry Dodwell, *Dupleix and Clive: The Beginning of Empire*, 1920, Methuen & Co. Ltd., London, Vishwavidyalaya Prakashan, Gorakhpur, reprint, 1962, p. 107.
23 Ibid, p. 108.
24 Ibid, p. 110.
25 Dodwell writes (*Dupleix and Clive: The Beginning of Empire*, p. 266): "His advent was hailed with an outburst of Oriental rhetoric. 'The flower of our wishes is blossomed in the garden of hope,' wrote one; to another his coming was 'as rain upon the parched earth.' And these expressions represented something more than mere compliment. Save those who feared punishment for their misdeeds, there was not a man, of any race or creed, in Calcutta, but felt the safer for Clive's coming."
26 Dodwell, *Dupleix and Clive: The Beginning of Empire*, p. 267.
27 "Only in 1766 was it decided not to complete the fort on its original plan, since if ever the English were cooped up within its walls their affairs might not be regarded as irrevocably ruined. This change of policy is deeply significant. It marks emphatically the point to which the force of circumstances had driven the English, and to which all had ignorantly contributed – Clive by his military success, Vansittart by his policy of re-establishing the Nawab's power, thus hastening the denouement of the piece, the Company's servants by their trade and the disputes occasioned thereby, until Clive returned to reap the harvest in whose sowing he had played so considerable part." – Dodwell, *Dupleix and Clive: The Beginning of Empire*, pp. 272–273.
28 The Nizam of Hyderabad was the subahdar.
29 Dodwell writes (*Dupleix and Clive: The Beginning of Empire*, p. 113): "Before the exploits of Dupleix and Bussy had produced their natural consequences, the position of Europeans in India had varied much. In the north they were at the uncertain mercy of the local Governors. At Calcutta, for example, the Council feared to condemn a Muhammadan to death; and neither French nor English were allowed to strengthen or enlarge their fortifications. But the government of Bengal under Alivardi Khan was comparatively vigorous and subordinate officials were closely watched. The governments dependent on the Subahdar of the Deccan, however, were much less strictly supervised during the later years of Nizam-ul-Mulk. He had adopted the custom of letting out the various

THE LOGIC OF URBANIZATION

offices for short terms to the highest bidder: and the local Nawabs were at liberty to recoup themselves as best as they could."

30 "Madras was a place of considerable wealth, a centre of trade and banking, not lightly to be meddled with, and there the English privileges were jealously upheld. When in 1744 a shroff, instead of applying to the English courts, dared to seek the aid of the amildar of St. Thome to procure payment from an English debtor, he was promptly fined 500 pagodas, and such representations were made to the offending amildar that he promptly offered apoligies, explaining that he had but recently come from a remote part of India and knew nothing of English privileges." – Dodwell, *Dupleix and Clive: The Beginning of Empire*, pp. 113–114.

31 For the details of the Plassey Plunder see N.K. Sinha, *The Economic History of Bengal*, Firma K.L. Mukhopadhyaya, Calcutta, 1965, pp. 12, 78, 103, 152, 221.

32 Dodwell, *Dupleix and Clive: The Beginning of Empire*, p. 130.

33 Cited in Dodwell, *Dupleix and Clive: The Beginning of Empire*, p. 158.

34 A detailed account of the operations is available in the introduction to C.R. Wilson's, *Early Annals of the English in Bengal*, Vol. I.

35 This point has been discussed in chapter IV entitled "The East India Company, 1600–1740" by Sir William Foster, in H.H. Dodwell, ed., *The Cambridge History of India*, Vol. V, British India 1497–1858, S. Chand & Co., New Delhi Second Indian Reprint, 1963, p. 107. Here is an excerpt from Foster: "The home authorities, who . . . were already persuaded of the necessity of adopting a bold policy, readily fell in with this view, and in 1686 they sent out orders that the Bengal factories should be withdrawn and an attempt made to seize Chittagong, for which purpose they dispatched several ships and a small force of soldiers. At the same time on the western side of India the Mughal coast as to be blockaded and the local shipping seized; while the Coast settlements were to assist with the full strength of their resources. The enterprise was a rash one, though all might have been well if the Company had left the control of affairs entirely in the hands of Job Charnock, its experienced agent in Bengal; not that fighting would have been entirely avoided, but an accommodation would have been reached more speedily and nothing would have been done as regards the absurd plan of attacking so distant a port as Chittagong." – p. 107.

36 "These failing, the English withdrew further down the Hugli river and fixed their headquarters on the island of Hijli, at its mouth; while, in reprisal for the injuries sustained, their ships sacked and burnt the town of Balasore." Foster, "The East India Company, 1600–1740", pp. 107–108.

37 "In their new station they were blockaded by the Mughal force, while fever made great havoc among the small garrison; but timely reinforcements enabled Charnock to effect an agreement under which, in the autumn of 1687, the English returned to Sutanuti, where they remained for a year unmolested." – Foster, "The East India Company, 1600–1740", p. 108.

38 "The home authorities, however, were obstinately bent upon the plan of a fortified settlement in Bengal." – Ibid.

39 Foster says that "in September, 1688, a fresh naval force arrived under Captain William Heath, who had plenary powers to carry out the projected attack upon Chittagong. Despite the opposition of Charnock the new settlement was abandoned, and in January the fleet arrived at

EARLY FORMATIONS

Chittagong, only to find it much too strong to be assailed with any chance of success; whereupon Heath decided to retreat to Madras." – Ibid.

40 "The approach of these raiders (the Marathas) created great consternation, for Fort William (finished in 1716) was of little real strength, and moreover its defensive capabilities had just been seriously reduced by the erection of warehouses against its southern face." – Foster, "The East India Company, 1600–1740", p. 112.

41 "Nevertheless Calcutta continued to grow in importance and wealth, and by the middle of the century its population was estimated at over 1,00,000 as compared with the 15,000 of 1704. This, it is true, was partly owing to a great influx about 1742, caused by the invasion of the province by the Marathas." – Ibid.

42 "The domestic history of Calcutta for this period [1700–1740] includes also the erection of a church (St. Anne's, consecrated in 1709): the building of a fine house for the governor in the fort and the organization of a judicial system under a charter granted by George I in September, 1726, which also provided for the appointment of a mayor, sheriff, and aldermen. The courts thus established were similar to those erected at Madras under the same charter, as described later, but they did not come into full operation." – Foster, "The East India Company, 1600–1740", p. 113.

8
MUNICIPAL ADMINISTRATION

Municipal growth a gradual phenomenon

The municipal growth of Calcutta in the eighteenth century was a gradual phenomenon. The Charter Acts of the British Parliament – dated 1727, 1753, and 1794[1] – created a municipal machinery for the town. The first effort towards the municipal organization of the city thus began within thirty-seven years since Job Charnock set his foot on its soil in 1690. In 1803 Lord Wellesley's Minute outlined a well-thoughtout scheme for promoting the health and welfare of the inhabitants of the town. This minute, it is said, "stands as a beacon of light in the misty path of municipal reform."[2] Although these four major Charter Acts were worked out in course of slightly more than one century of the city's life no tangible achievement is said to have been made towards organizing the municipal life of the city. The East India Company's government could not create a fund with which the municipal life could properly be given a shape. People paid various taxes, but they were credited to general revenues.[3] Lack of funds acted as a tremendous brake on the government's efforts to fulfil the major requirements of the town. Since the middle of the eighteenth century, bad hygiene had become a serious constraint on population growth.[4] After the famine of 1770 when the interior of rural Bengal showed a picture of misery people began to crowd in Calcutta. Because of the paucity of fund, "the efficiency of town administration suffered" and

> neither the standard nor the volume of municipal services improved. It was increasingly felt that the stringency of finance could hardly be got rid of without calling in the King Stork of Taxation. The people of Calcutta were already heavily taxed;

it appeared simply impossible to widen the tax net without soliciting the co-operation of the inhabitants in the working of the municipality.[5]

This however did not happen before the beginning of the fourth decade of the nineteenth century.[6]

For a long time since the beginning of the eighteenth century Calcutta was ruled by one of the civil servants of the company. He was called the *Zamindar*.[7] He had under him an Indian to assist him in the office and also to represent him in various activities. He was called the "Black *Zamindar*."[8] The main function of the *zamindar* was to collect rent and various other taxes and duties. But he usurped entire control over executive and revenue matters. He also exercised civil and criminal jurisdiction over the inhabitants of the town. This was in keeping with the Mughal tradition. According to the Mughal system of rule, *zamindars* were the lowest unit of the executive and judicial authority of the state. At the village level they collected revenue, policed over the interior and dispensed small justice at the local level. In a sense, they were the people who brought the might of the state at the doorstep of the peasants. At Calcutta, the zamindar appropriated the entire function of a rural zamindar. But the rural zamindar, partly by tradition and partly by the compulsion of his station, looked after the welfare of the people. But the zamindar at Calcutta had no regard for the people's welfare. "The regime of autocracy under the *zamindar* was ill-fitted for embarking on a policy of progressively improving the sanitary state of the town of Calcutta."[9] The result was that the city remained to be nothing better than "an undrained swamp surrounded by malarious jungles."[10] The Charter Act of 1727 set up a Corporation for the town, but it was "intended to exercise judicial rather than administrative function."[11] Under the Charter the main duty of the Corporation was to collect ground rents and town dues. Since the condition of roads and drains had become desperate, the Corporation at the most undertook some efforts to make necessary repairs in them. The town administration was weak, the finance was short, and the will to improve the condition of the town was absent. The Company's administration was anxious to whip up revenue because revenue provided them the sinews of commerce. The Company's stake at the Bengal trade and, through Bengal trade, its stake at the Asian trade were pressing and whatever revenue it could raise from the soil of the city would help them to provide for their investment in Bengal.[12] Moreover the expenditure incurred for the civil administration in the city was to be provided from the general revenue. Hence revenue that was forcibly raised was dearly conserved. There was no will to expend this revenue in the municipal renovation of the town. When the will to promote the city was absent at the government level, the creation of a Corporation by the Charter of 1727 was of little meaning. The Corporation entrusted the administration of the town in the hands of the zamindar who could not function in the absence of adequate funds. He failed and through him the Corporation failed.[13]

One of the main reasons why town administration suffered in the first half of the eighteenth century was the lack of coordination between the *White Zamindar* and the *Black Zamindar*. The White *Zamindar* was an autocrat and this autocracy began with Job Charnock[14] and persisted till such time as Siraj-ud-daullah's sack of Calcutta. The "Black Zamindar" under him was a scheming man who taking advantage of the ignorance of the white master of the intricacies of the land revenue administration sought to embezzle money. Nandaram Sen, the Black Zamindar of Calcutta in 1705, could not pull on well with his white master Ralph Sheldon. He was implicated in a charge of defalcation and was sacked from his office. But the Company's administration was in need of men who were trained in the revenue administration of the city. Hence Nandaram was reinstated in 1707. In no time he was again detected in a defalcation. But he somehow managed to escape from Calcutta and fled to the *Nawab*'s territory at Hugli. The *Faujdar* of Hugli seized him and eventually handed him over to the English authorities at Calcutta. He was ultimately forced to make good the loss to the Company.

Nandaram Sen was succeeded by two Black *Zamindars*, Rambhadra and Jagat Das. In 1720 one Govindaram Mitra was appointed "Black Zamindar" of Calcutta. Thus in course of fifteen years since the creation of the post in 1705, four persons were appointed *Black Zamindar*. Govindaram remained in the post for thirty long years, and his fall from his station took place when he failed to get along well with his white master John Zephaniah Holwell. Since Holwell's appointment as the *Zamindar* of Calcutta took place in 1752, one may say that Govindaram was in power at least till that year. He fell a victim to Holwell's suspicions that he had amassed huge money by defrauding government revenue. Govindaram's salary at the beginning was Rs. 30 a month and this was later increased to Rs. 50 per month. He also had income from his farms received from the *Nawabs* of Murshidabad.[15] Since Govindaram built the largest temple in Calcutta called the Navaratna Temple,[16] he became an object of suspicion to his superiors. Some historians are prone to accept the English version of the story that Holwell unearthed sufficient evidence of Govindaram's having screened the Company's revenue. Holwell's veracity was doubted by his own colleagues within the service of the Company. In any case, nothing was proved against Govindaram and he was acquitted of charges of embezzlement. But he was not allowed to remain in office as the "Black Zamindar" of Calcutta.[17]

The British charge of embezzlement levelled against successive Black *Zamindars* should not be accepted without scrutiny. It is said that the "Black Zamindar" was "accustomed by immemorial practice to supplement his inadequate salary by that he . . . considered as the perquisites of his office, emoluments which, on scrutiny, would be regarded by his employers as embezzlements."[18] Under the Mughals officers, remuneration consisted of perquisites. Thus a *qanungo*, a *patwari*, a *qazi*, an *amin*, or a *shiqdar* – all had enjoyed *russoms* or allowances drawn squarely from the interception of revenue.[19] The Mughal rule was a rule by devolution. The rulers at the top bartered away both revenue and authority to their representatives at subordinate levels and at the apex of power they remained as symbols of distant majesty. This point was not properly understood by the officers of the Company. When they complained about the corruption of the indigenous staff in their employment they invariably meant interception of revenue by them at their own stations. But the fact that this interception was an accustomed part of their living they could not understand.

In any case the absence of coordination between the *White Zamindar* and his subordinate *Black Zamindar* did not allow the town administration to take a proper shape. As years rolled on it was widely felt that the Zamindar could not be allowed to remain at the centre of the municipal administration of the town. In 1794 the municipal management of the town was taken out of the hands of the Zamindar.

The context that necessitated the take-over of the administration has been well analyzed by Goode. For a proper appreciation of the perspective of change we quote the following excerpts from his work.

> The municipal administration of the town (if such a conception can be accurately applied to the early days of Calcutta) was originally entrusted to one of the Company's Civil Servants, who was called the "Zamindar" and later the Collector of Calcutta. Under a Royal Charter issued in the twenty-sixth year of the reign of George I (1727), a Corporation consisting of a mayor and nine aldermen, with a mayor's court, was established, of which Holwell, the former "Zamindar" or Collector of Calcutta, afterwards became president. The Mayor's

Court was given civil, criminal and ecclesiastical jurisdiction over British inhabitants, and dispensed a kind of rough and ready justice, according to broad principle of equity. We hear of a tax being levied on the inhabitants of Calcutta for the construction of a town hall or court house to accommodate the mayor and his court. And in 1729 the building was erected on the site now occupied by St. Andrew's Church.[20]

The Corporation seems to have done little to improve the administration of the town; its charter was surrendered in 1753 and a new Royal Charter granted, by which the Mayor's Court was re-established, and an ineffectual attempt made to organise a municipal fund by the 'levy of a house tax of two or three lakhs of rupees, to defray the expense of cleansing and ornamenting the place internally'. The revenue from ground rents, tolls, and other town dues was partly employed in maintaining 'an undisciplined battalion of thanadars' and peons, constituting the only established guard or night-watch of the city[21]

We hear of orders from the authorities to the "Zamindar," or Collector, to "make the drains sweet and wholesome," and to cut down the jungle in and around the town, but little improvement in the sanitary conditions of the town appears to have been effected. The ditch to the east of the old Fort, into which the bodies of the victims of the Black Hole had been cast, was not filled up until 1766, nor the Mahratta Ditch until 1780, though both had been the dumping-grounds for all the filth and garbage of Calcutta.[22]

In 1790 Grandpre could still write that the public drains were regarded as the natural receptacles for all refuse and filth, that carcases were left to rot and putrefy in the streets, and that jackles had for two nights prayed on a human corpse thrown down at his gate. The need of drastic measures gradually forced itself upon the attention of the authorities.[23]

The unsoundness of a system which, in addition to his multifarious revenue and judicial duties, made the Collector responsible for public order, convenience, and health, became more and more apparent, as the area and population of the town expanded and aggravated the evils of over-crowding and imperfect drainage.[24]

Appointment of Justices – In 1794 under the Statute 33 Geo. III, the Collector was relieved of his municipal duties, the Governor General taking powers to appoint Justices of the Peace for the Municipal administration of the town, with authority to make regular assessments and to levy rates. This statute may be regarded as a landmark in the development of municipal government in Calcutta.[25]

Corporate control of the Justices of the Peace

Thus, by a Statute of George III, the town was placed under a corporate control of the Justice of the Peace. In this way the autocratic administration of the Zamindar passed away under the impact of a rightful application of law. It may be said that the municipal administration of the time came to be properly organized only in 1794. The institution of the Justices of the Peace was in existence for more than five decades. When the Mayor's Court was established in 1727, it was laid down that the five senior members of the Governor's Council would be called Justices of the Peace and they would dispense justice for all offences other than high treason. Through Justices of the Peace, efforts were made to extend the benefits of western institutions to the people in India.[26] But the number of Justices of the Peace was inadequate and their functions were not properly defined. These shortcomings were remedied by the Charter of 1794. The Act empowered the Governor General in Council to create new post of the Justice of the Peace. By commission to be issued from time to time the Governor General in Council might appoint or nominate covenanted servants of the Company or even private Englishman to act as Justices of the Peace. This provision removed the brake on the numerical strength of the Justices of the Peace.

The Charter of 1794 also organized the function of the Justices of the Peace.[27] Their administration was to take place through three departments – the assessment department, the executive department and the judicial department. The judicial department meant sessions of the justices. At the outset when business was small the sessions of the Justices were held once a year. Later on the volume of business increased and quarter sessions became a practice. The Justices in session had to hear appeals and decide complaints. That apart, they had to preside over such functions as assessment of rates, making arrangement for the execution of the conservancy works, the collection of the assessment, looking into the ordinary watch and ward of the town, ratification of assessments, and so on. Thus the function of the Justices of the Peace were properly organized.

Truly speaking, the Charter of 1794 brought about a great improvement upon the Charter of 1753. The latter Charter was "primarily judicial in its purport, it laid down elaborately the jurisdiction of the Mayor's Court and the rules and practices to be followed therein."[28] It did three things:

> It envisaged the establishment of the Court to be called the Court of Requests for the recovery of small debts (not exceeding five pagodas). And it conferred a general power on the President and Council for Fort William for making by laws and imposing penalties. It also contained a provision, as in the earlier Charter of 1726, of a Sheriff for Calcutta.[29]

These were broad administrative changes and nothing practically came out of these changes in the long run. Vis-à-vis the failure of the Charter of 1753, the changes brought about by the Charter of 1794 seem to be innovating.

> The Statute [of 1794 was], however, of great importance, in as much as it substituted corporated control and responsibility for the autocratic administration of the Zamindar. It bears the imprimatur of Government's faith in committees and in the transplanting of English Institutions on the Indian soil.[30]

Throughout the second half of the eighteenth century public health, in Calcutta suffered very much. "The unhealthy conditions of town life persisted, the amount spent annually to remedy these was insignificant and, though the population was increasing, few actual reforms were undertaken for the sanitation of the town owing to the acute shortage of funds."[31] Calcutta in all practical sense offered the picture of an undrained swamp, "filth lying in profusion everywhere, a cemetery in the very heart of the capital, and decoities within hark of Government house."[32] To remedy this situation, the Charter of 1794 specially enjoyed upon the Justices of the Peace "to appoint scavengers for cleansing the streets" and "also to order the watching and repairing of the streets therein as they respectively shall judge necessary."

There are two divergent views about the success the Justices of the Peace acquired in course of their function over years. The first

EARLY FORMATIONS

view holds that the office of the Justices of the Peace were effective and successful.

> The regime of the Justice lasted for many decades. At the beginning the Justices were largely Company's senior servants, but in due course, they included the leading citizens of the town. The Justices, we are told, set to their business in real earnestness and implemented certain reforms. One of their initial acts was the metalling of Circular Road.[33] Town conservancy also received some attention. The Justices adopted the system of inviting tenders for the supply of bullocks for the carts to be used in cleaning the drains and streets of Calcutta.[34]

Against this we have the other view. "It is true that before long, . . ., all real power began to concentrate in one person, the Chief Magistrate, responsible not to the people but to Government, while the Justices sitting in quarter sessions became for administrative purposes a mere nullity."[35]

Not an effective institution

The institution of the Justices of the Peace might not be an effective institution from a long-term point of view. But it formed a part of the general effort towards organizing the municipal administration of the town. As the offices of the Justices of the Peace came to be reinforced, the executive branch of the administration was also recognized. The executive branch of the municipal administration was manned by an engineer in charge of roads and conservancy, and an executive officer under him who also acted as the head overseer and a flock of clerks and menials who acted as the general staff of the office. In spite of the great reorganization of administration, nothing tangible was affected in terms of the improvement of roads and conservancy. Improvement in these directions was beyond the capacity of the Justices of the Peace.[36]

The institution of the Justice of the Peace had failed, but it showed that a milieu of change had been ushered in the city. With the English East India Company effectively saddled in power the administration came to be centralized more and more in Calcutta. The change had begun during the time of Hastings. He did three important things. Firstly, he transferred the exchequer, known by Mughal parlance the *Khalsa*, from Murshidabad to Calcutta. This was the most effective measure by which Calcutta became the capital of the financial world of Bengal. Secondly, he abolished the five provincial Revenue Councils

MUNICIPAL ADMINISTRATION

at Burdwan, Dacca, Dinajpur, Murshidabad, and Patna. Thirdly, he set up the Committee of Revenue in Calcutta. These measures not only brought about a centralization in administration but aimed at improving the collection and administration of territorial revenue. Revenue was in fact the main aim of the government. Consistent with this aim, the Justices in Session were authorized by the Charter of 1794 to appoint the Collector of Assessment.[37]

Thus it may be said that the Justices of the Peace were important instruments of change. At least a work culture had decidedly set in the metropolitan administration and the historian who regretted that the Justices in course of time were reduced to nullity could not help but appreciate this. "The Justices seem to have set to work at once to improve the town."[38] With this mood of optimism, the eighteenth century of Calcutta rolled on to the nineteenth. But the failure of the municipal administration in the city remained unredeemed throughout the course of the eighteenth century.

Notes

1 Keshab Chaudhuri in his *Calcutta: Story of its Government*, Chapter I, refers to the dates of the Charters as 1726, 1753, and 1793. S.W. Goode in his *Municipal Calcutta: Its Institution in Their Origin and Growth*, Edinburgh, 1916, pp. 8–10 gives the dates as 1727, 1753, and 1794. Goode's accounts appear to be quite reliable and Chaudhuri had depended on Goode to a very large extent. Except these dates, some of the staples of Chaudhuri's facts seem to be derived from Goode. Hence the dates given by Goode have been accepted here.
2 Quoted in Keshab Chaudhury, *Calcutta: Story of Its Government*, Calcutta, 1973, p. 4.
3 "Despite the earnestness of the Government to provide the town with Municipal services conducive to the well-being of the inhabitants, almost nothing could be done because the tax receipts from a wide variety of sources were credited to the general revenues of the state and not to the town fund." – Ibid.
4 See Ranjit Sen, *Calcutta in the Eighteenth Century*, Vol. I, Institute of Historical Studies, Calcutta, 2000, Chapter II.
5 Keshab Chaudhuri, *Calcutta: Story of Its Government*, p. 4.
6 In 1833 Mr. D.M. Farlan, the then Chief Magistrate of Calcutta, proposed a new scheme for the up gradation of the municipal Government of Calcutta. The scheme aimed at setting up a committee consisting of not more than nine members to look into the welfare of the town. Of these members not fewer than five members would be selected annually by the qualified voters in each of the four divisions of the town. This new scheme of town government however, did not succeed. There was a public apprehension that taxation would increase because of the activities of the committee. The public cooperation with the government was therefore absent and this eventually resulted in the failure of the Committee.

7. This adoption of the Mughal nomenclature does not seem unique in this case. In 1769, when the Supervisors were sent into the districts, they were given the Mughal title of *Amin*.
8. Mr. Ralph Sheldon and Holwell were the two most important *Zamindars* of Calcutta. Govindaram Mitra was the most important "Black Zamindar" in the Company's service in the eighteenth century. It is said that Sheldon was the first of the English Zamindars of the town. He was given appointment in 1700.
9. Chaudhuri, *Calcutta: Story of Its Government*, p. 18.
10. "The city was in fact little better than an undrained swamp, surrounded by malarians jungles and pervaded by a pestilential miasma." – Goode, *Municipal Corporation*, p. 9.
11. W.W. Hunter, *Imperial Gazetteer of India*, Vol. IV, p. 285.
12. For details of the E.I. Company's investment policy, see N.K. Sinha, *The Economic History of Bengal from Plassey to the Permanent Settlement*, Vol. I, Ch. II.
13. "The Corporation did little to improve the administration of the town" – Chaudhuri, *Calcutta: Story of Its Government*, p. 19.
14. "The Zemindar virtually turned out to be an autocract for the simple reason that there were no curbs on his power to collect rates and taxes." – Chaudhuri, *Calcutta: Story of Its Government*, p. 23.
15. About 1851, 100 years after the fall of Govindaram Mitra, the following was written about him. "Govindram was the Black Zamindar for 25 years and amassed an immense fortune. He also held large farms from the nawab of Murshidabad. There is still to be seen the remains of the largest Temples in Calcutta called the Navaratna or nine Jewels Temple built by Govindram. It was once crowend with a cupola visible from a distance of many miles." – Quoted by Chaudhuri, *Calcutta: Story of Its Government*, p. 16.
16. Ibid.
17. For further study on the subject of "Black Zamindars," see J.C. Marshman, "Notes on the Left or Calcutta bank of the River Hooghly", in *Calcutta Review, 1845–46*; J. Long's article in the Calcutta Review., 1851; Appendix XIV of the Census of India, 1951, Vol. VI, Part III.
18. The Fifth Report, from the Select Committee of the House of Commons on the Affairs of the East India Company, Vol. I Introduction, p. LXXIII.
19. These allowances were later resumed by the Government of the East India Company, see Ranjit Sen, *Economics of Revenue Maximization 1757–1793*, Ch. II, Nalanda Publication Pvt. Ltd., Calcutta, 1988.
20. Goode, *Municipal Calcutta*, pp. 8–9.
21. Ibid.
22. Ibid.
23. Ibid, p. 10.
24. Ibid.
25. Ibid.
26. Ibid.
27. "The administration of the justices was divided into three departments: (1) the assessment department, (2) the executive department, (3) the judicial department or the Justices in Session. The function of these departments were respectively (1) to assess the rates; (2) to provide for the execution

of the conservancy works, the collection of the assessment, and for the ordinary watch and ward for town; (3) to approve assessments and to hear and decide appeals or complaints against the assessors and the collectors. We are told that the sessions were at first held once a year, but as the volume of business increased, quarter sessions became necessary. The Justices were assisted by a Clerk of the Peace." – a post corresponding to that of a registrar or record keeper – Goode, *Municipal Calcutta*, p. 12.

28 Chaudhuri, *Calcutta: Story of Its Government*, p. 21.
29 Ibid.
30 Goode, *Municipal Calcutta*, p. 10.
31 Chaudhuri, *Calcutta: Story of Its Government*, p. 22.
32 H. Tinker, *The Foundations of Local Self Government of India, Pakistan and Burma*, p. 157.
33 "In 1799 steps were taken to effect a notable improvement – the metalling of Circular Road." – Goode, *Municipal Calcutta*, p. 12.
34 Chaudhuri, *Calcutta: Story of Its Government*, p. 26.
35 Goode, *Municipal Calcutta*, p. 10.
36 "It was however, soon evident that the most efficient conservancy could do nothing but mitigate in a small degree the ills under which the city laboured; in the absence of the wide roads and systematic drainage, conservancy itself was hardly practicable. Original works of a magnitude which placed them outside the resources of the Justices, were an imperative necessity." – Goode, *Municipal Calcutta*, p. 12.
37 In 1830, the post of the Collector of Assessment was attached to the office of the Superintendent of Police. The Justices were thus relieved of their duties of watch and ward. Henceforth they, as Divisional Magistrates, confined their attention to judicial works.
38 Goode, *Municipal Calcutta*, p. 12.

9

MAKING A PILGRIM CENTRE
Kalighat

Kali: a rallying force

Kali, the goddess of prowess and strength, had for many centuries been the rallying point around which the Hindu Bengali mind had taken its shape. Bankim Chandra Chattopadhyaya, the novelist, while writing *Anandamath*, made the transforming image of Kali a great symbol of the changing fate of the motherland. At one place of the novel Mahendra beholds the mother in presence of the *Brahmochari*:

MAHENDRA: Who is she ?
BRAHMOCHARI: She is the Mother.
MAHENDRA: Who is the Mother?
BRAHMOCHARI: She is the one whose children we are An awe-stricken Mahendra said: "*Kali*"
BRAHMACHARI: Kali, smeared with darkness and robbed of all her possessions and hence nude.

Thus the destitution of our motherland – the great *Bharatabhumi* – under the British rule has been compared to the denuded image of *Kali*. Bankim Chandra did not stop here. He built up a triad to describe the image of *Kali* – *Ma Ja Chhilen* (what the Mother was like – the Resplendent), *Ma Ja Haiachhen* (what the Mother has been reduced to – the Destitute), and *Ma Ja Haiben* (what the Mother will be like – the Prosperous).

From this, one will understand what powerful a force the concept of *Kali* is in the Bengali Hindu mind. Over centuries the icon of *Kali* has been worshipped by the Hindus in different forms and in different names.[1] One of these forms was *Dakshina Kali* in which it was worshipped at Kalighat. In some ancient literature relating *Sakta Pithas*, we come across the expressions *Kalighatta*, *Kalipitha*, *Kalikshetra* etc., but there is a great controversy among historians whether all these refer to Kalighat or not.[2] They, however, do certainly mean that the worship of Kali was universal in Bengal and the importance of Kalighat must be looked at from the general panorama of *Kali* worship in Bengal.

Kali-worship in the eighteenth century

In the eighteenth century, Calcutta witnessed *Kali* worship at two places – one at Chitpur and the other at Kalighat. Chitpur, at the beginning of the eighteenth century, was outside Calcutta but eventually at the end of the century it was incorporated as a part of the city and at present it forms a part of central and central-north Calcutta. A part of Chitpur now forms a part of the Burra Bazaar of Calcutta. At Chitpur the temple of *Chitresvari* or *Sarvamangala* was situated. The antiquity of this deity is unknown. The popular belief was that the icon of this *devi* was set up by one robber-chief called *Chite*. A biographer of Calcutta writes: "When they [the gangs of Chite] received the blessing of the devi in the form of consent they used to go out on land and on water for robbery."[3] He adds that the temple of this *devi* was originally by the side of the Ganga but later on the Ganga receded. There were thick forests around this temple and human sacrifices were very common there.[4]

There was another temple which in the middle of the eighteenth century captured much of the attention of the people in and around Calcutta. This was the *Navaratna* or *Nine Jewels Temple*[5] built by Govindaram Mitra, the "Black Zamindar" of Calcutta. This temple was richly ornamented and had a fine architectural structure. But it could never grow as a pilgrim centre. The Hindu Bengali sentiment from time immemorial capitulated to the attractions and spells of the mother goddess and hence this *Navaratna* temple in spite of having the glamour of its wealth and decoration, architecture and design, came to be overshadowed by the temples of *Dakshina Kali* and *Sarvamangala* or *Chittesvari*, respectively situated at Kalighat and Chitpur.

The point to be noted here is that, in the middle of the eighteenth century, there were three important temples in Calcutta vying for supremacy. Out of these the Kalighat temple emerged supreme. Two reasons account for this. The first was the pattern of belief of the Hindus. "Kalighat or Kalikshetra," writes an observer, "is reckoned by the Hindus as one of the holiest places of worship in Hindustan."

> To a Hindu, whatever sect he may belong to, be he a Saiva, a Sakta or a Ganapatya, this place is very dear. From remote times, vows have been made here for the attainment of objects,

and it is on record that in many instances the objects have been realized. Yogis and Sannyasis and saintly Hindus congregate at the place, and after quietly performing their worship of the great goddess go their own way. When the Feudatory Hindu Chiefs of northern parts of India happen to be in Calcutta they regard it as obligatory on them to offer Puja to Mother Kali before they return to their territories. The holiness of the temple has become to be known far and wide, and veneration for it is so deep-rooted in the minds of the Hindus that it may be compared to that of the temple of Bisweswar at Benares. It is that the East India Company in their early days used to offer Puja to the Deity at Kalighat. On the occasion of their Punnahas [*punyahas*] they participated in the ceremony, which they solemnized.[6]

Pattern of worship and support

Kalighat had a tradition of ritual worship. In this it received a very vast patronage of the richer sections of the community. It is said that Raja Nabakrishna of Shovabazar spent one lakh of Rupes "on the worship of this goddess." "Amongst the offerings were a gold necklace valued at 10,000 rupees, a rich bed, silver plates, dishes and basins; sweetmeat and other food sufficient for the entertainment of a thousand persons; and trifling presents of money to nearly two thousand of the poor."[7] Jaya Narayan Ghosal the Zamindar of Kidderpore (now in western Calcutta) "expended twenty thousand rupees at this place."[8] There are records showing that brahmanas and merchants at different times spent thousands of Rupees for the worship of the idol *Kali*. Thus ten years after Jaya Narayan's donation was made, a merchant from East Bengal spent 5,000 Rupees for the worship of the goddess here. In 1810 a brahman from east Bengal spent 4,000 Rupees, and in the following year another brahman, named Gopee Mohan, spent 10,000 Rupees for the worship of the deity but "Being a Vaishnava he did not offer any bloody sacrifices."[9] Animal slaughter was so rampant here that Jaya Narayan Ghosal "scarified twenty-five buffaloes, one hundred and eight goats, and five sheep, and presented to the goddess four silver arms, two gold eyes and many gold and silver ornaments" and ten years later the merchant from East Bengal paid "the price of a thousand goats which were slaughtered."[10]

This tradition of animal slaughter gave Kalighat the status of a centre where the ritual worship of *Shakti* could be done. *Shakti* worship in Calcutta gained great currency in the seventeenth and eighteenth centuries and continued till the twentieth. In the rich households of Calcutta, the *Shakti* was worshipped in different names – *Kali, Shyama, Jagaddhatri, Tara, Annapurna*, etc. One writer[11] has described how the *Kalipuja* was performed in the house of one Kalishankar Ghose, a very well-to-do man of Calcutta, with ghastly excitement. "The compound of this household," writes the author, "became submerged with blood at the night of Shyamapuja; streams of blood used to flow through the drains."[12] Such events were certainly later phenomena but they represented the culmination of a process which took shape over centuries and in the course of which Kalighat emerged as the central point of *Shakti* worship from where *Shakti* culture got its radiations. Vis-à-vis Kalighat *Chittesvari* temple at Chitpur could not grow there. This made the place somewhat desolate[13] in the early half of the eighteenth century.

Antiquity beyond the eighteenth century

It took Kalighat nearly three centuries to journey to fame. One of the earliest mentions of Kalighat dates back to 1495. That year Bipradas Pipalai wrote his Bengali poem *Manasamangal*. Bipradas' hero Chand Sadagar undertook a journey down the river Bhagirathi from Bhagalpur to the sea.[14] In course of the journey he passed by Chitpur, Calcutta, Kalighat and Betor.

> At Chitpur the king worshipped the goddess Sarvamangala.[15] . . . Rowing by the eastern Bank the great and heroic Chand passed by Calcutta and arrived at Betor. The pious Chand Datta worshipped Betai Chandi at Betor. Kind Chand having worshipped Kalika at Kalighat, passed by Churaghat and Jayadhali.[16]

The antiquity of Kalighat has also been proved by references from Mukundaram Chakravarti's *Chandimangal*, a Bengali text written between 1577 and 1592. In this book Kalighat is mentioned as one of the places visited by its hero, Dhanapati. Dhanapati is said to have worshipped goddess *Kali* at Kalighat. In "a third Bengali poem written by Khemananda a little before, the blessings of all the well-known local gods and goddesses are invoked in a prayer, and the goddess *Kali* at Kalighat is mentioned in the same breath with 'Betai' [as] at Betor."[17]

Three points are to be noted here. Firstly, goddess *Kali* at Kalighat had to compete with her rival goddess *Betai-Chandi* at Betor. In this competition goddess *Betai-Chandi* had an advantage over goddess

Kali at Kalighat. Bipradas in his poem *Manasamangal* observed that "Betor was a place of trade, and it seems to have had a market. It was to Satgaon, what jedda is to Mecca"[18] Thus it may be said that goddess *Betai* enjoyed the backing of merchants which goddess *Kali* at Kalighat did not enjoy before the eighteenth century.

The second point emerges out of this. If the evidences of Bipradas and Mukundaram are to be believed goddess *Kali* at Kalighat did not enjoy the patronage of the writers and bards to a very great extent. Between the sixteenth and eighteenth centuries the name of Kalighat-*Kali* was not a selling name. To those who wrote ballads and lyrics, poems, and verses, Calcutta and Kalighat did not denote the same place and this separation between the two places slowed the growth of the both – of the one as the leading urban centre and of the other as the leading pilgrim centre of the east.

> It will be observed that Calcutta had already come to be known as a place different from Kalighat and that Kalighat itself was a mere riparian village sacred to the goddess Kali, but not important enough to merit more than a word of mention. The goddess was deemed to be just sacred enough for a visit and an offering on the part of the traveller, but not nearly so great as the goddess Sarvamangala at Chitpore or the goddess Betai-Chandi at Betor, who had ancient temples. Nor was her renown such as to throw the poet into ecstasies over her adoration."[19]

From this it is clear that in the sixteenth and seventeenth centuries the worship of *Shakti* in the form of *Chandi* and *Sarvamangala* was more popular in Bengal than in the form of *Kali*, *Syama*, and *Tara* as were available in Kalighat and Tarapith in the eighteenth century. The worship of *Shakti* in the two forms *Kali* or *Shyama* and *Tara* became popular in the eighteenth century. The ascendancy of *Kali* to a dignified worship began since the days of Bipradas. But it took three centuries for this goddess to establish herself to popular worship, although during one century since Bipradas' time she was steadily emerging from her obscurity. This is the third significant point one should keep in mind before assessing the history of *Kali*-worship in Bengal. We quote from A.K. Roy's observation on this point.

> The goddess [*Kali*] had evidently acquired dignity since the days of Bipradas [the end of the fifteenth century]. In nearly a century's time she had reached the level of these

other goddesses [i.e. *Sarvamangala* or *Chittesvari* and *Betai-Chandi*]. As yet [till the time of Mukundaram, i.e. the end of the sixteenth century], however, she had not attained that fame in Tantric rites which evokes the enthusiasm of later votaries. In the works of Bipradas and Khemananda, Kalighat is dismissed with a passing allusion to it and its goddess; in the *Ganga Bhakti Tarangini*, published about the year 1740 A.D., it is described as a wonderful place where the Brahmins chant hymns, while the worship of the goddess accompanied by the "Homa" ceremony [*Havana*], is celebrated with much pomp and sacrifice.[20]

From this, Roy arrived at the unavoidable conclusion that Kalighat rose to complete fame not before the middle of the eighteenth century, although in the earlier centuries its rise was noticed in literature. He writes: "It seems therefore, tolerably certain that, although Kalighat had become known before 1495 A.D. its fame did not spread till 1592 A.D., but was well established before the middle of the eighteen century."[21] The eighteenth century was the period when Calcutta became the seat of a power, trans-oceanic and commercial in nature namely the English East India Company. This was also the century when the rudiments of urbanization of Calcutta began. We shall now, therefore, see to what extent the growth of Kalighat as a pilgrim centre was a determinant factor for the growth of Calcutta as an urban centre and vice versa.

Could Calcutta grow as a religious centre?

Calcutta was not a place of traditional worship as Madurai was. Nor did it undergo the process by which Ramadaspur eventually became Amritsar. Yet Calcutta had the potentiality to grow as a pilgrim centre for, as it has already been said, it was the seat of *Kali*, the goddess of prowess and aggressiveness around which the Hindu Bengali mind had traditionally veered. "The ancient Hindus," writes a biographer of Calcutta, "called it by the name of Kalikshetra. It extended from Bahula to Dakshinasar. According to the puranas a portion of the mangled corpse of Sati or Kali fell somewhere within that boundary whence the place was called Kalikshetra. Calcutta is a corruption of Kalikhsetra."[22] This association with the puranic mythology was enough in itself to give Calcutta a boost towards its growth as a religious centre or as a pilgrim town. Historians say that cities which grow as religious and pilgrim centres have a slow growth, but their growth is stable and lasting. As compared to this, cities which grow as commercial and political centres grow quickly, but their growth is unstable and is likely to be impermanent.[23]

Calcutta had great potentialities to grow as a stable and permanent pilgrim centre, a vast religious town that could have added much to the pilgrim heritage of India. But in the long run it did not. Why it failed to derive its inspiration for urbanization from its being a pilgrim spot will be our subject of study here.

Calcutta's potentiality to grow as a religious centre developed out of three factors. The first factor was the belief of the people that Calcutta had an association with the puranic past of this holy land of ours – *Pavitra Bharatbhumi*. It is one of the fifty-one *pithas* or scared spots which were sanctified by the receipt of the cut-off limbs from *Sati*'s body. It is said Kalighat, a place in the southern part of Calcutta, received the little toe of the right foot of *Sati*. Wilson, one of the earliest biographers of Calcutta, points out that according to *Pithamala* (meaning the garland of holy places) of *Nigama-Kalpa* the actual site where *Sati*'s toe fell was *Kalikshetra* and not Kalighat. According to a version of the *Pithamala* "Kalikshetra extended over two joyanas from Behala in the south to Dakshineswar in the north, forming a sort of triangle, standing on the Ganges and containing the three primeval Gods of the Hindu Trinty – Brahama, Vishnu and Siva – at its three angles, with the goodess Kali at its centre."[24]

Kalighat in Calcutta thus could have grown into a substantially Hindu Tirtha before the rise of Calcutta as an urban centre of the east. That it did not grow into a full-fledged prime point of subcontinental fame before the eighteenth century may be due to the fact that its pull factors were extremely weak. The status of a pilgrim centre depends upon its heritage. Kalighat did not get sufficient time to grow its heritage. A very informative research volume on the *Sakta Pithas* of India makes this point clear. It says: "The sixteenth century author Vamsidasa of Mymensing does not regard Kalighat as a Pitha."[25] In a further passage the same author observes that the name of Kalighat does not occur in a "list prepared in Southwest Bengal possibly a little later than the composition of the Chandimangala. The popularity of Kalighata is probably later than the foundation of Calcutta by Job Charnock in 1690."[26] The coming of the English thus proved beneficial for Kalighat. Whatever little flourish it had acquired over years must be dated to the period when the English were building up their commercial capital in Calcutta. The attraction of Calcutta as a centre for commerce was greater than its attraction as a pilgrim spot. Being situated in Calcutta Kalighat suffered two setbacks. Firstly, it had to compete with another pilgrim centre at Chitpur, not very far from Kalighat, where the temple of *Chittesvari* or *Sarvamangala* was located. Secondly, since Calcutta had no natural endowment like scenic beauty etc. the pull factors of Kalighat did not grow. If we keep Benaras in mind we can understand how natural factors tend to contribute towards building the status of a pilgrim centre. We may quote the following passage to show how nature helps towards building up the antiquity of pilgrim centre.

> Of the antiquity of Benares there can hardly be any question. From its peculiar situation on the banks of a splendid river, with its eastern boundary converted by the current into a magnificent natural amphitheatre, facing the rising sun, it is not unreasonable to conjecture that even before the Aryan tribes established themselves in the Ganges valley, Benares may have been a great centre of primitive sun-worship.[27]

It has been pointed out by an Indian scholar that the structure of pilgrimage must be understood in terms of three analytical tools: the sacred geography, the sacred performance and the sacred specialists.[28] Pilgrim centres like Benares, Hardwar etc. have sacred geography because they were situated by the side of the Ganga: to the Hindus, the Ganga is a holy river. In this sense also the location of Kalighat was holy because it had the water of the Ganga flowing by its side. Sometimes sacred geography becomes only a concept by virtue of a touch with mythology. If a place is mentioned in the *Puranas*, then it is considered sufficiently old to common veneration. If a place has connection with any Puranic episode then it is said to have enough attributes to be holy. Both Kalighat and Tarapith became holy because they are mentioned in the *Puranas* as having received the small toe and the pupil of the eye of *Sati*,[29] respectively. Sacred performances are matters of practice. The worship of *Kali* in Bengal is based on bloodshed which is done by animal slaughters. Previously the worship of *Durga* used to have the highest ritual hallmark in a *balidan* – ritual slaughters of animals, particularly sheep and lamb. From this standpoint Kalighat had a unique record of sacred performances. Ghastly human slaughters, which were practised near the *Sarvamangala* temple of Chitpur, were never in vogue at Kalighat. The pattern of worship there was much more humane and this attracted, since the eighteenth century, a host of merchants and political magnates who gave the place a status of sanctuary. If epic heroes – the heroes of the *Mangalkavyas* – had worshipped *Betai-Chandi* at Betor and *Sarvamangala* at Chitpur, then the eighteen-century political heroes and the opulent magnates, like Maharaja Nabakrishna of Shovabazar and Raja Jayanarayan Ghosal of Kidderpore had worshipped the goddess at Kalighat. In the heritage of sacred performances Kalighat was weighing heavy since the eighteen century. With the rise of Calcutta synchronized the fall of Hooghly. Chitpur being not directly controlled by the English it became one of the badly administered places near Calcutta. To ensure the tranquillity of the place Md. Reza Khan appointed a *faujdar* at Chitpur. But Chitpur did not prosper because of being outside Calcutta. For these reasons, from the eighteenth century onwards, the importance of Kalighat increased and good and effective performances in worship became a regular feature at Kalighat. As time went on, the worship of *Dakshina Kali* of Kalighat became so popular that before any important domestic and social ceremony – like marriage, *upanayana, sraddha*, commencement of business, signing of contracts, digging of ponds, and even celebration of the Bengali New Year – as *punyaha*, people used to go to Kalighat and give their offerings to the goddess. The image of *Durga* and *Kali* in Bengal like the image of *Ganapati* or *Ganesha* in western India and the image of *Hanuman* or *Bajrangvali* in north India became not only symbols of divinities but also symbols of great truths in life – inner strength, dedication, purity, and felicity. They became poetic shorthand for the inspiration and elevation of mankind. The importance of *Kalipuja* encroached in other pujas as well. It is said that during *Gajan*, a ceremony connected with the worship of Lord *Shiva*, "the sannyasis of Calcutta used to go Kalighat very early in the morning and got them pierced with nails."[30] Kalighat was the rendezvous for all sannyasis willing to take part in the *Gajan*. From Kalighat they used to spread out to every locality and every bazaar of Calcutta. They inserted needles and nails in their tongues, ears, palms, and stomachs, made themselves up a *Shiva* and *Durga* and lost themselves in dance and music.[31] These were crude merriments but extremely popular ones. In these merriments took part not only men of caste Hindu families, but also a vast multitude of low caste men like *Hadi*, *Muchi*, *Bagdi* etc. Thus during the time of *Gajan*, Kalighat and, as a matter of fact, every *Kalimandir* and *Shivamandir* in Calcutta and around became rallying points where distinctions of caste and class temporarily vanished.

MAKING A PILGRIM CENTRE

Absence of sacred specialists in Kalighat

From the earlier text, it is clear that Kalighat had enough attributes to score on two major points – sacred geography and sacred performance. But it has been deficient on the third point, namely sacred specialists. Two other *Shakti-pithas* in Bengal – Dakshineswara and Tarapith – were sanctified by the name and presence of two sacred specialists: Sri Sri Ramakrishna Paramahansa Deva and Sri Sri Thakur Bamakhepa. Such extraordinary specialists have never been found to be available in Kalighat. Those who were there failed to build up legends around them. As one of the early mohants of Kalighat said:

> Kamadeva Brahmachari is traditionally known to have worshipped her in Calcutta, where his ground is said to have come subsequently to be known as the "Fakir's ground." This ground was north of Kali's temple and had five sacred trees, from two of which Nimtala and Bat-tala are said to be named.[32]

Prof. Wilson speaks of one Jungle Gir Gossain[33] and credits him with discovery of goddess *Kali* in Calcutta. Some associate Maharaja Pratapaditya's family with the discovery and eventual introduction of the worships of *Kali* in Calcutta. Bhubaneswar Chakrabarti, the first priest of *Kali*'s temple, was known to the family of Maharaja Pratapaditya of Jessore. It is said that at one time he was the priest of Pratapaditya's uncle Basanta Roy.[34] In any case none of these early leaders of *Kali* worship in Calcutta and Kalighat could assume for themselves the status of sacred specialists such as the one assumed in the later days by men like Ramaprasad of Halishahar, the composer of excellent *shyamasangeet*, Bamakhepa, or Ramakrishna Deva. Prior to the coming of these men the *Kali* worship in Bengal was the worship of the Impersonal Absolute – the omnipotent and omniscient *Shakti*. But these men by their own identification with the goddess transformed her into an omnipresent power, a personal Divinity. "To the *Saktas*, no idea can be more sublime than the conception of the personal God as the Divine Mother – the source, support and end of the entire empirical universe."[35] This worship of *Kali* in the form of a personal goddess was brought to its logical finish by Ramaprasad and Ramakrishna Deva. Theirs was a kind of worship where *Kali* was seen not in any of its classical forms – *Chandi*, Chamunda, *Kali*, *Mahakali*, *Bhadrakali*, *Kapali*, *Karali* etc.[36] – but in a different human form where there was a kind of equation between

EARLY FORMATIONS

the worshipper and the goddess that was worshipped. With these men, *Kali* was coming out of the *tantric* mode of worship as a result of which humanity and divinity came much close to each other and was eventually compounded into a unity out of which the worshipper's halo grew. This had made Ramakrishna Deva and Ramprasad appear in public eyes as sacred specialists of *Kali* worship. Such sacred specialists Kalighat never had. Being devoid of the human mobilizer Kalighat had to depend upon other factors for its eventual promotion and growth. This was the eventual incorporation of Kalighat into Calcutta. The journey of Calcutta along the path of urbanization opened the doors for the rise of Kalighat into real prominence. Kali as the goddess of Kalighat did not get much support from literature so much so that, prior to the founding of the city of Calcutta as an urban centre, the people of Bengal did not get charged with the devotion for Kalighat. Until date no season in Bengal has come to be earmarked as the season of the worship of *Dakshina Kali* at Kalighat. Vis-à-vis this some other deities of Bengal – for example *Taraknath* of Tarakeswar and *Tara* of Tarapith – had a well-defined season of worship. "Pilgrims to Tarapith," writes an author, "in the month of Pausa stated that they had chosen this time to make their pilgrimage because worship of Kali in Pausa is especially favoured and the goddess of Tarapith was 'Pausa Kali.'"[37]

That apart the worship of *Kali* did not enter into any order of religious belief. Vis-à-vis *Kali* "Tara is one of the Mahavidyas, the ten most important goddesses of the Tantras. These are the Manifestations of Sakti representing transcendental knowledge (Maha: great, Vidya: wisdom). She is described in the Kalika Purana (Chapter 63, lines 64–9)."[38] Between *Kali* and Tara, *Kali* is a mellowed goddess, Tara is fierce. "Tara is terrible to look one and fierce. Her fierceness is emphasized in her epithet Ugratara."[39] The result of this was that *Kali* eventually entered into the pattern of domestic worship, became a domestic goodess and was eventually identified with *Shyama* the Mellowed Blue. In this capacity she became the mother goddess of the Bengali household and any Hindu opened his mind with an acceptance of her as "Ma" – the Mother. Vis-à-vis *Kali*, Tara was relegated into a pattern of tantric worship with her icon located at a definite *pitha* where annual pilgrimage became a part of her ritual worship. As against this *Kali* was less demanding, a holy domestic deity, her *pitha* being a sanctuary for all she was not particularly emphasized as the one whose ritual annual pilgrimage could be a formalized part of ritual worship. Once a deity becomes accepted in routine household worship her demand as an icon of a *pitha* decreases. On the other hand, she became the sovereign subject of a system of songs called

MAKING A PILGRIM CENTRE

Shyama-Sangeet – "The songs of the Dark One."[40] This helped spreading her glory but not her demands. Her presence became universal.

From this discussion, it is clear that Kali was a universalized deity in Bengal. This universalization destroyed her potentiality to be made up into a core of a pitha-based worship where pilgrimage could be a ritual – at least as much a ritual as a pilgrimage to Tarakeswar and Tarapith was. The result was that the growth of Kalighat as a profound pilgrim centre was overtaken by the process of urbanization of Calcutta. The majestic performances of the English in Calcutta was a part of the conspicuous history of the Empire. In the din and bustle of this conspicuous history, what prospects could Kalighat hold for the potential recreation of life? In the eighteenth century, as Calcutta reared into its new political and socio-economic life, Kalighat became resplendent. *Kali* of Kalighat became the goddess of Calcutta – *Kali Kalkattawali* – the deity presiding over the pristine religious genius of the people. The status of Kalighat rose and *Kali* became the symbolic essence of the new rise which Calcutta had begun to attain.

Notes

1 For details, see D.C. Sircar, *Saktha PIthas*, pp. 39–42. Some of the forms in which Kali was worshipped or is still being worshipped in Bengal are given here. Lot others were there.

Name of the place of worship, i.e. region   Name of the Devi
i   Bahula (Modern Behala in   Bahula south-western Calcutta)
ii   Vakresvara (in Birbhum District)   Vakresvari (The corresponding male deity is Vakresvara Shiva – this is essentially a Shivapith)
iii   Kalighat (in Calcutta)   Kalika or Kali or Dakshina Kali
iv   Yasora (in Jessore, now in Yasoresvari Bangladesh)
v   Nalhati (in Birbhum District)   Sephalika, Tara, Ugratara
vi   Chitpur (in Calcutta)   Chittesvari or Sarvamangala
vii   Tripura (in modern Tripura)   Tripuresvari, Tripurasundari
viii   Kshiragrama (Near Katwa in Yogadya Burdwan District)
ix   Adyapith (near Dakshineswar)   Adyashakti or Adyama
x   Dakshineswar (near Calcutta)   Kali
xi   Balidanga (in Hooghly district)   Chandi
xii   Dhaka (in Bangladesh)   Dhakesvari
xiii   Shrihatta (Sylhet in Bangladesh)   Sadhana
xiv   Tarapith (in Birhbum district)   Tara
xv   Betor (in Hooghli)   Betai-Chandi

2 See Sircar, *Saktha PIthas*; P. Thankappan Nair, *Calcutta in the 17th Century*, Firma Klm Private Limited, Calcutta, 1986, Part I, Ch. 2; Raja Binaya Krishna Deb, *The Early History and Growth of Calcutta*, Rddhi edition, Calcutta, 1977, pp. 21, 63; Prankrishna Datta, *Kalikatar Itibritta*, Chapter under the title "Kalighat," Pustak Bipani, Calcutta.

3 Datta, *Kalikatar Itibritta*, p. 10.
4 Ibid.
5 See Keshab Chaudhuri, *Calcutta : Story of Its Government*, 1973, p. 16.
6 Krishna Deb, *The Early History and Growth of Calcutta*, pp. 63–64.
7 Ibid, p. 65.
8 Ibid.
9 Ibid.
10 Ibid.
11 Datta, *Kalikatar Itibritta*, pp. 135–34.
12 Ibid, p. 134.
13 Ibid, p. 50.
14 A.K. Ray, *Calcutta Town and Suburbs: A Short History of Calcutta*, Census of India, Calcutta, 1901, Vol. VII, Part I, Rddhi-India edition, Calcutta, 1982, pp. 16–17; Nair, *Calcutta in the 17th Century*, pp. 29–20 "Notes on the Banks of the Hooghly", *Journal of the Asiatic Society of Bengal*, 1892, p. 1893.
15 Sarvamangala was the other name of goddess Chittesvari.
16 Thankappan Nair, *Calcutta in the 17th Century*, p. 30.
17 Roy, *Calcutta Town and Suburbs: A Short History of Calcutta*, p. 18.
18 Quoted by Roy, *Calcutta Town and Suburbs: A Short History of Calcutta*, p. 18.
19 Roy, *Calcutta Town and Suburbs: A Short History of Calcutta*, p. 18.
20 Ibid, pp. 18–19.
21 Ibid, p. 19.
22 This statement of Pudma Nav Ghosal was originally published in *The Indian Antiquity*, 1873, p. 370. Also available in W. Newman & Co's *Handbook to Calcutta*, 1875, p. 1. Krishna Deb, *The Early History and Growth of Calcutta*, 1905, Rddhi—India, Calcutta 1977, p. 21, note & also in Thankappan Nair, *Calcutta in the 17th Century*, Firma KLM Private Limited, Calcutta, 1986, p. 28.
23 "Out of different dominant growth factors, which may be identified as mainly religious, economic and political, the first two were more stable and secure. The religious faith of the people and their traditions of pilgrimage remained unchanged for centuries. There could be gradations in the popularity of religious centres – centres of local importance, regional importance, and national importance. But these gradation were, more or less, fixed. Also there was rarely any sharp rise or decline in the fortune of a religious city" – V.D. Divekar, "Political Factor in the Rise and Decline of Cities in Pre-British India – with Special Reference to Pune", in J.S. Grewal and Indu Banga, eds., *Studies in Urban History*, pp. 92–93. To understand why political and commercial cities are unstable, see Ibid, p. 93–94.
24 Nisith Ranjan Roy, *Calcutta: The Profile of a City*, K.P. Bagchi & Company, Calcutta, 1986p. 3.
25 D.C. Sircar, *Sakta Pithas*, Calcutta, 1948, p. 34 note.
26 Ibid, p. 34. Note.
27 E.B. Havell, *Benares: The Sacred City*, 2nd edn, 1905, p. 2.
28 See L.P. Vidyarthi, *Sacred Complex in Hindu Gaya*, Asia publishing House, Bombay, 1961. Since Vidyarthi was one of the pioneer Indian

Scholars to make a systematic study of the places of Hindu pilgrimage it is advisable to read the following along with the one mentioned above:

   i   Vidyarthi, L.P., M. Jha & B.N. Saraswati, *The Sacred Complex of Kasi: A Microcosm of Indian Civilization*, Concept Publishing Company, New Delhi, 1979.
   ii Vidyarthi, L.P. & M. Jha, eds., *Symposium on the Sacred Complex in India*, Council of Social and Cultural Research, Ranchi, 1947.

29 "Only one classical source – the Sivacarita – considers Tarapith as a Mahapitha (great seat) of the goddess, where the eye of Sati fell." – E. Alan Morinis, *Pilgrimage in the Hindu Tradition: A Cast Study of West Bengal*, Oxford University South Asian Studies Series, Oxford University Press, 7984, p. 165. Also see Sircar, *Sakta Pithas*, p. 39.
30 Datta, *Kalikatar Itibritta*, p. 150.
31 For details of Gajan, see Datta, *Kalikatar Itibritta*, pp. 150–151.
32 A.K. Roy, *Calcutta Town and Suburbs: A Short History of Calcutta*, Census of India, Calcutta, 1901, p. 26, note also see C.R. Wilson, *The Early Annals of the English in Bengal Being the Bengal Public Consultations for the First Half of the Eighteenth Century*, Thacker Spink & Co., Calcutta, pp. xlix–lii.
33 Wilson, *Early Annals*, Vol. I, Part 7, p. 130.
34 Roy, *Calcutta Town and Suburbs*, p. 27 note.
35 D.C. Sircar, ed., *The Sakti Cult and Tara*, Calcutta, 1967, p. 16.
36 G. Sastri, "The Cult of Sakti", in D.C. Sircar, ed., *The Sakti Cult and Tara*, p. 15, For details of Shakti worship in ancient India, see Ch. VI of D.C. Sircar's Studies in the Religious Life of Ancient and Medieval India. 1971.
37 Alan Morinis, *Pilgrimage in the Hindu Tradition*, p. 175.
38 Ibid, p. 172.
39 Ibid, p. 171.
40 Ibid, p. 170.

10
CHALLENGES OF AN URBAN GROWTH

Planned insulation of a garrison town

The urbanization of Calcutta began in the first decade of the eighteenth century. As early as October 1707, the proposal was mooted that a hospital should be built so that the health of the soldiers could be adequately taken care of.[1] Along with this there was a proposal to keep the city properly fenced. A ditch was also to be dug.[2] The instruction of the Court ran thus:

> That this Ditch will contain about 2000 yards in the whole length and that the Earth taken out of it would fill up the lower parts of the ground thereabouts that the water should not lie and stagnate there but might be made with a shoot or a little slope so as to carry the rain into the Ditch as our Ground in London Streets from which the water runs into the Kennell with ease.[3]

The intention with which this was done was clear. Calcutta was to be an insulated city and the army that defended the city and the interests of the Company there were to be properly protected. As a matter of fact one of the major aims of the Company in acquiring the revenue rights of the three villages in Calcutta-Govindapur-Sutanuti was that their revenue would help maintaining the army settlement of the Company on the eastern bank of the Ganga. The territorial revenue of the three villages will finance the charges of the Company's garrison there.[4] As soon as the three villages were actually acquired the Company set its aims to two things – first to stimulate its revenue and then to strengthen its fortifications. "We shall now expect to see an Instance of your zeal and skill for our service by the advancement of our revenues there."[5] This was the general instruction which ran from the

CHALLENGES OF AN URBAN GROWTH

Court on 21 November 1699. Concurrent to this there was another instruction: "Besides . . . you may go on now in making any necessary additional strength to our fortification without fear of giving Umbrage to the Moors because they can't pretend to make an inquisition in a place where they have nothing to do withal."[6]

The position was thus clear. Calcutta and its surroundings formed a place where the *Nawabi* administration had "nothing to do withal." Taking advantage of this the Company's administration tried to strengthen their fortification and make the place an insulated one. It was widely believed that the proper administration of these places will help in the growth of population. The Court's confidence in this was unique. It said: "due care kind treatment of the Natives will make those Towns flourish under the mild Government of the English."[7] The Company's administration also knew this. It was clear to the English that the revolt of Sova Singh had shaken the confidence of the people who insured the efficacy of the *Nawabi* rule. The people longed for protection and peace. If the Company's administration provided protection why should it not take levy from the people on this account. With confidence, therefore, the Court instructed the Calcutta Council:

> Protection being the true foundation on which all pretences for raising Customs Subsidies and other Taxes are originally built, for this it is Tenants swear fealty to their Lords, and all subjects owe Allegiance to their Princes, and on this Ground, and to Reimburse us our great charge [of building fortifications] we recommend to you the raising a standing Revenue by the Methods above mentioned, or any other you shall observe more adapted to the Genius and Custom of the inhabitants.[8]

In a further communication the Court's advice seems to be firm: "raise a Standing Revenue."[9]

The logic of urbanization grows out of insulation

This attitude of the Court of Directors gives us an insight into the question as to what led to the urbanization of Calcutta. Calcutta was to be protected and insulated. A proper fortification was to be raised. People were to be given protection and security. They were to pay more tax to finance all arrangements of security. And once security was assured in a condition of general turmoil people will throng in and around Calcutta. This is the idyllic condition in which the urbanization of Calcutta could be thought of. From the beginning the Court of

Directors was after revenue. They wanted to increase the demographic strength of Calcutta because more and more population meant more and more revenue and profuse revenue would, it was believed, help them to cover the cost of their own military establishments in and around Calcutta. The military might of the Company was the mainstay behind all their activities in trade and commerce in this country. Thus trade needed military support. Military establishments involved great expenses. These expenses could be met through revenues derived from people. In the early years of the eighteenth century the Company's administration in Calcutta did not have any settled plan of urbanization. They met eventualities. At the outset there were two things to which the Company's administration responded as primary points for consideration. In the first place, those who settled in Calcutta and paid "Ground Rent to the Right Honorable Company for the compounds they live in" desired "liaces [leases] for ground as customary in other places."[10] The Calcutta Council appreciated the problem and wrote to the authorities at Fort St. George for necessary permissions in this matter. The second thing that called the attention of the administrators in Calcutta was that mud-built houses did not satisfy the necessities which situations had created about this time. For example, when in 1705 the prison in the Burra Bazaar area was destroyed partially by fire, it was ordered that "the same are rebuilt with brick, the charge not to exceed one hundred and fifty rupees."[11] In any case the concept that Calcutta was being built anew had already come into air. Only eight months after the Burra Bazaar fort was ordered to be rebuilt with brick the Court of Directors in London informed their men at Calcutta: "We are told you are about new building Calcutta and making it more regular."[12] Thus the idea "about new building Calcutta" and "making it more regular" had been so current that it reached the ears of the Court and so powerfully influenced them that they quickly sent their instruction to Calcutta: "we recommend to you to order the streets so as that the fort Guns may be brought to bear on the Several Streets to beat out an Enemy."[13] The instruction did not stop here. It added further: "houses may be at such a Distance from the fort as not to prejudice any part of it in case by accident or design they should be set on fire."[14] But Revenue was the terminal point to which all discussions were directed, and immediately after this instruction the Court made their position absolutely clear: "It is a pleasure to us to understand the Revenues increase at Calcutta which is no wonder since you add the people increase there and though the Revenues don't yet we hope they may in time by a prudent management be improv'd to pay the charge of Fort William."[15] Thus the point was made clear that Calcutta was to be rebuilt and this was to be done so that military mobilizations through it became easier. Calcutta was also to be rebuilt so that more and more population would come and settled there, yielding more and more revenue to the coffers of the Company.

A fort-centric growth pattern with private collaboration

While all these were taking place reports were there that "the Towne buildings increased"[16] in Calcutta and the "Revenues especially the Rent of the 3 Towns encrease yearly people flocking there to make the neighbouring zemidars envy them."[17] This report was sent to the Court to stimulate their confidence in their agents in Calcutta. In this report the authorities in Calcutta did not miss ensuring the most sensitive point to their authorities in London. The following expression was cautiously inserted in the report: "the Streets regular that the Guns can bear on those near the fort and the fort secured if the town should be fired." Thus the town was of no importance to the English. The fort was to be preserved at moments of catastrophe and the interest of the town was subservient to that of the fort.

This extraordinary sensitivity to the fort was because in it resided the military and civil personnel of the company. The time had not come when the officers of the Company would begin staying outside the area of the fort and the factory. If the safety of the fort was important to the authorities in Calcutta then they were equally keen to maintain the safety of the factory as well. In 1706 orders were issued to pull down the old factory and rebuild a new one in that place. The "Carpenters and Bricklayers with several other" were set in the work.[18] Apart from the factory, the church building was newly built and in 1707, as soon as the news came that the Emperor was dead,[19] the Company thought it proper to build new bastion to the fort.[20]

These civil activities could be properly undertaken if there was a fund of revenue assured. The Company's authorities had always an eye to this. In July 1705, orders were issued to measure the "Three Towns and Buzar" and "inspect into the revenues of these."[21] From the beginning efforts were made to establish landholding rights on clear legal basis.[22] Measures were also taken to check screening of lands by those who were associated with land management.[23] Those who had thus screened lands and withheld revenue from payment were to be expelled from the Company's service on the charge that they had defrauded the Company of its revenue.[24] The Company's authority knew that it was not possible for them to understand the intricacies of the Mughal revenue system. Hence as early as 1703 "Bannarse Seat" [Banarasi Seth] was appointed in place of "Muda Metter" [Madan Mitra] to look into the revenues of the town. This was because it was found that 131 houses and 288 *bighas* of land were not assessed to revenue.[25] Four years later the Company realized the importance of the collaboration which the Seths offered to the English. Therefore it was decided that Janardan Seth, Gopal Seth, Jadu Seth, Baranasi [Banarasi] Seth and Jaykrishna Seth would "keep in repair the highway between the fort and land mark to the Norward on the back side of the Town."[26] For this they were allowed a rebate in their garden rent to the tune of eight *annas* in a *bigha*. Behind this rebate the considerations were primarily low: "they being possessed of this Ground which they made into Guardens [Gardens] before all had possessions of the Town and being the Company's Merchants and Inhabitants of the place."[27] Thus the entire area between the fort and Chitpur was brought under the care of the Seths. This was perhaps the first major instance to maintain and upgrade the town with private enterprise and investment.

In 1709 plans were made for additional constructions. In its letter to the Court, 18 February 1709, the Calcutta Council informed the Directors in London that two new bastions to the fort had already been constructed and "a what next the River" (meaning what next was required between the river and the fort) was to be built.[28] Side by side with this, "a small Tank to the Eastward" of the fort was to be enlarged and deepened to keep the water good and constantly in it."[29] Instructions came from the Court to improve Calcutta-Sutanuti area because that was the most inhabited place at that time. The Court wrote:

> Our reason for mentioning only Chuttanutte was because we understand the principall Native Merchants as well as our own people lived there and all were unwilling to put you on too much work at one time but when that is once done well . . . you shall have our directions about Govinpore and Soota Loota.[30]

Commenting on this Wilson says that the Court actually wanted to promote the growth of Calcutta and "Chuttanutte" in the letter, "is a mistake for Calcutta."[31] Wilson adds that the Court in their letter of 7 April 1708 "spoke of making a wall and ditch round Calcutta town."[32] Apparently from the last part of the observations of the Court it is clear that they wanted to promote the development of

"Soota Loota" and "Goinipore" after they had promoted the growth of Calcutta. In any case Calcutta, Sutanuti, and Govindapur were not far from each other. The growth of the one was bound to improve the condition of the other. What is important was that the Court was definitely contemplating urbanization of these places for they wrote: "Whatever building you make of Brick it be done of Pucker [Pakur tree or wood?] work which though chargeable is cheapest on account of its duration."[33]

Introduction of bricks in civil construction and supersession of timber

In any case the nucleus of all developments in Calcutta at this time was the fort area. On 17 August 1710, the administration at the Fort William decided that the ground in front of the fort was to be cleared because it was "very much choked up and close sett [set] with Trees and small country thatched houses and standing pools of stinking water."[34] These were to be cleared, the water was to be drained out and the holes were to be levelled. This world, it was hoped, "contribute very much to the making of the Town wholesome and healthful."[35] In doing this, the following question arose: how would the water be drained out of the area if the pool was to be filled up? The answer was simple – by "cutting small Trenches on each side to carry the water clear from the adjacent places into the large Drain."[36] In 1714 when the river broke its banks near the Perrin's Garden threatening "the loss of great part of the Town,"[37] it was ordered that "a Drain be made of Brick."[38] Thus there was a tendency to use brick in every construction as far as possible. The reason became apparent when the ditch that was proposed to be dug around the town became a subject of discussion because of the high cost involved in it. A letter from Calcutta to the Court said this: "The Soil of Bengal being two or three foot clay then sand and clay and sand can't make a Ditch to last unless faced with brick and cemented with good Mortar for turfing or planting tree will not do and it would cost 2000,000 rupees."[39] There was another reason why bricks were increasingly used in the construction of buildings about this time. Rats had increased in the town and in the British records we find frequent mention that rats were making holes in the mud or clay walls.[40] On account of the damage caused by rats, a long row of buildings in the fort near the river was to be pulled down and rebuilt.[41] Yet there was another reason why brick was preferred in the constructions in Calcutta. It was seen that fire did not affect brick buildings. A letter from the Court said: "we find a terrible Account in your Copy Book of Letters received where in Mr. Ange's Letter from Cassimbuzar dated 19th March he writes that the Fire at Muzodavad had consumed all the houses within three Miles round except Brick work."[42] Hence came the instruction to their agents in Calcutta "Be sure don't use any of the Oalie Timber which by your account is subject to rot take care to get the most durable."[43] The instruction was more clear than this "suffer no Buildings within the Fort what are of Brick and well secured from Fire for fear of Accidents."[44]

The area around the fort was to be made clear of thatched huts. Fire was certainly the primary fear, but this had given Calcutta a tremendous push towards urbanization. In 1717, the order was given to the zamindar of Calcutta to demolish all the thatched huts "on the Rivers edge" "before the rains set in."[45] While doing all this, the company was cautious to see that the eyes of the *Nawab* did not fall on Calcutta.

For this reason they tried to remove the influence of the *Nawab* and the *Faujdar* of Hughli as far as possible. About this time there was an "Octogon" built on a plot of land near Sutanuti. The "Octogon" was strategically placed so that "it overlooks the river up and down a great way." For this reason "the collector of Hughly Customs has several times attempted to get it into his hands in order to fix a Chaukey there." Thinking that this would cause great inconvenience to the Company's "Affaires both Publick and Private at this place" the company decided to buy it at a price of "four hundred Madras Rupees."[46] The Company's administration wanted to build up Calcutta as an insulated zone where the influence of outsiders would be marginal. This was one of the primary conditions necessary, they thought, for the eventual growth of Calcutta. In any case they had to handle all their transactions with the *Nawabi* government very cautiously because they needed revenue for which more and more land and population were required. No land could be acquired without the sanction of the government. In 1718, they were trying to "obtain the possession of the 38 towns" because it was hoped that "these would in a few years raise Revenues sufficient to bear all the charges and the necessary encrease of Military to defend them against the Moors."[47]

Revenue was required and the company's administration wanted to save revenue by reducing expenses. They thus steadily went for slightly less expensive materials for building houses than those which were used earlier. They were particularly sensitive about the kind of wood that was being used in different constructions in the town. "Oaley [Oily] timbers rot so soon and are subject to breed white Ants"[48] and hence their positive instruction was not to use them. Their instruction was clear about this: "we hope you will use no more of them."[49]

They advised the use of Teak and in the event of this not being found "Salty and Corea" which are "both durable and will bear all weathers" and are said "to be had at Ballasore."[50] This certainly increased the expenses of the company. There were thick wood around Calcutta but here cutting and felling of trees were not to the liking of the Company's administration. The so-called oily timber was perhaps more expensive than the new ones prescribed by the Court either at its original cost or for the treatment that it required in order to last. The Court positively said "Oaley Timber . . . creates much more charge than the buying of New."[51] From a report sent from Bengal to the Court it is learnt that the oily timber got rotten by nineteen years where as "saltee timbers" "may last for 60 or 70 years."[52]

Road construction – not yet a phenomenon

It is vital to note that in course of the first two decades of the eighteenth century there was seldom any reference in English records to roads being built in Calcutta. In a record of 1721 we came across an account of a proposal to build a road from the English factory near the fort to Govindapur. On this account subscriptions were raised from the merchants or the place.[53] The Company's government in Calcutta always depended on whatever resources it could pull by levying extra taxes on the merchants. It was either because the merchants were the only resourceful persons available in Calcutta or the Company's administration thought it improper and unethical to tax ordinary people who were not very used to taxations for public works. Moreover about this time the government was trying hard to make Calcutta habitable so that population might increase. After all, population was the potential source of revenue. Therefore the government at this stage did not want much to tax all the people who had newly built up the inhabitations in the three villages of Calcutta, Sutanuti, and Govindapur.

This explicit purpose for making the new road from the factory at the fort to Govindapur has been detailed out in a record of 1720. "The reason for making the new roads was to drain Govindapur to bring Inhabitants thither this in time will increase the Revenues."[54] The ultimate purpose was to increase revenue. Govindapur was a low land and slightly marshy with tendencies for water-logging. Unless the water was drained out from there it was not possible to make it habitable. On the low-lying areas of Govindapur, these new roads were strategic: "by these roads [one] can see into the Neighbouring *Zamindars* Country who attack'd them two years since and March better to support the out guards if insulted by him."[55] Right from the beginning of their possessions of the three villages of Calcutta, Govindapur, and Sutanuti the English East India Company were in conflict with the neighbouring *zamindars*. Therefore the English had to take guards against all possible attacks from their neighbouring *zamindars*. Even a cursory look into the first 150 pages or so of Wilson's *Old Fort William in Bengal*, Vol. I, will reveal records that show how much for strategic reasons the Company's administration in Calcutta went in for the urbanization of the city. The company's administration had a good artillery and this gave it the military superiority over the country powers. They knew that their guns gave them a sanguine capacity to fight with the hostile *Nawabi* administration around. Whatever roads they made, whatever building they had constructed were done with the ulterior purpose of making mobilization possible. One very important reason for discarding the so-called oily wood and switching over to new ones was that the new wood either teak or anything else, could support their heavy guns. Demolition of mud and thatched houses was prompted by the desire to get rid of fire. Mud huts were vulnerable, and the enemies could set fire on them at any time. In any case the desire was there to keep the three villages insulated from enemy attack. For this, army mobilization was to be made effective and hence these roads and buildings became necessary.

The third reason why new roads were built towards Govindapur was to make the place healthy. As a result of the construction of new roads, "the place is now made healthier by the wind's free passage to the town."[56] The marshy lands were drained out, unnecessary jungles were cleared, mud huts were demolished, and the new look of Calcutta and Govindapur became very apparent. In another letter dated 31 January 1721, the effect of the construction of the new road has been discussed: "For last 4 months the Revenues have been encreasing again since finishing the new Road and draining the Grounds the Inhabitants encreasing,[57] so that waste ground is now inhabited. In the same report a hint was there at draining Govindapur further because that would "make Calcutta healthier" and "will bring inhabitants."[58]

The land which was actually drained was situated between Calcutta and Govindapur. It was a "low ground."[59] It was made habitable by thoroughly draining the place and also "by making a high road across it."[60] The government could now write confidently to the court: "ground now tenantable the people begin to build and enclose about it."[61] Those who settled in this ground were allowed to be there four months rent-free so that "they raise the Ground fit to live on."[62] The demographic policy of the Government in Calcutta was shaped by its need for revenue. In 1721–1722 the ground rent suffered from Rs. 13,476.49 in 1721 to Rs. 13,020.411 in 1722. This "was occasion'd by the Cowries falling from 5 to 6 Pan in a Rupee, customary to take them of the tenants at 40 pan, for a sicca Rupee, Ground rent for Tennants settled in 1722 will come in next years account being collected in October."[63]

The Govindapur area seemed to be of great concern to the government. In 1724 the water of the Ganga inundated a part of the market place in Govindapur. Immediately there was instruction to repair the *gunj*.[64] In 1725 the roads near Perrin's Garden were damaged and these were also ordered to be repaired.[65] These repair works were charged as the expenses of the government. To this the court reacted very sharply. On 17 February 1727, the court wrote to their agents in Bengal:

> we shall not at this time object to the repairing of the Bridges and Roads, but at fort St. George the Inhabitants are at the charge of Building and Repairing theirs. And we hope you will take care in future to engage the Inhabitants to contribute there to, for though all was done at our charge in the Infancy of the settlement, there is not the same reason it should always be so.[66]

Immediately on receiving this instruction the company's administration in Calcutta tried to translate this into practice, and, on 28 January 1728, they informed the Court that henceforth "The Inhabitants contribute to the mending the Roads and repairing the Bridge."[67] In 1730 the Council at Fort William reported to the Court of Directors in London that "The Repairing the Roads, Bridges and Drains, amounting to Rupees Seven thousand nine hundred and ninety nine fifteen Annas, Order'd that the Inhabitants of Calcutta pay the sum of Five thousand Rupees and the Honorable Company the remainder."[68]

The principle was thus steadily coming into shape that the inhabitants must share a part of the expenditure which was being incurred to keep the roads and bridges in their right conditions. Among the inhabitants the merchants were under the highest fiscal pressure. Very often it was found in records that merchants were placed under certain fiscal levies in order that they shared a part of the government's burden in respect of repairing and upgrading roads or undertaking any other public works. As a matter of fact, between 1700 and 1740, bricks were increasingly being used in public constructions. Godowns, storehouses, warehouses, *Kachhari* buildings, hospitals, jails, offices of the guards, *chowkies*, banks, and many other such buildings which were in the past made of mud, bamboo, straw etc. were demolished because they were worn-out, and in their place new brick constructions came up. Bamboo and straw constructions had to be repaired every year and this involved a recurring expenditure. To avoid this brick construction was also insisted upon. For example, in 1733, the old *Kachhari* building "built of all Bamboo and straw and being fallen down and having cost a great deal of money to repair every year" it was ordered that "a substantial one be built of Brick for the Jamindars Business (i.e. what Wilson says 'the Calcutta Collectorate') and that no New one be hereafter built."[69] Brick constructions were resorted to because of security reasons. In 1733 there were certain murders and robberies committed in the town. People were scared and fled out of the fear that the outgates of the town were damaged and the robberies might take place any day.[70] Immediately the authorities ordered the gate to be repaired. In May, the government ordered that the *Kachhari* house of the zamindar should be built and in December the report came that the building was complete and for this an expense of Rupees 1,836.13 was incurred.[71] The same report said that the factory house was repaired with teak timber and it had become so sound that even the President of the Council may live in it. These public works certainly involved heavy expenses. Attempts were made on every occasion to squeeze some money out of the Indian inhabitants so that the government was relieved of some part of these expenses. One occasion when some roads and bridges were repaired, levies were imposed on the "Black Merchants." But they resented it because they "reckon'd it Oppression if anything had been levied on them so soon after their Assessment to the Town Hall and Gaol [Jail]."[72] As a result of this the entire expense had to be borne by the government. In their letter dated 29 January 1739, the Court of Directors took exception to this and left a clear mandate for their agents in Bengal: "we expect that for the future you find out some Method to ease us of that and all other Burthens, which ought to be bore by these who reside under our protection."[73]

Tensions over public works

Thus expenses for public works had always been a point of tension for the company's government in Calcutta. On the one hand the Court of Directors were reluctant to spend their revenues which had been so strenuously raised. On the other the native inhabitants of the town, particularly the merchants were reluctant to pay any subscription or levy for they thought that they were overtaxed. There was no compromise between those two viewpoints. But the government had to make expenses because necessity demanded that. For example, in 1735, it was "necessary for one of the Doctors to reside at the Hospital for the Attendance of the sick." In response to this it was agreed to "build a couple of upper rooms and a shop for the Medicines at one of the ends of the Hospital."[74] Sometimes government revenues were expended to meet eventualities, but often it was found that the purpose was not served. For example the "outgate" of the town which was repaired to prevent robberies did not serve its purpose and a report of 1735 says that it was still "full of Robbers."[75]

One reason why robbers could not be suppressed was that there were no good roads through which quick mobilization could be easily made. Every year roads came to be damaged heavily because of rains and the Company's administration had little money to undertake the jobs of repair. Sometimes commodities could not be brought into the city owing to the roads being damaged, and this led to a serious crisis in the supply of food staff. The government revenue suffered because of this. A record from 1736 substantiates this point:

> Mr George Mandeville Jemindar representing to the Board that the unusual heavy Rains that fell last Month and the beginning of this Month has so Damag'd the ways and blown up several of the Bridges in the avenues to the town, particularly in the Roads at the Northerly End of Town, that the country people all prevented bringing Provisions, Grain and Merchundize usually brought to the Bazars and Marketts of this town, and thereby are Obliged to carry their Goods to the Adjacent Towns out of the Honourable company Bounds by which the Revenues are daily decreasing. Therefore we think it for our Honourable Masters Interest that the Roads have a thorough Repair and the Bridges mended.[76]

As the revenue of the government suffered it was instantly ordered that "the zamindar do immediately set about it."[77] Next year, when a great storm took a heavy toll on the population of Calcutta, the same situation arose. People were about to desert the town and there was the apprehension that the government might lose revenue. The government decided to give them exemptions from payment of rents so that the people felt an incentive to stay back in the city. The company's administration on Calcutta wrote to the court on 31 December 1737: "Inhabitants in as low and wretched condition by the violent storm so that we remitted them part of the Arrears to prevent their Deserting the Towns."[78] The people got remissions in their payment of revenues of August, September, and October. The storm caused great devastations to the town. It is said that the storem "Levelled most of the walls in the town, shattered and threw down many of the Buildings and blew up the Bridges, the Tide some days after broke in upon and carried away some of the wharfs slips and stairs ... church steeple was overthrown."[79] Sutanuti was greatly damaged. "A sad effect of the Hurricane was a Famine that raged all-round the country best part of the year."[80] The government "[was] obliged to forbid the exportation of rice on the 5th June which affected Private Trade, more particularly Mr. Elliot who had two ships laden with rice."[81] To remedy this situation the government "Took off the Duty on all rice brought into the Town the 12th June, Hooghly Government (the *Nawabi* government) had done the same."[82] At this time of distress revenue from the town decreased "but when the famine was over revenues arose as usual."[83]

Out of the fear that revenue would fall the Company's administration decided to repair "several Bazars and Market places" in the city.[84] As a matter of fact after the great storm of 1737 some construction works were undertaken. By December 1739 it was reported that "Part of the Buildings shattered by storm are repaired."[85] Yet the need was great and the Calcutta authorities, it was urged, "must build some New ones."[86] After the storm it was felt that there should be a granary for rice to be kept for extraordinary situation. A vast granary for 20,000 maund of rice was laid on 26 March 1739. But later it was found to be of no use. Hence the granary and the stock were sold out.[87] All these constructional activities involved a lot of expenditure. The authorities in Calcutta was under the fear that the Court of Directors would not sanction this expense. On 21 March 1740, the Court wrote to their agents in Calcutta: "we shall grudge no Expense so necessary, provided that you lay out our Money in a frugal manner, and see that we are not abused either in the price or quality of the Materials, and the day Labourers do not loiter away their time."[88] But the Court was tremendously angry that civil constructions did not keep the time schedule properly. The "Repairs being Delayed for above a year till the 18th January 1738–39." The court suspected that there "was wrong management." They complained that "everything grows worse and worse where Repairs are postponed." To their agents in Calcutta their insistence was clear: "Your Assurance that we many depend the work shall be done in a frugal and secure manner must be complied with and made good."[89]

The general cause why the Court became angry with their agents in Calcutta was that, for some time, past revenue raised from the city was not upon the expectation of the authorities. At the beginning of

1741 the Calcutta Council admitted that "Revenues are a small matter more than last year." And the cause behind it was laid down in equally simple terms: "Ground Rents are difficult to collect – Tenants poor."[90] On the top of this reports were frequently sent to the Court that fire had consumed the assets of the Company. In December 1739, the report was sent to the Court that "A Fire entirely consumed Patna factory in March, 1738 with Broad Cloth Godowns."[91] In January 1791, another news was sent to London that the "soldiers Barracks at Cossimbuzar were damaged by a Fire."[92] The authorities in London developed the impression that their agents in eastern India were not looking after their business well. This impression had persisted right from the beginning and over years it gained momentum. What the Company's authorities in London dreaded most was the loss of revenues. Revenue could not be increased if property was damaged and habitation was unsettled through frequent fire and other dreadful events like banditry, which in their turn had led to a general deterioration of the security of the place. In any case the management of the town in the first half of the eighteenth century did not give any impression to any one concerned with administration that there was any conscious effort on the part of the government to build up the three villages into any form of organized township.

A mirror from the south

In the previous section we have analyzed at random some basic data that show what factors shaped or slowed the coming into shape of the process of urbanization. Calcutta's image as an English town vis-à-vis the *Nawabi* towns of Dacca, Murshidabad, and Hooghly appeared to be the only fixed point paving the way for its urban form. Other factors – an undefined boundary, fluctuating population, and a dynamic revenue – were all variable factors. The four fixed factors were available in south Indian urbanism – namely, geography, inhabitants, pattern of trade, and patterns of pilgrimage – could counteract one variable factor there – namely, unstable political boundaries.[93] Hence the process of urbanization did not suffer much set back there. Truly speaking, in south India variable factors did not ever gain any upper hand in the process of urbanization. Fixed factors had always remained sound at the backdrop. "The economic nodal points did not change"[94] and hence till the eighteenth century the economic content of urbanization remained very sound. "In the nineteenth century, there was to be a significant modification in this – the geography, the inhabitants and the pilgrim pattern remained fixed points, so also the political control. The content and pattern of trade became a variable factor."[95] Once again the fixed factors coagulated into a system which could contain the variable factor within its bounds. In Calcutta in the eighteenth century the situation was the reverse. The English control of Calcutta stimulating its image as an English town highlighted the only stable political factor in the process of urbanization. All other factors remained variable. Its boundary was not settled till the end of the eighteenth century. Its population had a chance of increase only during the time of the Maratha invasions, but such temporary demographic gains were quickly offset by repeated famines that visited the city every decade from the middle of the eighteenth century, by rise in the incidence of banditry because of which people fled the city, and also by bad hygiene and job scarcity that did not allow the morphology of the town to grow. The weakness of the government had always been at its purse. The revenue yield was never commensurate to the level at which the authorities at London had fixed their expectation. Moreover in the eighteenth century Calcutta remained to be a garrison town and the interests of the garrison remained as the uppermost factor dictating routes for the passage of goods and armies. Sustenance of the military manpower at the cost of the general population at times of famines and general scarcity was one factor from which the demographic stability of the city had always suffered. If Calcutta was a bandit-ridden and fire-afflicted city, it was equally a city of rice-scarcity and labour shortage. These were certainly not conducive for a congenial habitation. People who very often came to the city from outside were attracted mainly by the pattern of service available at the colony and that being highly temporary they had very little chance of getting permanently domiciled here. The service of the colony in the context of Calcutta in the eighteenth century meant, at a lower level, jobs of ill-paid labour in civil and military constructions or employment in the cramped entourage of domestic retinues of luxury-addict Europeans. At a slightly higher level it meant the function where *banians, munshis, dalals, do-bhasis, gomastas*, and the like competed with each other for meagre favour that might trickle down from the closed fists of their European bosses. The English from the beginning wanted to build Calcutta in a way that would bridge the distance in space and time to an English home.[96] But the influx of lower men did not allow their dream to come true. The English records in Calcutta throughout the eighteenth century are replete with evidences wailing on the fact that Calcutta was increasingly becoming a den of destitute and vagabonds, men of dignity being kept away from it.

Haphazard morphology

With plenty of bazaars spreading haphazardly here and there in an utter hotchpotch of construction, Calcutta's chance of getting a European tone was becoming steadily blurred. The early attempt to transfer the native population of Khiderpur to Shovabazar in the north was designed to keep the racial cut-out of the city clear. The intention behind this was that the racial segregation of the European part of the town in the south would maintain its characteristic distinction if the natives were pushed to the north. But hitherto the calculation misfired because a palpably growing native suburb in Kalighat and Bhowanipur had destroyed the ease of a quiet neighbourhood of the English town in the south. As a matter of fact, Calcutta in the eighteenth century gave the English a frustrating experience of town-building. The racial segregation of the natives was not possible because of the lurking of Kalighat and Bhowanipur in the immediate neighbourhood. The maintenance of the cultural identity of the tough island race of the English by keeping them insulated in the south was equally impossible because a cosmopolitan town with a mixed population existed as a buffer between the natives of the north and the whites of the south. From the beginning the English in Calcutta tried to build up a culturally modified environment for themselves with which the English behaviour could interact. But the influx of unsubstantial men, European vagabonds and native destitute, did not provide the congenial atmosphere in which ethos could grow. The paradox lay here. The English administrators had before them their vision London, their idyll. That idyll was to be sustained by the cooperation of the large labouring Indian population, and this was the most unwelcome a factor to them. They wanted the city to thrive with substantial men, but in its stead a large unsubstantial crowd formed the bulk of the population mix of the city. This was that seemed to be most frustrating to them. This was one reason why the Englishmen in Calcutta in the eighteenth century came to throng more and more around Chowringhee in the south. They certainly sought a distance from the Indian population in the north, but, in course of time, they became painfully aware that they could not further expand to the south where Bhowanipur and Kalighat had created a native barrier. The result was that they lived in an encapsulated colonial world of an exile. This feeling of living in exile in Calcutta had stifled their incentive for town-building. Calcutta grew with the misery of a checkmated soul.

EARLY FORMATIONS

Notes

1. The following is an extract from Bengal Public Consultations, Fort William, 16 October 1706, Range I, Vol. I. "Having abundance of our Soldiers and Seamen Yearly Sick and this year more particularly our Soldiers, and the Doctors representing to us, that for want of an Hospital or Convenient Lodging for them is mostly the occasion of their Sickness, and Such a place will be highly necessary as well for the Garrison and Sloop as the Company's Charterparty Shipping to keep the men in health.
    This therefore AGREED that a Convenient spot of ground near the ffort be pichted upon to build an Hospitall on, and that the Cashiers pay out of the Companys Cash for the said occasion." – quoted from C.R. Wilson, *Old Fort William in Bengal*, John Murray, London, 1906, Vol. I, p. 68.
2. The proposal was "that a Strong wall should be build [built] at the end of de [dihi] Calcutta town between that and Chuttanuttee with one Gate to go in and out at which may have a redoubt or Small ffortification near it to beat off any Enemy ... and at the End of that wall to the Land Side there should be cut a Ditch of 16 or 18 broad and 12 foot or more deep which should run from thence round Calcutta town" and should eventually "fall into the River." – General Letters from the Court to Bengal, London, 7 April 1708, paragraph 37, Letter Book No. 13; quoted in Wilson, *Old Fort William in Bengal*, p. 69.
3. Ibid, paragraph 38, Wilson, *Old Fort William in Bengal*, p. 70.
4. "We have gained the Princes Neshan for a firme Settlement in this place with the rent of three towns which will be revenue sufficient to bare the Charge of the Garrison & ca." –General Letter from Bengal to the Court, Chuttanutte, 22 February 1699, Original Consultation (O.C.) No. 6,617, Wilson, *Old Fort William in Bengal*, p. 42.
    In the General Letter from the Court to Bengal, London, 21 November 1699, para 5, Letter Book No. 10 [Wilson, *Old Fort William in Bengal*, p. 44] it is stated that the grant of the three villages was made against an annual rent of 1,200 hundred rupees. Wilson in the further note observes: "In the parawana of the diwan, Izzat Khan dated Shaban 2, in the forty-second year (British Museum Additiona MSS, 24,039, No. 39), the annual rent is given as Rs. 1,194,14,11. In the Bengal public consultations, May 4,1714, the annual rent is stated to be Rs. 1,281.6.9 The increase is in the rent of Govindpur in Paiqan" (p. 44 note).
5. General Letter from the Court dated 21 November, 1699, Wilson, *Old Fort William in Bengal*, p. 44.
6. Ibid.
7. Ibid.
8. Instructions from the Court to Charlles Eyre, London, Dec. 20, 1699. Letter Book No. 10. C.R. Wilson, *Old Fort William in Bengal*, p. 47.
9. Ibid.
10. Calcutta Consultations 3 May 1703. Factory Records, Calcutta No. 4. Wilson, *Old Fort William in Bengal*, p. 55.
11. Bengal Public Consultations, Fort William 4 May 1705. Wilson, *Old Fort William in Bengal*, p. 60.
12. General Letter from the Court to Bengal, London, 18 January 1706, paragraph 48, Letter Book No. 12, Wilson, *Old Fort William in Bengal*, p. 61.

13. Ibid.
14. Ibid.
15. Ibid.
16. General Letter from Bengal to the Court, Fort William, 31 December 1706, Wilson, *Old Fort William in Bengal*, p. 63.
17. Bengal Public Consultations, Fort William 18 April 1706, Range I, Vol. I, Wilson, *Old Fort William in Bengal*, p. 62.
18. Both bricklayers and carpenters were not easily available in Calcutta at that time. Some of them had to be brought from England.
19. Wilson, *Old Fort William in Bengal*, p. 63.
20. Ibid, p. 64.
21. Bengal Public Consultations, 12 June 1707, Wilson, *Old Fort William in Bengal*, p. 65.
22. "We therefore do think it equitable according to the custom of the Country and agreed that the Inhabited, tilled or mannured land or such ground as any one possesses do annually pay the following Rents. . . . and that the rent gatherer or Jemidar do give each Inhabitant a Putta or Ticket with a No. affixed to it, for the certain sum he shall annually pay and what received in monthly to be endorsed on said Tickett and the Ticket to be renewed once every year for which Putta, or Ticket the Tenants are to pay the Company as formerly." Bengal Public Consultation, 12 June 1707. Wilson, *Old Fort William in Bengal*, p. 65.
23. "The Putwarrys or black rent gatherers & ca. are found to have taken Clandestinely considerable quantities of land and formed it out notwithstanding they received monthly wages from the Company agreed therefore that all such land be taken from them or any other black officer and farmed out for the Company and that the Putwarrys be accounted with for the time they have possessed it." – Ibid.
24. Wilson, *Old Fort William in Bengal*, pp. 65–66.
25. Calcutta Consultations, 10 June 1703, Factory Records, Calcutta, No. 4, Wilson, *Old Fort William in Bengal*, p. 55.
26. Bengal Public Consultations, 11 September, 1707, Range I, Vol. I, Wilson, *Old Fort William in Bengal*, p. 67.
27. Ibid.
28. General Letter from Bengal to the Court, 19 December 1709, Wilson, *Old Fort William in Bengal*, p. 77.
29. Bengal Public Consultation, Feb. 28, 170, Range I, Vol. I, Wilson, *Old Fort William in Bengal*, p. 77.
30. Letter from the Court, paragraph 65, 9 January 1701, Letter Book No. 13, Wilson, *Old Fort William in Bengal*, p. 79, note.
31. Wilson, *Old Fort William in Bengal*, p. 79, note.
32. Ibid.
33. Vide 29, paragraph 68.
34. Bengal Public Consultation, 17 August 1701. Range I, Vol. II. Wilson, *Old Fort William in Bengal*, p. 82.
35. Ibid.
36. Ibid, p. 83.
37. Bengal Public Consultations, 12 October 1714, Range I, Vol. II, Wilson, *Old Fort William in Bengal*, p. 94.
38. Ibid.

EARLY FORMATIONS

39 Letter from Fort William to the Court 11 December 1714, Wilson, *Old Fort William in Bengal*, p. 95.
40 A letter from Fort William to the Court, 11 December 1714 speaks of the "Walls [of a long range of lodgings near the river] being ready to fall by Rats eating in and the timbers being rotten." Wilson, *Old Fort William in Bengal*, p. 95.
41 Bengal Public Consultations, 7 March 1715, Range I, Vol. II, Wilson, *Old Fort William in Bengal*, p. 97.
42 General letter from the Court, 18 January 1717, paragraph 53, Letter Book No. 16, Wilson, *Old Fort William in Bengal*, p. 100.
43 Ibid.
44 Ibid.
45 Bengal Public Consultations, 24 January 1717, Range I, Vol. II, Wilson, *Old Fort William in Bengal*, p. 101.
46 Bengal Public Consultations, 14 November 1717, Range I, Vol. IV, Wilson, *Old Fort William in Bengal*, p. 101.
47 General Letter from Bengal to the Court, 6 December 1718. Wilson, *Old Fort William in Bengal*, p. 103.
48 General Letter from the Court to Bengal, 9 January 1719, paragraph 57, Wilson, *Old Fort William in Bengal*, p. 105.
49 Ibid.
50 Ibid.
51 Ibid.
52 General Letter from Bengal to Court, 14 May 1719, Range I, Vol. IV, Wilson, *Old Fort William in Bengal*, p. 106.
53 Bengal Public Consultations 1 May 1721, Range I, Vol. IV, Paragraph 167, Wilson, *Old Fort William in Bengal*, p. 111.
54 General Letter from Bengal to the Court, 2 December 1720, paragraph 119 Wilson, *Old Fort William in Bengal*, p. 111.
55 Ibid.
56 Ibid.
57 General Letter from Bengal to the Court, 31 January 1721–1722 (?), paragraph 84, Wilson, *Old Fort William in Bengal*, p. 112. In our writing we have accepted the date as 31 January 1721.
58 Ibid.
59 Letter from Bengal to the Court, 18 January 1723, para 86, Wilson, *Old Fort William in Bengal*, p. 113.
60 Ibid.
61 Ibid.
62 Ibid, para. 89.
63 Ibid. para 89, Wilson wrote "A pan is 80 cowries" – *Old Fort William in Bengal*, p. 113 note.
64 Bengal Public Consultations, 16 November 1724, Range I, Vol. V, Wilson, *Old Fort William in Bengal*, p. 116.
65 Bengal Public Consultation, 13 December 1725, Wilson, *Old Fort William in Bengal*, p. 118.
66 Letter from the Court, 17 February 1727, para 39, Wilson, *Old Fort William in Bengal*, p. 120.

67 General Letter from Bengal to the Court, 28 January 1728, Wilson, *Old Fort William in Bengal*, p. 123.
68 Bengal Public Consultation, 11 May 1730 Range I, Vol. VIII Wilson, *Old Fort William in Bengal*, p. 132.
69 Bengal Public Consultation, 7 May 1733, Range I, Vol. VII, Wilson, *Old Fort William in Bengal*, p. 139.
70 "There being severall Murders and Robberies committed in the Town and the people making their Escape by reason of the Outgates being out of Repair. Agreed that they be repair'd" Ibid, 13 August 1733, Wilson, *Old Fort William in Bengal*, p. 140.
71 General Letter from Bengal to the Court, 26 December 1733, para 78, Wilson, *Old Fort William in Bengal*, p. 140.
72 General Letter from the Court, 29 January 1734, para 69, Wilson, *Old Fort William in Bengal*, p. 140.
73 General Letter from the Court, 29 January 1734, para 69, Wilson, *Old Fort William in Bengal*, p. 141.
74 Bengal Public Consultation, 26 March 1735, Range I, Vol. VII, Wilson, *Old Fort William in Bengal*, p. 141.
75 General Letter from Bengal to the Court, 28 December 1735, para 97, Wilson, *Old Fort William in Bengal*, p. 143.
76 Bengal Public Consultations, Wednesday, 29 September 1736, Wilson, *Old Fort William in Bengal*, p. 143.
77 Ibid.
78 General Letter from Bengal to the Court, 31 December 1737, para 73, Wilson, *Old Fort William in Bengal*, pp. 147–148.
79 General Letter from Bengal to the Court, 29 January 1739, para 76, Wilson, *Old Fort William in Bengal*, p. 150.
80 Ibid.
81 Ibid.
82 Ibid, Wilson, *Old Fort William in Bengal*, pp. 150–151.
83 Ibid.
84 Bengal Public Consultation, 14 August 1739 [Wilson, *Old Fort William in Bengal*, p. 152] says: "Mr John Halsey Zemindar acquaints the Board that the Several Bazars and Market places not having been Repaired for these three years past are so much out of Order that the People cannot conveniently come to their stalls with Provisions and Other necessaries for the Town which if not duly taken care of much inevitably lessen the Honourable Companys Revenues." "Agreed that the Zamindar do see them Repaired forthwith and to do it with all possible Frugality."
85 General Letter from Bengal to the Court, 24 December 1739, paragraph 134, Wilson, *Old Fort William in Bengal*, p. 152.
86 Ibid, para. 135, Wilson, *Old Fort William in Bengal*, p. 152.
87 Ibid,, para. 140, Wilson, *Old Fort William in Bengal*, p. 153.
88 General Letter from the Court to Bengal, 21 March 1740, para. 58, Wilson, *Old Fort William in Bengal*, p. 153.
89 Ibid.
90 General Letter from Bengal to the Court, 3 January 1731, paras. 133 & 135. Wilson, *Old Fort William in Bengal*, p. 154.

91 Ibid, dated 24 December 1739, para 136.
92 Ibid, dated 3 January 1741, para 127.
93 Narayani Gupta, *Towers, Tanks and Temples: Some Aspects of Urbanism in South India Eighteenth and Nineteenth Centuries*, Occasional Papers Series: 5, Urban History Association of India, 1983, p. 3.
94 Ibid.
95 Ibid.
96 The expression has been borrowed from Pamela Kanwar, *The Changing Image of Shimla, Occasional Papers Series: 10*, Urban History Association of India, 1989, p. 5.

11
THE CITY ASSUMES FORM

The eighteenth century: a period of poor urbanization

For Calcutta, the eighteenth century was a period of poor urbanization. From the site of Hindu *Kalikshetra* it had inherited two things: the absence of broad brick laid and stone laid streets[1] and the uncleanliness of a filth-strewn habitation. The result was that when Lord Wellesley came to rule India as an empire of the British, he missed in Calcutta the marks of an imperial town. When his famous Minute of 1803 was drawn, Calcutta lacked roads, drains, water courses, well-arranged market places, corpse-disposal arrangements, burial grounds, law-regulated sites for animal-slaughters and effective system of town-cleaning.[2] In this situation, Wellesley's Minute came as a mark of deliverance, or as A.K. Ray says, it "stands out, as a beacon of light in the misty path of municipal reforms."[3]

The work of municipal reforms in Calcutta properly began in the last decade of the eighteenth century. From the dawn of that century, the East India Company's administration in Calcutta had rarely concerned itself with municipal reforms. It was not that municipal welfare schemes were not there. From time to time, the agenda of improvement of the town was drawn up, but they were more in the nature of patch work than of any systematic and planned action in the matter. The zamindar of the town from the beginning was entrusted with the charge of collecting ground rents. In addition he "was entrusted with the care of public order, convenience and health."[4] The zamindar's office had no competence of town management. It was not adequately manned and its purse was much too thin to cope with the problems of an expanding town: its extension of area, increase of population, over growth of houses (many of which were still thatched and mud-built ones), and its multiplying municipal and sanitary needs. Hence in 1794 under a statute of George III the management of the town was taken off the zamindar's hands and entrusted with a set of new officials, Justices of the Peace, who were appointed as authorized men to take charge of the town. They were to make regular assessments of the needs and duties to be discharged for the town.

Along with this change in Calcutta's administration two more things happened. "By the proclamation of 1794, the boundary of the town was fixed to be the inner side of the Mahratta Ditch."[5] The area was thus specified within which the Justices of the Peace were to function. With this the second thing got into a start. "In 1793 the practice of raising money for public improvements by means of lotteries first came into fashion"[6] The lotteries removed the crunch for money and the brake on city improvement was lifted. In the agrarian world a new order was ushered in with the enunciation of the Permanent Settlement. Now it was time to round off the British possessions in Bengal and create a centre from where the growing empire of the British in India would be ruled. It was with this urge that the nineteenth century set off for Calcutta's urbanization.

Urbanization was certainly not the idea which possessed the minds of the city fathers in the early years of the nineteenth century. The concept was one of improvement. The Act of 1794 commissioned the Justices of the Peace to two set functions – collection of revenue and their proper utilization for the improvement of the town. The Act specified what it meant by improvement – "principally repairing, watching and clearing the streets." The approach was to meet eventualities and not to create a planned urban structure.

In the eighteenth century planning for a sprawling urban location was never in the mind of the city-builders in Calcutta. A fort-centric politico-military castle-town resembling the castle-based urban centres of medieval Europe was hastily built up by the early English settlers in Calcutta. The precise model of Islamic town-building, which we see in northern and north-central India, was absent in Bengal. The Muslim rulers in general had never shown any enthusiasm for town-building in this part of the country. The only exception was Shujauddin Khan (1727–1739), the son-in-law of Murshid Quli Khan (1700–1708, 1710–1727) who raised some haphazard buildings and gardens in Murshidabad during the period of his governorship in Bengal and exhausted in the process the revenue reserve his father-in-law had left for him. The trade nexuses of the bigger Indo-Islamic world of commerce that connected the imperial cities of India's heartland, Delhi and Agra, with the coastal cities of Surat and Cambay and maintained tangential links with central Asian and west Asian trades through Lahore and Kabul could not rope into their system far-off parts of India's interior in the east.[7] The result was that *Subeh* Bangla remained secluded on its consolidated agricultural base protected by its village kinship and rural commodity production system. It was in such an economy that the English attempted to build up their urban base in Calcutta.[8]

Security and protection: the main urge

From the time of the purchase of three villages of Kalikata, Sutanuti, and Govindapur the main urge behind the growth of Calcutta was security and protection, mainly from the *Nawabi* interference and also from rebel zamindari upsurge like that of Shova Singh in 1696. The concept of a fort grew out of this – the need for protection. Screening the settlement from the eyes of other European competitors was another necessity that inspired English exclusiveness. The fort was thus an outcome both of a need shaped by geopolitics and of a fancy fashioned by islanders' isolationist inclination.

The White Town of the English in Calcutta which grew around the fort was thus intriguing. It had no semblance of an oriental town and to a European observer in 1727 – Alexander Hamilton – it seemed to be patterned after the baronial castle of medieval Europe.[9] It shows that planning at this early stage was determined by the need of security and the irregular clusters around the fort were hangovers of old and irresistibly stubborn habitations of the past.[10] Sheltered in the hub of security, the English settlers felt no need to look beyond the periphery of their own settlement. The southern part of their settlement was unexplored almost till the end of the eighteenth century and the eastern part was either covered by the Salt Lake or dotted by an intense jungle covering the modern territory of Sealdah (the then Srigaldaha)[11] and Beliaghata. The result was that only the northern part of the settlement remained open for habitation and the town-improvement in the early nineteenth century thus directed itself irresistibly to the north and partly to the south-west along the axis of the river towards modern Khidirpur.

The fort-centricity of this circumscribed settlement did not require any great planning for it. But the castle-like bearing of the whole town must have some planned setting inside it which has gained confidence with a modern historian. It "had" writes Pradip Sinha, "a powerful element of planning in it." "In basic design," he adds, "the settlement was in line with European urban transplants on the maritime belt of Asia, arising out of the needs of defence, hygiene and exclusiveness, growing round the semblance of a medieval baronial castle."[12]

EARLY FORMATIONS

Techniques of space utilization

Time was not ripe for spacious, preconceived town planning and a quick-settlement motivation within a secured habitation called for techniques of space utilization which was otherwise not known to Mughal settlement with Islamic structures. "The technique of utilization," Sinha goes on: "highly limited space proceeded from pragmatic considerations rather than from preconceived notions of planning that can be related to contemporary urban development programmes in Europe."[13] Coming in the wake of a war with the Emperor and the tremor of a formidable rebellion (that of Shova Singh in 1696) the purchase of three villages was marked by the exigencies of time. The English needed a foothold in Bengal where the commercial interests of the Company had to be cushioned by adequate security measures. Thus planning, if there was any, was for exigency. In such circumstances the map of a baronial castle complex was a readily available design that possessed the minds of the town planners. "The European urban transplant," Sinha further adds, "is a highly interesting historical phenomenon but strikingly free from complexity. It was an interesting form, but even at the height of its elegance, its should lay in the vaults of a commercial house."[14]

Motivation changed in the nineteenth century

Security was not a predominant motivation in town planning with the dawn of the nineteenth century. The *Nawabi* rule had sunk. European competitions had been beaten. Chances of a local rebellion were all defeated. Overriding security now emerged two other factors – requirements of a port and the necessities of a seat of administration. To address to these needs, the first essential prerequisites in town planning were drawn up. One of these was to clean the town. Dilapidated structures, abandoned houses, thatched huts grown of irregular and haphazard habitations, ghettos of men belonging to the work force, slums of domestic menials, shelters of Hindu idols, roadside butcheries, improvised shops and market places had filled the city at the dawn of the nineteenth century. In a letter to the Governor General[15] in council on 31 August 1804, the Committee for improving the Town of Calcutta urged the necessity of removing "the existing nuisances" in the town.[16] Three measures were immediately recommended by the Committee – the removal of the Dharmatala Bazaar to a situation "eligible and contiguous," building a Town Hall or "any large Ornamental Building which Government might have occasion for" in the place thus vacated which was 'central and commanding' and finally "pulling down all the remaining original works of the Old Fort." Trade in the city had increased manifold and larger space was required for import and export wares which needed to be properly housed. The export warehouse keeper had been representing on this point for a long time and the Committee for improvement now drew the attention of the Governor General in Council to the "heavy annual expense which is incurred by renting store Houses for the Export and Import Establishment."[17] The Dharmatala Bazaar was situated to the "North East Quarter of the Esplanade."[18] The Committee for improvement wrote the following: "The ill-judged construction of this Bazar, and the consequent uncleanly state of it added to the central and exposed situation of the place induce us to represent it as a grievous nuisance." They continued: "To the South East of the present Bazar there is a considerable piece of Ground perfectly well calculated both by situation and extent, for the erection of a new Bazar and on which there are no Buildings of any consequence at present."[19]

From the immediate vicinity of the fort the town planners' gaze moved a little far to the north and south of the city – but certainly on the line along the axis of the river bank. To the south the road to the Alipore and Kidderpore (Khidirpur) Bridges had to be overhauled. "The rapid descent from the top" of these bridges had "occasioned dangerous accidents" in recent times. Therefore, it was recommended that the ground on the northern side of both the bridges be raised and the rails on both sides be continued.[20] The entire zone from the Chandpal Ghat to Khidirpur was taken within the purview of improvement and improvement then meant diverse things: from raising, levelling, and dressing grounds just as what was recommended for the Khidirpur area to filling ditches, a very imperative need of the time; from widening of roads and road-crossings to removal of debris of dilapidated structures; from shifting of ineffective and shabby government offices to erecting new ones; from shutting old burial grounds to providing new places as substitutes; and from pulling down thatched huts to substituting them with tiled ones. Necessities were big and recommendations were great but the work was very slow and it took a long time to bring Calcutta to an order which might be called fit for an imperial headquarters.

Effective and planned measures from 1805

In July 1805 the Town Improvement Committee recommended the following measures.[21]

EARLY FORMATIONS

Measures to Avoid Accidents: The landing slopes on the northern side of the Alipur and Khidirpur bridges had to be properly raised and dressed up. The "sharp angle formed by Park Street and Chauringhee (Chowringhee) Road on the South side [had to] be removed." "Carriages proceeding in different directions frequently run against each other at this point in consequences of the view of each other's approach being obstructed by the angle of the compound to the House lately occupied by Colonel Garstin." "Ditches in the North East quarter of the Esplanade [had to] be dressed up by sloping the sides," and "their inequalities in the Ground in that quarter [had to] be filled up."

Removal of thatched houses: It was "proposed that none but Tiled Houses be allowed in the Cooley Bazar, and that the sheds belonging to the Garrison Store Keeper and other military Officers in the vicinity of the Bazar be tiled." This measure was recommended to prevent fire in the city. This recommendation was very urgent. Fire was rampant in the city that was covered from end to end with "thatched bungalows and straw hovels."[22]

Removal of obstructions which served to impede "the free Navigation of the River": The bank of the river between Chandpal Ghat and Chitpur had to be cleared. Innumerable huts and sheds were built on the western part of the bank. Many of them were unauthorized and irregular and had obstructed both the sight of the river and a passage to it. They had to be removed.

"This measure is recommended," the Special Committee wrote to the G.G. in Council,[23] "with a view to the removal of Huts and the sheds which may be found improperly situated to promote the free Navigation of the River, and to afford to Boats an easy access to the shore at all places."[24] There were a good number of bathing ghats and an innumerable pathways, narrow and serpentine which had connected them with the town in the interior on the eastern part of the road. Habitations in this region have already become congested and this had choked the business arteries into the river.

Spatial expansion for army drill and public work: The area between the fort and the Chandpal Ghat[25] provided the space for routine army drill. Therefore, the Town Committee recommended that "the quarter of the Esplanade, on the river side adjoining to Chandpaul Ghat be cleared of the brick rubbish, Timbers and Old Guns, which are scattered upon it and that instruction be given to the officer in charge of the Engineer Department to level the ground and to keep it in a good order for the Militia Parades, and Public Walks, and that a Rail be put upon the East side of the bridge at the water shed to prevent accidents."[26]

THE CITY ASSUMES FORM

The whole area around two kilometres in radius centring the Fort had become congested. The congestion was caused not only by thatched huts and improvized sheds but also by the godowns of the Company. Thus "the passage from Hastings Street to the River" was covered by a "range of godowns" commonly called "Vrignous Godowns." The Hastings Street was then a "narrow passage" which served as

> the principal thoroughfare for goods and passengers proceeding from Chandpal Ghaut and Kootchagoody Ghaut into the town consequently [because of the godown obstructions] carriages, hackeness [hackney carts] and palanquins are frequently interrupted in their progress and detained to the great inconvenience of the inhabitants and obstruction to the commerce of the Town.[27]

White men's bunglows often created bottleneck points in some important thoroughfares in the White Town. Thus at the bankshall houses occupied "by Mr. Hare the watchmaker and Mr. Torry" made the Lane "narrow and irregular passage" for traffic. The Lane had to be widened.[28]

Sometimes the official buildings occupied large plots of land and obstructed passages to the river and the town. One such building was the Marine Paymaster's Office which occupied "upwards of 3/4th of the Ground which formerly constituted the approach to one of the principal Ghauts of the Town." In the judgement of the Committee "the disuse into which Quouillah Ghaut [present Koila Ghata Street area] has of late years fallen for commercial purpose may fairly be ascribed to the obstructions occasioned by encroachment above adverted to you."[29]

Creation of burial grounds: The old burial grounds had become a source of nuisance in the city. There were separate burial grounds for the Portuguese, Greeks, the English and the Muslims. There was a separate burial ground called the Hospital Burial Ground. These were mostly in the eastern part of the city and adjacent to areas around the modern Circular road. Of these the condition of the Hospital Burial Ground and the Muslim Burial Ground was the worst. The Hospital Burial Ground was "represented as being one entire Mass of Bones." "It appears from the testimony of the Reverend Mr Brown that one quarter of it has been filled four times over (the Graves have been regularly marked out close to each other) within the period of his remembrances." The Muslim Burial Ground was considered to be one of the filthiest parts of the town. It was "represented as being during the rains a perfect Marsh." The Bodies are generally interred in a negligent manner, sometimes within two feet of the surface and the jackals constantly prowl in the place. In a memorial presented to the Government in 1804 the families in the vicinity of the 'Mussulmen's Burying Place' represented it 'as being a precarious nuisance, particularly at the later end of the rains.' In view of all these the Town Improvement Committee recommended that the Muslim, the Christian and the Hospital Burial Grounds "be shut up" and "that [for the English] a site for a new place of Internment be selected somewhere between Boitaconnah and the Portuguese Burying Ground in the east side of the Circular Road." What is significant is that the burial grounds were to be shifted to the eastern part of the town parallel to the Circular Road that not only marked the eastern boundary of the town but also provided new space to the town in the east. "It is objectionable," the Committee wrote to the Government, "that the Repository of the dead should be on the South East quarter of the town."[30]

Measures to ensure free air circulation: The removal of burial grounds was a part of the sanitizing efforts resulting directly from Wellesley's Minute of 1803. The circulation of free air was another necessity that was taken care of. The old fort was the greatest obstruction to the passage of free air in the city coming from the river. The "decayed and ruinous state" of the fort "building," its "high walls equally useless to the proprietors and disfiguring to the appearance of the principal quarter of the Town serve to obstruct a free circulation of air and must also from their being strongly impregnated with saltpetre and extremely damp, occasion noxious and unwholesome vapours." This was one reason that was causing distress to the entire site where the Fort and the Esplanade were situated. To get rid of poisonous air blowing into the town it was advisable to pull down the entire structure. The old fort and the Maritime Paymaster's Office occupied a vast area which the Town Improvement Committee considered 'a very valuable piece of Ground' which should be retrieved and utilized for other purposes. The Committee's recommendation was that "if the approach were widened by the removal of this [Paymaster's] house the Ghaut [the Koila Ghat] in question would in consequence of its local advantages become one of the most convenient and popular Ghauts in Calcutta."[31] These recommendations were tentative plans which needed the support of experts' opinion. Hence Mr. Taylor, the export warehouse keeper, was consulted by the Committee. His concurrence was secured. He advised that the old fort must be pulled down and the Paymaster's office should be removed.[32] The proposal to erect a "range of spacious godowns" in the place of the old fort did not seem to be sound as a measure of town planning. The predominant motive behind change was to meet trade requirements and the prime places at the heart of the White Town were not considered as sites necessary for the construction of stately edifices which otherwise would have added to the dignity of the town. This narrow utility-oriented commercial vision did not reflect any planning deficiency on the part of early planners. It only showed that a commercial company did not have the mind to adjust its commercial ends with the majesty of a ruling authority that was endowed with the function of governance of a growing town. The First Report of the Special Committee instituted for the town envisaged at one point measures for free air circulation and at other point planned to erect dirty constructions which obstruct passage of free air from the river and add to the filth of the town. It was this desire to extract service-utility from the natives which led extravagant and luxury-prone early British officers to permit the growth of menials' quarters around their apartments, which eventually took the shape of slums in the town.

Measures for the beautification of the town: The Special Committee for Town Improvement recommended measures for the renovation of the great tank in the White Town. The renovation was to proceed on a two-fold plan consisting of clearance and construction as follows:

> That the ground on all sides adjacent to the Great Tank be cleared away and that the present Buildings of every description as well as the gardens on the North side be removed and measures be taken to prevent further encroachments of the like nature.
> That a wall, Railing and chain similar to those which encompass the South side of the Government house be constructed all-round the Tank and a spacious gravel walk for Public accommodation be made immediately within the enclosure and that Handsome substantial Benches or Garden Chairs be placed in the centre of each of the walks which enclose the great Tank.

Along with the great tank the Holwell monument raised in remembrance of the so-called Black Hole victims was to be taken care of. The recommendations said:

> That the Monument situated at the west and of the Writers' Buildings be thoroughly repaired and handsomely decorated and that an ornamental Iron railing be erected around it.

The First Report of the Special Committee laid out a bare programme for the development of the White Town. The riverbank area of the fort complex was to get a face-lift and eventually turned into a nucleus from where the town planning for nineteenth-century Calcutta would start. Trade requirements, military needs and public utility demands were all present in the recommendations made in the report. The basic aim, however, was to make the White Town habitable with comfort and dignity, or, as the eighteenth-century parlance went "flourishing, sweet and wholesome."[33]

Constructions of roads: While these recommendations were made the town planners seemed to be equally aware that roads were necessary for promoting the town. For the construction of roads, land was necessary and the Committee drew the attention of the Government to this most essential element "for the improvement of the Town" namely land. The earliest note in this regard was sent to the Governor General in Council on 22 January 1805 stating the necessity of "the purchase of the ground requisite for opening the new roads from North to South and from East to West."[34] The Chitpur-Chowringhee axis which led to Halisahar to connect this holy place with the pilgrim spot of Kalighat was the only and major axis along which the town in the eighteenth century grew. This road was to the western part of the city and ran parallel to the river bank. It was on this street that the ancient Sutanuti Hat, which was turned into Bura Bazaar by the Marwari and Gujarati traders in the eighteenth century, was situated. There were innumerable bathing and ferry ghats on the bank of the river and the lanes which connected them with the habitations in the interior criss-crossed with this road. The pressure of habitation and the rush of ever-increasing business transactions met at every point of this criss-cross and made life difficult. Therefore, an alternative to this road had become a dire necessity. Out of this necessity later grew the parallel arteries of the town running north to south – the one was the College Street-Cornwallis Street corridor and the other was what later came to be developed as the Central Avenue link between Shyambazar and Esplanade. To the north and the east of these newly conceived arteries was situated the Circular Road which formed the eastern boundary of the town and was called at that time as Boithakkhana Road.[35]

The east-west roads which the planners had in their contemplation would be parallels to the road which went from the zamindar's cutchery near the Fort to Srigaldaha in the east which is known as Sealdah in modern times.

THE CITY ASSUMES FORM

The city becomes compact

The main thrust of the city planners was to construct north-south arteries funded by the money raised from lotteries. With the coming of these arteries the white and the Black Town came to be compacted. Till the end of the eighteenth century, the Government did not open its purse for public welfare. The upkeep of the army and the fort, the cost of administration and the system of policing the town and syphoning money as sinews of commerce consumed the bulk of revenue of the town. In the first part of the eighteenth century, Calcutta was a money-short economy. But after the battle of Palasi situations changed. Krishnadas, the son of Raja Rajballabh, the *dewan* of Dakha, had already fled with vast treasure to Calcutta before Palasi. After Palasi, the *Nawab* Mir Jafar was fleeced. No one could say with certainty which one was bigger in terms of extractions – the private squeeze by the Company's officers of the *Nawab* or the restitution money donated by the *Nawab* as a stipulation of the conspiracy contract. Big *zamindars* of the interior then began to deposit their wealth in Calcutta because Murshidabad had sunk. This was also because Calcutta offered security to people – an experience people had enjoyed since the time of the Maratha incursions in the 1740s. Previously men in the interior used to bury their wealth under earth because of fear from robbery. Now these treasures were lifted from their hidden shelters and men, money, and family all henceforth shifted to Calcutta. Moreover this was the city where the *banians* used to stay. They were the men who amassed wealth through their trade with the foreign East India Companies and through their own individual business. This was how they turned into the greatest capitalist class in the country superseding the Jagat Seths now in a state of decline. By the time Cornwallis came to rule, Calcutta had already become an affluent city. The tendency to pump out money from private sources thus began to gain momentum. In the next three decades it came to be called *Kamalalaya*: the abode of goddess Lakshmi, urging one writer of the city Bhabani Charan Bandyapadhyay to write his famous tract *Kalikata Kamalalaya*. In view of all these the government up to the time of Lord Cornwallis had never had the urge to open its purse for public use. This administrative miserliness had held Calcutta's development in check for a long time. Situations changed only in the nineteenth century after the assumption of the administration by Lord Wellesley. No major street was built up to that time. But certainly Calcutta developed its aspirations. The public opinion was steadily formed and public pressure was mounted on the Government. To this the Government yielded and planning was set into action with the turn of the nineteenth century.

The evolved process of internal town formation

This was how the internal town formation of the city began to take place. The original idea was that Calcutta was to have a planned insulation of a garrison town. After the battle of Palasi the idea did not hold away any more. The *Nawabi* vigilance over Calcutta was over and the Company's officers came out of their crammed life within the fort. A new fort was on the way to being constructed and the confidence was grown that any menace from outside could be thwarted. Since the life of a sprawling existence now started for the English, new roads and drains necessary for the cleanliness of the city became essential for a settled urban life. The town in the nineteenth century grew in response to this.

By the end of the eighteenth and the beginning of the nineteenth century, the urbanization of Calcutta, it may be said, had already shed much of its early hesitations. In 1803, to a European visitor, the white part of the city appeared to be a full-grown urban settlement. The picture of Calcutta's urban growth was a point of pride to a European visitor looking at the White Town from the side of the river. The pride was not an unjustified exuberance. Its unmatched superiority vis-à-vis the Black Town provided its own *raison d'etre*.

A visitor observed the following:

> The town of Calcutta is at present well-worthy of being the seat of our Indian Government, both from its size and from the magnificent buildings which becorate the part of it inhabited by Europeans. The citadel of Fort William is a very fine work, but greatly too large for defence. The Esplanade leaves a grand opening, on the edge of which is placed the new Government House, erected by Lord Wellesley, a noble structure, although not without faults in the architecture and upon the whole not unworthy of its destination. On a line with this edifice is a range of excellent house chummed and ornamented with verandahs. Chowringhee, *an entire village of palaces*, runs for a considerable length at right angles with it and altogether forms the finest view beheld in any city.[36] [Italics ours]

With all its splendour Calcutta was still a village – considered by a beholder as "an entire village of palaces." This was because of two reasons. Calcutta had no roads and was still a mud-strewn place without any specific system of drainage. A series of brick-built structures had come up, giving a wonderful view of the city from the river-end but they could not efface the rusticity of the neighbourhood. A little away from upcoming quarters of the Europeans there was, one could see, the Black Town coming up with equal speed with the white. This was the second cause of irritation in the otherwise placid surface of a new-found urbanity. A congested interior now contrasted with a sprawling white habitation with a mesmerizing picture of a riverfront. Affluence and misery, growth and stagnation, elegance and ugliness of the city were now marked features in the entire stretch of the river bank from the south to the north. Vis-à-vis the White Town, the black settlement was picture of settled gloom around a clustered habitation. The visitor's impression on it was this:

> The Black Town [i.e. the Indian quarter], is as complete a contrast to this as can be well conceived. Its streets are narrow and dirty, the houses of two stories, occasionally brick and generally mud, and thatched, perfectly resembling the cabins of the poorest class in Ireland.[37]

This was colonial Calcutta available in the year the famous Minutes of Lord Wellesley were drawn. Intrinsically its character was defined. Externally it resembled Madras of a little later date. In span of less than fifty years since the battle of Palasi, its internal lay-out was marked. Chowringhee was to be the European civil line slightly away from the new fort and it touched the Esplanade at the right angle. This Esplanade was a vast space dividing the European civil settlement from the fort on the one hand and on the other it separated the White Town from the Black Town allowing a small grey town of mixed population of natives, Portuguese, Greeks, moors, Chinese, and Armenians to emerge in the middle. It acted as a buffer between the white and the Black Town. Looking from the standpoint of town morphology Madras of 1813 resembled Calcutta of 1803.

Madras is divided into two parts, the Forte or White Town, and the Black Town.... The Black Town is to the northward of the Fort, separated by a spacious esplanade.... The town is the residence of the Gentoo, Moorish, Armenian and Portuguese merchants.... Some of the merchants at Black Town (own) large and elegant buildings."[38]

The city form, the segregation of the blacks from the whites, which Calcutta assumed even in the beginning of the nineteenth century, had apparently resembled Madras in its outward formation.[39] The existence of Esplanade as an imposing buffer separating the white from the Black Town gave the two towns the shape of apparent similarity but there were enough differences between the two. In the beginning of the nineteenth century, the Black Town in Calcutta was yet to witness the coming of palatial structures which in Madras had already started making their appearance, giving the Balck Town its own distinction. In Calcutta the Black Town had its surreptitious penetration in the White Town. Calcutta ceased to be a paradise in a mid-nineteenth century report.

"But with all its advantages," goes the report, "do not imagine that Chowringhee is a paradise, one of those localities that every person desires to live in." Bishop Haber, in a cursory note of Moscow, informs us that in that city the palace and the hut are often close to each other. This may be said to be the case, though most probably not so often, in Chowringhee. The road has on its eastern side many fine colonnaded mansions in the Grecian style and which have indeed a fine effect when viewed from the river, but it has also in the very front of it a cluster of miserable native huts, tenanted by some 200 natives. This incongruous neighbourhood of huts and lowest Soodras to palaces and European magnates speedily banished from the mind of the near spectator the paradisiacal notions he may entertain about Chowringhee. The splendid mansion loses half of its architectural attraction when it is besides a collection of mud and bamboo huts. For the good of the fair name and for the "sake of the fair ladies of Chowringhee, it would be desirable that a north-western would one of these days blow down every hut in this and in other parts of the district, and if this sweeping away can be done by a north-western without injury to the persons and goods and chattels of the native who settle down in these places, it will be consummation most earnestly to be wished by every white face in Chowringhee."[40]

Interpenetration between the white and the black settlements

The greatest feature of this upcoming city in the beginning of the nineteenth century was, therefore, not the seclusion of the white from the Black Town but the slow and steady interpenetration between the two. The white population of the city, particularly the officers and servants of the Company, had developed the eastern habit of living in idleness with a touch of luxury and comfort in the routine of their life. They needed menials to serve their domestic chores but seldom were these menials allowed to stay inside the residence of their masters beyond their service hours. Naturally they built their own quarters, their hovels and huts, in the proximity of their masters' residences. Moreover from the time of the construction of the new fort there was an influx of coolies and a vast workforce associated with the business of construction, both government and private. A cooly habitation, called the "cooly bazaar," grew near the fort along the lower circular road axis at a point known to us a present as Hastings. The cooly workers and the domestic menials had a free exchange of their population so that their slum residences spilled over beyond Chowringhee and marred much of the organized smartness of the white city. What, therefore, attracted the attention of the authorities most was the mud and swamps and the filth and undrained water that choked the animation of an otherwise vibrating town. Lord Wellesley's first concern was, therefore, streets and drains the improvement of which eventually led to the first and real beginning of the town as an imperial city.[41] Lord Wellesley's rule initiated the third phase of the growth of Calcutta. In the first century of British rule in India, Calcutta as a city grew in three stages. In the first stage, between the purchase of the three villages of Sutanuti, Govindapur, and Kalikata in 1698 and the battle of Palasi in 1757, Calcutta was territorially static and had no sovereignty of its own. With a will to grow yet to be born, it was in all real sense a stagnating city rooted in its fort-centric existence. Its impulse to grow began when the fear of *Nawabi* impingement was removed and the English had started experiencing a sprawling life outside the crammed existence of the fort. That was the time when Calcutta acquired the space for expansion up to the sea and renovations of internal infrastructures of old possessions began. The entire phase of the administration of Clive (1757–1760 and 1765–1767), Vansitart (1759–1764), Verelst (1767–1769), and Cartier (1769–1772) was oriented for stability and was unmarked by ambition. The momentum for change was developed under Warren Hastings followed by incentives acquired during the rule of Cornwallis. That was a new age and new constructions and innovative structures were ushered in. Hastings took over as the Governor General of the British possessions in India, and Calcutta began its career as the seat of British administration. The ambition to convert Calcutta into an imperial city took off under Lord Wellesley.[42] Calcutta became the seat of British administration in 1773 only with the passing of the Regulating Act in that year. Lord Wellesley's Minute came in 1803. In course of these intervening thirty years, the city character of Calcutta was formed but its imperial majesty was still unborn. That majesty came firstly by the initiation of the practice of raising money through lottery in 1793, which removed the money constraints from urbanization and secondly by the Minutes of Lord Wellesley, which set the town to a new career free of filth and marshy lands laced with beautiful roads and streets running through north to south making the white and the Black Town clubbed into one imperial urban unit which in course of time would acquire the entitlement to be called the second city of the Empire.

With Lord Wellesley, one may say, Calcutta's city formation really took off. In the first eight decades of its existence, Calcutta resembled a village with no sign of modernization. A.K. Ray, one of the early biographers of Calcutta, observes that even in 1780 Calcutta was a compound of swamps and jungles unfit for habitation. He writes: "Calcutta at this time [1780] was little better than an undrained swamp, in the immediate vicinity of a malarious jungle, 'the ditch surrounding it was, as it had been for thirty years previously, an open *cloaca*, and its river banks were strewn with the dead bodies of men and animals.'"[43] This was the situation in which Calcutta was placed even after the city was declared to be the seat of the growing British Empire in India. The post-Palasi years witnessed the first British experience of moving out of a crammed life into a sprawling existence. This experience was a bewildered process – one of a simple stretching out from the fort in search of new space where there would be an escape into a kind of a free and individual residential existence. The need then was to be a little away from accommodations where the garrison was sheltered. Moving out from the fort, the first concern of the English was to rearrange their ramshackle shelters – godowns, barracks, workshops, offices, residential quarters, and the like – and there was little urge to improve the municipal life of the city in general. The result was catastrophic:

> From 1780 and onwards, correspondents in the newspapers make frequent complaints about the indescribably filthy condition of the streets and roads. This is fully confirmed by the account of Grandpre in 1790, who speaks of the canals and cesspools reeking with putrefying animal matter, of the streets as awful, of the myriads of flies, and of the crowd and flocks of animals and birds acting as scavengers. Often the police authorities are reproached for suffering dead human bodies to lie on the roads in and near Calcutta for two or three days.[44]

THE CITY ASSUMES FORM

How stagnation was lifted: emergence of public opinion

This was entirely a picture of a stagnating city. Two things lifted it from its condemned existence. The first was the practice of raising money through lottery and the second was the vision of Lord Wellesley to make the city an imperial seat of power. In the 1790s, there was the real beginning of change effected in Calcutta. In 1794, the first advertisement for lottery for "benevolent and charitable purposes"[45] went out. It was a "lottery of 10,000 tickets, at Rs. 32 each, and some of the best streets and churches were constructed out of these funds."[46] Reverend James Long gives us a major insight into the benefits of the lottery. He writes:

> Lotteries were the order of the day; large houses fetching Rs. 10009 monthly rent were sold by lottery tickets of Rs. 600 each, also garden houses, a *Howrah house is put up to lottery*, situate on the bank of the river where the bore has no effect. The Harmonic house, a celebrated Tavern, was put up to auction by lottery in 1780, and won by the Hon'ble Mr. Justice Hyde. A garden house in Entally was raffled in 1781 for Rs. 6,000 prize tickets Rs. 75 each. Some of the best roads in Calcutta were subsequently made by the sale of lottery tickets.[47]

If the lotteries, commonplace as a practice and officially commenced in 1794, opened a new vista of urbanization in Calcutta, another important event then took place in the same year which marked the beginning of the most productive phase of urbanization in the city. This was the replacement of the zamindar of Calcutta by Justice of the Peace in the management of the town. Since the foundation of the city the civic management of the town was in the hands of a zamindar but in none of his administrative fields his achievement could match the rapid expansion of the town with its expanding sanitary needs.[48] Hence this drastic measure was taken in 1794. An institution of nine decades was scrapped. The management of the town was entrusted to a body fashioned after western institutions, the Justice of the Peace.[49]

"The Justices set to their business in real earnestness and effected various reforms," writes A.K. Ray and he adds: "One of their first acts was the metalling of Circular Road."[50] The Circular Road was the major thoroughfare which encircled the entire city from north to south starting near Baghbazar where the Maratha ditch was dug and ending at the bank of the river near Govindapur. The soil that was dug out of the Maratha ditch was used in filling up the road and elevating its surface. Five years after assumption of charge the Justices issued the following notice in the *Calcutta Review* dated 24 October 1799:

> Notice is hereby given that His Majesty's Justices of the Peace will receive proposals of contract, which must be delivered sealed to their first clerk, Mr. John Miller, within one week from this date, for levelling, dressing and making in pucker, within the least possible time, the road forming the eastern boundary of the town, commonly called the Bytockunah Road and commencing from the Russapugla Road at the corner of Chowringhee and terminating at Chitpur bridge.[51]

Dressing the streets, filling the obnoxious drains and taking care of the conservancy of the streets were measures that had already gone into the civic agenda of the Company's authorities in Calcutta long before the Minutes of Lord Wellesley were drawn up but they were adhered to as small improvements for meeting eventualities and not as any part of a planned scheme of urbanization. Meeting eventualities was a routine exercise of the eighteenth century. Planning was an event of the nineteenth century as it descended from the top in the form of an advice from the Governor General. From 1780s public opinion was pressing for reform and more planned improvements. Filth, mud, undrained water, and street nuisances had become colossal obstacles to the growth of township. Public opinion roared against it. Calcutta had assumed a status with the foundation of the office of the Governor General, the Supreme Court, and the new fort. The civil residences of the Company's servants had been separated from the army quarters in the fort. The Chowringhee Road had established itself as a new civil line.

New men of the interior, rich and solvent, had shifted to the city with their treasures. And with them expectations were on the rise, but the city landscape had very little signs of planned urbanity. Naturally, therefore, the *Calcutta Review* on Thursday, 19 October 1766 had expressed its concern thus: "the nuisances in the streets are of late loudly and generally complained of dirt and rubbish of every kind are permitted to lie before the doors of the inhabitants in a most slovenly and offensive manner."[52]

This was how public opinion was taking care of the need for overhauling the defects of the city. This public opinion was new

THE CITY ASSUMES FORM

phenomenon in the city. A civil society was slowly emerging in Calcutta and the civic life was slowly being taken under public address. A.K. Ray writes:

> These and similar Press notices of the prevailing un-healthiness and insecurity of different parts of the town put the authorities on the alert, and they planned and effected various little improvements. Some old drains were filled up and the wretched old bazar in the Fort – the ancient Govindapur bazar of mud and thatch – was demolished.[53]

Removal of bazaars created space and filling up of drains had provided the city a levelled surface of grounds on which roads, streets, and constructions could be built. Removal of ugliness from the face of the city was not only a part of beautification but also a deliberate move to create convenience in which plans of development could be ushered in. The demolition of the Govindapur bazaar was informed to the public in the Gazette of Thursday, 30 August 1787 thus :

> The old bazar composed of an irregular and confused heap of straw huts, not only collected filth and threatened contagion, but proved in fact an asylum for every theft that escaped the hands of justice in Calcutta : robberies were, of course, daily committed without the possibility of detection.[54]

The city inconveniences called for redress not only because they were related to civic sanitation and hygiene but also because they were conducive for crimes to flourish. Urbanization was a form where shortcomings of life had to be overcome with organized facilities of existence. Towards that Calcutta started moving from the end of the eighteenth century. In the course of that century the three villages of Sutanuti, Govindapur, and Kalikata slowly gave up their rustic orientations. Their city formation was yet to come in their configuration. The process to that end started from the time of Lord Cornwallis. Under Lord Wellesley it was consummated. In the first three decades of the nineteenth century, Calcutta received its first formal city form.

Appendix

LORD WELLESLEY'S MINUTE ON CALCUTTA, 1803 REPORTS OF THE FEVER HOSPITAL COMMITTEE 1839 APPENDIX – F PAGE – 301 NO. 100

Minute of the Governor General on the improvement of Calcutta

The increasing extent & population of Calcutta, the Capital of the British Empire in India, and the seat of the Supreme authority, require the serious attention of Government. It is now become absolutely necessary to provide permanent means of promoting the health, the comfort, and the convenience of the numerous inhabitants of this great Town.

The construction of the Public Drains and Water-Courses of the Town is extremely defective. The Drains & the Water-Courses in their present state neither assume the purpose of cleaning the Town, nor of discharging the annual inundations occasioned by the rise of the River, or by the excessive fall of rain during the south west Monson. During the last week a great part of this Town has remained under Water, and the drains have been so offensive, that unless early measures be adopted for the purpose of improving their construction, the health of the inhabitants of Calcutta, both European & Native, must be seriously affected.

The defects of the climate of Calcutta during the latter part of the rainy season may indeed be ascribed in a great measure to the State of the drains & Water Courses, and to the stagnant water remaining in the Town & its vicinity.

The health of the Town would certainly be considerably improved by an improvement of the mode of draining & cleaning the Streets, Roads & Esplanade. An opinion is generally entertained that an original error has been committed in draining the Town towards the River Hooghly. And it is believed that the level of the country inclines towards the Salt Water Lake, and consequently that the principal channels of the Public Drains & Water Courses ought to be conducted in that direction.

Experience has manifested that during the rainy season, when the River has altered its utmost height, the present drains become baseless; at that season the main continues to stagnate for many weeks in every part of the Town, and the result necessarily endangers the lives of all Europeans residing in the Town, and greatly affects our Native subjects.

Other points connected with the preservation of the health of the inhabitants of the capital, appear also to require immediate notice. No general regulation at present exist with respect to the situation of the Public Markets, or of the places appropriated to the slaughter of cattle, the exposer of Meat or the burial of the Dead. Places destined to these purposes must necessarily increase in number with the increasing population of Calcutta. They must be nuisances wherever they may be situated, and it becomes an important branch of the Police to confine all such nuisances to the situation wherein they may prove least injurious and least offensive. It must however have been generally remarked, that places of burial have been established. In situation wherein they must prove both injurious & offensive, and Bazars, Slaughter-Houses & Markets of meat now exist in the most frequented parts of the Town.

In those quarters of the Town occupied principally by the Native inhabitants the houses have been built without order or regularity, and the streets and lanes have been formed without attention to the health, convenience or safety of the inhabitants. The frequency of Fires (by which many valuable lives have been annually lost, and property to a great extent has been destroyed) must be chiefly attributed to this cause.

It is a primary duty of Govt. to provide for the health, safety & convenience of the inhabitants of this great Town, by establishing a comprehensive system for the improvement of the Roads, Streets, Public Drains, and Water-Courses, and by fixing permanent rules for the construction and distribution of the Houses & Publick Edifices & for the regulation of nuisances of every description.

The appearance and beauty of the Town are inseparably connected with the health, safety & convenience of the inhabitants, and every improvement which shall introduce a greater degree of order, symmetry and magnificence in the streets, Roads, Ghats and Wharfs, Public Edifices, and Private Habitations, will tend to ameliorate the climate and to promote & secure every object of a just & salutary system of

EARLY FORMATIONS

police. These observations are entirely compatible with a due sense of the activity, diligence and ability of the present Magistrates of Calcutta, by whose exertions considerable improvents have been made in the general Police of the Town. The Governor General in Council has frequently expressed his approbation of the conduct & services of the present Magistrates of Calcutta, who have jealously and judiciously employed every effort, within their power to mitigate the effects of the evils described in this Minute. But the Magistrates of Calcutta must be sensible that the establishment of a more comprehensive system of permanent regulation, is indispensably necessary for the purpose of security to the Town the full benefit of the laudable service of the Officers to whom the administration of the Police has been entrusted by Govt.

With these views, the Govt. proposes that the under mentioned gentlemen be appointed a Committee to consider & report to his Excellency in Council the means of improving the Town of Calcutta :-

Major General Fracers	Mr. Ross
,, ,, Cameron	Mr. Alexander
Mr. Speke	Major Colebrooke
Mr. Graham	Captain Wyatt
Mr. Brooke	Mr. Dashwood
Mr. Taylor	Captain Aubury
Mr. R.C. Birch	Captain Preston
Colonel Pringle	Captain Blunt, of Engineers
Mr. S. Davis	Captan Sydenham
Mr. G. Dowdeswell Suptd. of Police	Messrs. C.F. Mastin
Lieutenant Colonel Harcourt	W.C. Blaquiere
Captan Shawe	E. Thorlon
Colonel Garstia	and
Mr. Tucker	A. Macklew, Justice of the
Mr. Farlie	Peace for the Town of Calcutta
Mr. Colvin	and Mr. R. Bleclynden

The Governor General further proposes that Mr. Tiretha be directed to attend the committee and that Captain Blunt of Engineers, be appointed to officiate as their secretary.

The Governor General further proposes that the following special instructions be issued to the Committee – 1st To take the level of the Town of Calcutta and the adjacent country and ascertain & report what alternative may be necessary in the direction of the public Drains & Water-Courses.

2nd ly To examine the relative level of the River during the rainy season compared with the level of the Drains & Water Courses.

3rd ly To suggest what description of Drains & Water Courses may be best calculated 1st to present the Stagnation of rain water in Calcutta & the vicinity thereof and 2nd ly to cleanse the Town.

4th ly To consider & report what establishment may be necessary for cleaning the Drains & Water Courses and for keeping them in constant repair.

5th ly To take into consideration the present state of all places of intervent (?) in the vicinity of Calcutta and to propose an arrangement for the future regulation of those places in such manner as shall appear to be best calculated for the preservation of the health of the inhabitants of Calcutta and its vicinity.

6th ly To examine the present state & condition of the Bazars & Markets for Meat and of the slaughter Houses in Calcutta and to propose such rules & orders as shall appear to the Committee to be proper for the regulation of these already established for the removal of such as may have actually become nuisances – and for the establishment of New Markets or Slaughter Houses hereafter.

7th ly To inquire into all existing nuisances in the Town & vicinity of Calcutta, and to propose the reasons of removing them.

8th ly To examine and report for the consideration of Government the situation best calculated for appearing new streets & Roads, leading from East to West from the new Circular Road to Chowringhee and to the River, and from North to South in a direction really parallel with the New Road.

9th ly To suggest such other plans and regulation as shall appear to the Committee to be calculated to promote the health, convenience and comfort of the inhabitants of Calcutta and to improve the appearance to the Town & its vicinity.

10th, To form & submit to the Governor General in Council an estimate of the expense required to complete all such improvements as may be proposed by the Committee.

The means of raising the funds for the purpose of defraying the expense which must attend the execution of the important, improvement suggested in this minute, will claim the early & deliberate consideration of Government. The Governor General in Council entertains no doubt, that those funds may be raised without subjecting the Honourable Company to any considerable expense and without imposing a heavy tax on the inhabitants of Calcutta; – it will certainly be the duty of Government to contribute in a just proportion to any expense which may be requisite for the purpose of completing the improvements of the Town.

FOR WILLIAM
June 16th, 1803.
(Signed) WELLESLEY
(The Governor General in Council)

Notes

1 "Hindu Kalikashetra boasted of only two roads. One of these, with an avenue of trees at its sides, led eastwards from the zamindar's cutchery, which was at the site of the present Collectorate, to a ghat at the Adiganga, at its confluence with the Salt Water Lakes on the south of Sealdah, then called Srigaladwipa. The other, wider than this, was the immemorial Pilgrim Road to Kalighat, which was dignified by the British with the name of Broad Street, where it bounded their first Settlement." – A.K. Ray, *Calcutta Town and Suburbs: A Short History of Calcutta*, Census of India, Calcutta, 1901, p. 220.
2 See Ray, *Calcutta Town and Suburbs*, p. 157.
3 Ibid.
4 Beverley's, *Report on the Census of Calcutta*, 1876, p. 41.
5 Ray, *Calcutta Town and Suburbs*, p. 110. Calcutta's territorial dynamics got a boost twice in a hundred years' time. First in 1757 when by the secret treaty with Mir Jafar Khan when lands as far as Kulpi in the south near the sea was granted to the English. Then in 1857 when the "suburbs" of the city by Act XXI of 1857 "were defined to include all lands within the general limits of Panchannagram. It is important to remember that they included from the very beginning mauzas Dallanda, Dhaldanga, Sealdah, Serampore and parts of Kamapara and Simla, Dakhin Paikpara, bahir birji and Bahir Serampur." – Ibid.
6 See Ray, *Calcutta Town and Suburbs*, p. 158. Beverley's Report on the Census of Calcutta, 1876, p. 47.
7 To know more about this trade pattern, read Ashim Dasgupta, "Trade and Politics in 18th Century India", in D.S. Richards ed., *Islam and the Trade of Asia*, Oxford, 1971, p. 183.
8 "In the context of the developed bazaar economy of the 16th to 18th century it is possible to speak of a rough quadrilateral of trade – the two coasts and the two axes which connected the extremities of the coasts with the heart-land of imperial cities like Delhi and Agra. This hinterland was further connected with central Asian trade via Lahore and Kabul. Major Indian cities crowded round these routes and the hinterland of each felt the pull of the market to some extent. But this pull naturally disappeared after a point, as the cost of land transport became prohibitive. This interior India with its innumerable villages remained distinct from these other areas of trade and administration." – Pradip Sinha, *Calcutta in Urban History*, Firma KLM Private Ltd., Calcutta, 1978, Introduction, p. xvi.

THE CITY ASSUMES FORM

9 Alexander Hamilton, *A New Account of the East Indies*, 1727 cited in H.E.A. Cotton, *Calcutta, Old and New*, W. Newman & Co., Calcutta, 1907, pp. 5–10.
10 In the neighbourhood of the fort, two bazaars flourished in the eighteenth century – within one and a half kilometre was situated Dharmatala Bazaar just at the spot where the Town Hall stands today and within three kilometres that spot grew the Burra Bazaar. The slums of the minerals gradually raised their heads near the modern Chowringhee road and took the shape of crowded bazars. To the south of Dharmatala Bazaar there was another bazazr called the Govindapur Bazar which was later demolished.
11 Sealdah region was also called the Srigaladvipa.
12 Sinha, *Calcutta in Urban History*, p. 4.
13 Ibid, pp. 4–5.
14 Ibid, p. 5.
15 Marquis of Wellesley was the Governor General at this time.
16 "The First Report of the Special Committee for considering the Nuisances which exist throughout the Town of Calcutta and proposing the best means of removing them." Judicial Criminal Consultation No. 22 and 23 dated 31 August 1804 and 25 July 1805.
17 Ibid.
18 Ibid, 110.23.
19 Ibid.
20 Ibid.
21 Ibid. In the records The Committee for improving the Town of Calcutta has often been referred to as Town Improvement Committee, Town Committee, Special Committee, etc.
22 See Ray, *Calcutta Town and Suburbs*, pp. 161–162.
23 Judicial Criminal Consultation, No. 23, 25 July 1805.
24 Ibid.
25 Ghats were places with flights of stairs or general slopes on the ground by which people descended on the water of the river to take bath in the morning and afternoon and perform their religious rituals and other rites in the early morning and evening.
26 Ibid.
27 Ibid. For further details of Chandpal Ghat and Kootchagoody Ghat see Ray, *Calcutta Town and Suburbs*, p. 245.
28 Ibid. The tendency of the white men to build their own houses at the riverfront often created dislocations in building up thorough fares. This was one constraint from which it was difficult for Calcutta to recover.
29 Ibid. Koileghata was situated at the centre of the main business hub of Calcutta. Therefore, both crowd and commerce encroached upon this area making it less and less habitable.
30 Judicial Criminal Consultation No. 23, 25 July 1805.
31 Ibid.
32 The opinion of Mr. Taylor, the expert warehouse keeper was this: "I entirely concur in the observations made by the Spacial Committee on the state of remaining original Buildings of the Old Fort. It would be desirable that the whole of those buildings should be pulled down and a range of spacious Godowns erected in the room of them which from the great additional accommodation they would afford, would enable the Board of

EARLY FORMATIONS

Trade considerably to reduce the annual expense incurred for the hire of Godowns for the use of the Export and Import Warehouse Departments amounting on an average of the last three years, ending 30 April 1804 to nearly 12,000 Sicca Rupees per Annum." – Ibid.

The warehouse keeper further said: "For the reasons urged by the Committee I am of opinion that the Marine Paymaster's Office should be removed I think it proper however to state for the information of Government that the office in it's present situation being contiguous to the Bankshall, is extremely convenient to 150 Europeans and 70 Natives employed under the master attendant who receive their wages from the Marine Department." "The Marine Pay Office was purchased by Government in April 1788 for the sum of Sicca Rupees 10,000 and a further sum of Sicca Rupees 4000 was afterwards expended by Government in repairs and in building an additional upper room in the office." – Ibid.

33 Sinha, *Calcutta in Urban History*, p. 1.
34 R.W. Cox and S. Davis to the G.G. in Council, Fort William, 22 January 1805, Judicial Criminal Consultation, No. 25, 25 July 1805.
35 Ray, *Calcutta Town and Suburbs*, p. 198.
36 This picture of Calcutta was drawn by Lord Valentia who visited Calcutta in 1803 the year when Lord Wellesley's famous minutes were drawn. Lord Valentia's statement has been cited in Dr. P.C. Bagchi, ed., *The Second City of the Empire (The Twenty Fifth Session of the Indian Science Congress Association*, Calcutta, 1938, p. 42.
37 Ibid.
38 Milburn, *Oriental Commerce* (1813), Vol. 2, p. 1.
39 This racial division determining the morphology of a town was hallmark of urbanization in the colonial age. The Esplanade in Calcutta or Madras became the imposed buffer that separated the residence of rulers from the ghettos of the ruled. But in Calcutta the splendour of the white town was not an unmixed grandeur.
40 Griffin (pseu), *Sketches of Calcutta*, Edinburgh, 1843, p. 315.
41 See Appendix to this chapter under the title Lord Wellesley's Minute.
42 Among the early Governors whose labours in this direction are of a more systematic character may be mentioned the Marquis of Wellesley. He appointed a committee of experts, both Indian and Europeans, and their reports embodying schemes of reform exhibit the anxious care which the noble Marquis bestowed on its improvement. He opened the Government purse, and his attentions were early paid to the defects of the drainage system. It is worthwhile quoting here his own observations: " 'The defects of the climate of Calcutta during the latter part of the rainy seasons may, indeed, be ascribed in a great measure to the state of the drains and the watercourses, and to the stagnant water remaining in the town and its vicinity'. It was the desire of the noble Lord that 'India should be governed from a palace, not from a counting house, with the ideas of a prince, not with those of a retail dealer in muslin and indigo'. Governor Vansittart, Lord Clive, Governor Verelst, Governor Cartier and Governor General Hastings have also rendered services towards cleansing the town and making it wholesome and convenient." – Raja Binay Krishna Deb, *The Early History and Growth of Calcutta*, ed. Subir Ray Choudhuri, Rddhi, India, Calcutta, 1977, pp. 40–41.

THE CITY ASSUMES FORM

43 Cited in Ray, *Calcutta Town and Suburbs*, p. 152.
44 Ibid.
45 The expression is cited from Krishna Deb, *The Early History and Growth of Calcutta*, p. 38.
46 Ibid.
47 Cited in Krishna Deb, *The Early History and Growth of Calcutta*, pp. 38–39.
48 See Beverley's, *Report on the Census of Calcutta*, 1876, p. 41. Also see Ray, *Calcutta Town and Suburbs*, p. 156.
49 "The management of the town was, therefore, taken off his [zamindar's] hands, and in 1794, under a statute of George III, Justices of [the] Peace were appointed for the town and regular assessments authorised. The first assessment under the Act was made in 1795 by Mr. Mackay." –Ray, *Calcutta Town and Suburbs*, p. 156.
50 Ibid.
51 Seton Carr, *Selection from the Calcutta Gazette*, Vol. III, p. 37.
52 Ibid, p. 159.
53 Ray, *Calcutta Town and Suburbs*, p. 156.
54 Cited Ibid.

12

THE CITY IN HINDSIGHT
Some observations in conclusion

Calcutta's growth was a phased out development. From a territorially clustered village settlement its journey to a modern town was an event of chance – slow and unperceived at the outset but later quick as it picked up momentum since the end of the eighteenth century. The chanced victory of the English at the battle of Palasi truly ensured its destiny. Prior to that, about six decades since the purchase of the three villages of Sutanuti, Govindapur, and Kalikata, the English settlement at Calcutta had no territorial dynamism. The English had the permission to purchase thirty-eight villages around Calcutta. But it did not materialize because of the opposition of the Bengal *Nawabs*. The vigilance of the Bengal *Nawabs* put a cordon around it. Robbed of a chance of expansion, Calcutta had little prospect of growth. The Company's personnel lived in the fort, the nucleus of the town. Suffering from a crammed existence Calcutta's early fate was to grow as a garrison town. The fort had a small garrison essential both for defence of settlement and security of trade. Emerging out of a war with the Mughals (1686–1690) and the turmoil of a massive zamindari revolt (Shova Singh's revolt of 1696), the logic of a fort-based settlement never left the English mind.

The more the English became fort-centric the more they became suspect to the *Nawabs*. Four things made them objects of suspicion and finally accounted for Calcutta being under the *Nawabi* scanner. An island people, the English had a river inclination. To this they added a fort inclination as well. The Mughal rulers knew that they were weak at the sea. They also had the knowledge that stationed at Madras the English could move out to the sea with command. This had always scared the Mughals. When such people, redoubtable as they were with command at the sea, developed an inclination for forts and territory, they became suspect in the eyes of the rulers. This was Calcutta till the middle of the eighteenth century – a suspect territory that had little chance to develop itself.

THE CITY IN HINDSIGHT

The English were suspect because of many reasons. They claimed a jurisdiction which was contrary to Mughal Principles of governance. They imposed their own will and applied their own law in Calcutta. This practice was initiated by Job Charnock himself who ordered offenders to be lashed in the evening so that, it is said, their groans served to be the music of his dinner. As time went on, this practice gained momentum and the Company's authority claimed exclusive jurisdiction for their settlement in Calcutta. Residents in Calcutta were to be tried by their own laws and not by the laws of the government. This was opposed by the *Nawabs*. Subjects of the *Nawab* committing mischief in *Nawabi* territories escaped to Calcutta and got shelter there under the Company's authority. The Bengal *Nizamat* and the Company's government in Calcutta had always been at loggerheads on this issue, and their conflict since the time of Murshid Quli Khan cumulatively mounted to an open conflagration in the time of Siraj-ud-daullah over the custody of Krishnadas, alias Krishnaballabh, son of Raja Rajballabh of Dhaka, who fled to Calcutta with a huge amount of unauthorized wealth. Disapproving this, Siraj invaded Calcutta in 1756 and the English were routed. The Company's war with the Mughals in the years 1686–1690 was the second round of incidents when the English seemed to be on the path of war with the Mughals. In 1690, after the end of the war, the English were invited back into the Mughal territory of Bengal by the then Mughal Governor of the *Subah*. This time in 1756 they were driven out. The English entry back again into the city was forced through a war. This time the Mughals were routed. The defeat of the *Nawab* changed the status of Calcutta and inaugurated series of further changes that ensured Calcutta's rise to power. Calcutta became the station from where the English could coordinate the rise of the British Empire in India.

In Calcutta, the English combined a position of reality and vision. The reality was that the Company was a small assignee of revenue – a *talukdar* of three villages within the framework of Mughal system of governance. The vision was that their *taluk* was their property. From the beginning they construed it as their 'estate' where they could exercise their own authority. This conjured image of a possession had blurred Calcutta's constitutional position from the beginning. The result was that the *de facto* authority the English enjoyed and exercised in Calcutta was mostly appropriated and hence unauthorized. In order to defend its entitlement to this authority, the Company always needed to be in a state of preparedness for war. For this they required very urgently the defence of a fort. Immediately after the battle of Palasi their first duty was, therefore, to raise a new fort and

EARLY FORMATIONS

discard the old one. To this effect a new site was selected at the village Govindapur near Calcutta which was immediately vacated and its residents were transferred to Similia (later known as Simla) in north Calcutta. This was the first major case of mass transplant of population in Calcutta. This demographic resettlement was a prelude to a set of bigger changes in Calcutta. Three major institutions were installed in Calcutta in the aftermath of Palasi, which gave stability to the Company's regime in Calcutta and consolidated the Company's claim for an extra-territorial jurisdiction in the three villages in lower Bengal – Kalikata, Sutanuti, and Govindapur. These were the construction of the fort, the installation of the office of the Governor General, and the setting up of the Supreme Court – three major institutions of power in one city, Calcutta, and at one given time – the immediate aftermath of Palasi. From the 1770s, one may say, Calcutta began its career as an imperial city. With an imperial status newly acquired, Calcutta seemed to have no infrastructure. As a city it was really a bundle of inconsistencies and its inherent contradictions continued till the time of Hastings. The new Governor General was too busy in arranging the internal consolidation of power in Calcutta and coordinating from there the formation of the British possessions into a British Empire to make any planning of city improvement tangible in terms of contemporary requirements. The result was that, up till the time of Cornwallis, the city seemed to have been desperately trying to patch up its acquired imperial status and balance it with its sham infrastructural reality.

Students of the English rise to power in eastern India in the eighteenth century know that the conflict between the Company's authority in Calcutta and the *Nawab*'s government at Murshidabad blocked Calcutta's rise to power and its early colonial city formation up to the battle of Palasi. The English command over the sea with a powerful navy, their pretension to extra-territorial jurisdiction, their craze for a fort, and finally their lust for territory and commercial privileges were the four major factors which had always made the English suspect to the Bengal *Nawabs*. The English had cleverly extracted concessions on the acquisition of new territory and trade privileges from the Emperor of Delhi in 1717. They gained permission to purchase thirty-eight villages near Calcutta. The villages were spread on either side of the river. It meant that the English were planning to assume a pervasive influence on both sides of the river banks. If they could do it extra-territorial enclaves would be formed bordering on the *faujdari* of Hugli with Calcutta as their centre. The *Nawabs* always dreaded this. Therefore, they put barriers to all English efforts to acquire new territories anywhere in Bengal. Calcutta thus lost its territorial dynamism during the first six decades of its foundation by the English.

The Company's relations with the *Nawabs* grew out of antithetical adjustments. So did Calcutta's fate. The *Nawabs* fleeced the English whenever they were in need of money. This was because they were traders and had money. Contrary to fleecing they were also placated because they brought bullion to Bengal without which money could not be minted and Bengal's economy would run dry. The English were aware of this. Within the context of this relationship Calcutta and Murshidabad developed their cross-political adjustment. As early as the time of Murshid Quli Khan they engaged themselves in two serious adventures which made Calcutta all the more suspect to the *Nawabs*. They tried to build a more formidable structure in the site of the present fort. This was promptly thwarted by Murshid Quli Khan. Parallel to this they consolidated their own jurisdiction by setting up the Mayor's Court in 1726. With the fort and the Court operating together as units of exclusive existence, Calcutta became, much to the annoyance of the *Nawabs*, an enclave of the English outside the structure of Mughal governance in Bengal. The Mayor's Court continued till 1774 when it was taken over by the Supreme Court of Judicature that had of late come into existence.

By the time the Maratha invasions took place in Bengal in the 1740s Calcutta had become a consolidated zone resembling a sanctuary. People in distress took shelter there and its population increased. Calcutta could be considered now as one of the most important military strongholds in south Bengal. It was likely, therefore, that men of Calcutta and around had begun to repose faith on the English and accommodate the city in their confidence. Calcutta was now slowly emerging out of its garrison status. It had begun to gain political importance. Krishnaballabh's flight to Calcutta in 1756 was a milestone toward this. As an asylum of a fugitive, Calcutta now assumed a kind of political importance. It was a new reality for Calcutta. The city was now considered as an alternative seat of power by those who went for defection in the *Nawabi* camp and joined the English in a conspiratorial alliance before Palasi. Political gravity now seemed to have been slowly shifting to Calcutta.

From the beginning the English in Calcutta had a set of ambitions to fulfil. These were an accession to mint (which they got in 1757), a fort, compact territories of villages, trade privileges and extra-territorial jurisdiction in the form of imposing their own law in dealing with natives who otherwise were subjects of the *Nawabs*. All this was tantamount to claiming an entitlement to autonomy for Calcutta. Many new things happened now which helped Calcutta's rise to prominence. First, Clive on his way to Calcutta bombarded Hugli and Chandernagore, thus disabling the prospective Mughal-French alliance in a moment of crisis for the Mughals. This also destroyed the capacity of the two cities to rise ever as competitors of Calcutta. The status of Calcutta was also now changed. For so long, its status was that of a purchased city based on the grant of the Emperor. Now it added a new feather to its status. It was a conquered city – a spot where the *Nawab* was made to surrender to the English. In many ways it had anticipated the bigger Mughal surrender at the battle of Buxar in 1764 where the combined army of the Emperor and the two *Nawabs* of Bengal and Awadh surrendered to the English. The whole movement was manoeuvred from Calcutta. Between Clive's victory in Calcutta in early 1757 and the English victory at Buxar in 1764, there took place the battle of Palasi where a chance victory changed the status of Calcutta. In the treaty of Alinagar (Calcutta was renamed by Siruddaullah in 1756 as Alinagar), a defeated *Nawab* surrendered many marks of sovereignty to the English. The English now achieved an accession to mint. This *de facto* authority over currency making gave Calcutta a new boost. Within three months' time, after the battle of Palasi, the English gained access to territories as far as Kulpi, near the sea in the south. This was a concession the English gained because of their participation in the conspiracy against the *Nawab*. This lifted the brake on Calcutta's territorial space for expansion. Immediately after the battle of Palasi a new fort was constructed. This completed the status of Calcutta as a garrison town. This positioning of Calcutta as a military station provided new benefits to Calcutta in the long run. After the battle of Buxar the Mughal army that guarded the eastern flank of the Mughal Empire was crushed. In the vacuum that was created a militarily upgraded Calcutta stepped in. This helped Calcutta to emerge as the arbiter of the post Mughal situations in the east.

The coming of Krishnadas to Calcutta was important. It signalled the alliance between the English on the one hand and the country's power elite on the other. From this point onward started Calcutta's defiance of Murshidabad which was both political and constitutional. This defiance became an institution after the battle of Palasi when the English changed the protocol of addressing to the *Nawab*. Previously the governor of Calcutta as the authority of the Fort William Council or any of his agent operating through the Resident at the *durbar* met the *Nawab* at Murshidabad. Now the *Nawab* had to come down to Calcutta to meet the governor and his council members in Calcutta. Later Calcutta's defiance changed its target. From the *Nawab*

THE CITY IN HINDSIGHT

the Governor General in Calcutta – Hastings – turned his attention to the Emperor whose annual tribute he stopped. Thus one of the most unconstitutional events took place in order to boost up Calcutta's imperial arrogance to the point of defying the apex imperial authority in the country.

Hastings placed Calcutta in an all-India perspective of power. His participation in the First Anglo-Maratha war, his Rohila war, his treatment of Chait Singh of Benaras and the Begams of Awadh, and finally his tribute-defiance of the Emperor all made Calcutta a station of concern for everyone who either contested to be the successor of the Mughal Empire or wanted to remain as a sovereign splinter of that fractured overarching structure. Positioning Calcutta in power was a mammoth job and, being engrossed with it, the new Governor General did not get much time to rivet his attention to town planning.

Yet remarkable things happened in the process of town development. After the battle of Palasi the Company's officers influenced by the newly acquired confidence of victory over the *Nawab* moved out of their clustered existence in the fort. The age of Clive and Hastings in Calcutta saw Englishmen spreading out into the sprawling zone of Chowringhee. English residences began to grow along this new axis beyond the rampart of the fort. This was the new civil line that had grown up about this time. As this had happened the English officers, merchants and people of rank and file became accustomed to new ways of life fashioned after the leisurely styles of the orient. They became accustomed to domestic service offered by Indians. Cheap labour and its abundant supply transformed the European life in Calcutta. This was the beginning of the appearance of what was later called "nabobs" – Englishmen free of occidental rigours, rich with oriental wealth, and given unmistakably to the luxurious comfort of leisure.

From the middle of the eighteenth century conversion from mud hut to brick-building started in Calcutta. Calcutta was very much afflicted with fire and pests – rants and white ants. Naturally the trend was ushered in that clay structures had to be substituted by brick structure. Two things happened in consequence. Brick kilns developed around Calcutta and jungles began to be cleared in the city proper so that kilns could be provided with wood as fuel. There was so much demand for wood in the kilns that domestic supply of wood became short, creating an uproar in the European households. As jungles were cleared, new space was available within the city providing scope for house-building and real estate growth. Calcutta developed as a security zone – the greatest, perhaps, in south Bengal. This was also the time when there was a colossal rise in banditry in Bengal. Those in the interior who had wealth and a stable family and whose invariable practice it was to bury their wealth for safety began to migrate to the city. As a result, the native sector of the town, technically called the "Black Town" in the north, swelled with population and became congested. Slavetrade was still in vogue. The lifting and kidnapping of young girls and boys was a common practice. To escape this horror many solvent families left their home and hearth in the districts and settled in Calcutta and its immediate neighbourhood. This process of migration doubly benefited Calcutta. Because of the rise in population, the Company's revenue increased. With the coming of rich families, the wealth so long accumulated into the interior now found its way to Calcutta. In next seventy years' time, so much wealth poured in Calcutta that, toward the end of the first quarter of the nineteenth century, Calcutta was considered to be the abode of Lakshmi – *Kalikata Kamalaya* – by Bhabani Charan Bandyopadhyay. Toward the building of this wealth, much was also contributed by the *banians* who traded with foreign Companies and acted as the liaison men of private European traders and amassed conspicuous wealth out of their business, particularly their connections with men of power. After the battle Palasi, another new trend was seen in Calcutta. *Zamindars* in the interior began to deposit their wealth in Calcutta. Calcutta now became the focus of the interior. This elevation of Calcutta was surely the achievement of the Clive-Hastings regime that spanned nearly three decades after the battle of Palasi.

The geopolitical elevation of the city did not necessarily mean that the city was also keeping up morphologically. During the first twenty years since the battle of Palasi, the thrust of the Company's city planning was renovation and not innovation and new construction. Ramshackle structures, shades, barracks, godowns, storehouses factories, and the like which had become dilapidated or worn-out were sought to be either overhauled or substituted by alternative accommodations. The Company's administration in Calcutta always received instructions from the home government advising them to be frugal. Operating under a ban from superiors, the Calcutta administration practised economy and all planning for constructive improvement was set aside as extravagant. One may say that the Clive-Hastings phase of Calcutta's growth was broadly a phase of transformation. It was a period of Calcutta's geopolitical elevation. Only in the nineties of the eighteenth century was it was realized that the morphological growth of Calcutta did not match its geopolitical elevation. Then attention was paid to town planning. It was a turn to a new direction for which money was needed. The city's boundary was not yet determined. It was to be done

THE CITY IN HINDSIGHT

on the basis of an urgent necessity. After the digging of the Maratha ditch in 1742, it became the fashion to describe it as the boundary of Calcutta. Later on the Maratha ditch was filled up and along its axis the Circular road was constructed. By a proclamation of 1794, the inner side of the Maratha ditch was declared to be the boundary of Calcutta. The previous year, in 1793, the system of public lottery was instituted for public improvement. Thus a new phase began. From the proclamation of 1793 to Wellesley's Minute of 1803, one may say, the real phase of town planning for Calcutta started.

The massive spate of building construction in the city took place since the time of Wellesley. It means that Calcutta's take-off started with the turn of the nineteenth century. Prior to that situation in Calcutta was not conducive for urban construction. The Company itself was in financial crisis. There was famine in 1770 and also in the middle of 1780s. Calcutta was also affected by famine. Moreover there was a dearth of building materials. *Chunum* had to be brought from distant places like Sylhet. The supply of soil to brick kilns was also a factor. Random and clandestine digging of soil was destroying the face of the earth around Calcutta. Up to the beginning of Hastings' rule the major supply of brick and labour went for the construction of the fort. Poaching of labour for private construction was not, of course, uncommon. But none could thwart the irresistible pull with which the fort had drawn labour and building materials to its site. The work of fort construction was so vast that at one point the Company's authorities in Calcutta requisitioned masons and bricklayers from England. The labour force necessary for construction was drawn from among the peasants. After the famine of 1770, one-third of the population in Bengal died and one-third of the arable land returned to the jungle. As a result, agriculture suffered. It was difficult to procure men from the interior who would work as construction labours in the city. This was one reason why city construction did not take off in the second half of the eighteenth century. Secondly, there was paucity of public funds which could be invested in the construction of the city. The East India Company itself solicited loan from the Parliament and there was talk in England that those at the helm of affairs in Calcutta and the districts had squandered money. There was a picture of spoliation everywhere. The profits of the "Plassey Plunder" – the huge money extracted from the *Nawabs* – enriched officers allowing them to grow as owners of private wealth. This spoliation was the event of the Clive-Hastings regime. In this phase Calcutta's urbanity suffered. Every English house needed domestic labour. Every English officer was surrounded by service attendants. These men lived in the slums that grew behind the residences of the Europeans in the White Town. A big "cooli bazaar" grew near the fort itself. Streets had not been developed and no drainage system was there to keep the city free of filth. The city ambience of Calcutta was yet to grow under active government patronage. That patronage came only under Lord Wellesley. As a preparatory to that, preliminary works like boundary fixation and fund-raising through lottery were done under Cornwallis. That much only was the city achievement. A capital city with bare infrastructure: that was Calcutta in the eighteenth century.

In 1789 one observer, Grandpre, noted that the "roads were merely made of earth; the drains were ditches between the houses, and the sides of the road, the receptacles of all manner of abomination."[1] "Even in 1803," A.K. Ray observes, "the streets in the 'Blacktown' as the Indian portion of the town was called, were, according to Lord Valentia, narrow and dirty and the houses generally of mud and thatch."[2] There was no sign of take off before 1803 when Lord Wellesley declared that Calcutta was to be improved so as to suit the majesty of an empire. "We have it, however, on the authority of Mr. H.E. Shakespear, that up to 1820, the improvements sanctioned by the Government had not been carried into effect, and the streets were, with four or five exceptions, kutcha, and the drains mere excavation by the roadside."[3] The real improvement of the town began with the coming into force of the system of lotteries. Although started in 1793 nothing much was achieved from the lottery fund till 1805. Some important works were executed by lotteries between 1805 and 1817. Finally, in 1817, the Lottery Committee was appointed and the balance of the previous seventeen lotteries was made over to it. The Lottery Committee existed till 1836. During these twenty years, tangible benefit was accrued to the city. A.K. Ray says that "the town improvements ceased with the abolition of the Lotteries." And then "with the establishment of the Corporation of the Justices in 1871, under Act VI of that year, a fresh era of Town improvements dawned, and streets, lanes, tanks, landing and bathing ghats, drains, markets, houses and all other matters connected with the sanitation and ornamentation of the metropolis obtained considerable attention."[4]

Given this, it is clear that the urbanization of Calcutta was essentially a phenomenon of the nineteenth century. Its eighteenth century career was one of mixed developments. The first sixty years of its foundation were absolutely non-dynamic. It experienced a geopolitical elevation in the aftermath of the Palasi. But then its city formation did not match its political rise. There was little government patronage for town-building during this period. The major concern for town-building came when the fort gave security to the settlement. Business within and outside the city increased. The need for boundary demarcation was felt. Means were devised to raise money for civil construction. What was now needed was the political will which would spur visions into action. This came early in the nineteenth century, in 1803, with the minutes of Lord Wellesley. With the political will taking shape Calcutta now set in for its destination to be the second city of the Empire – the city of palaces in the east. Under Hastings, Calcutta began her career as the capital of the British Empire. Under Lord Wellesley, she became enthroned, assuming the imperial majesty of a capital.

Notes

1 Cited by A.K. Roy, *Calcutta Town and Suburbs: A Short History of Calcutta*, Census of India, Calcutta, 1901, p. 221.
2 Ibid.
3 Ibid.
4 Ibid, pp. 221–222.

BIBLIOGRAPHY

In addition to the books, documents, Journals, periodicals, newspapers, essays and articles mentioned in the text and the notes of the book the following bibliography is given for further information, perspectives and perceptions in the subject.

Part I : Original Sources

I. Persian Sources
II. Official Records
III. Miscellaneous official Literature
IV. Miscellaneous Books
V. Literature Relevant to 18th Century Calcutta
VI. Censuses
VII. Maps.
VIII. Documents & Reports
IX. Official Manuscript Records

Part II : Secondary Sources

X. Books
XI. Journals & News Papers.
XII. Articles.
XIII. Bibliographical Supports.

Primary sources

I. Persian literature available in English

These books are important for building up the perception of European Settlements vis-à-vis the *Nawabi* rule in Bengal. These books also give us an insight into the nature of Mughal rule when the Europeans were planning their adventures in the east. They are required for background studies.+

BIBLIOGRAPHY

Abul Fadl. *Ain-i-Akbari*, Vol. I, translated by M. Blochman, 2nd edition, revised by D.C. Phillott, Bibliotheca Indica, Calcutta, 1939, Vols. II & III, translated by H.S. Jarrett: Revised and further annotated by Sir Jadu Nath Sarkar in 1949 and 1948 respectively in Bib. Ind. Text ed. by H. Blochmann and published in Bib. Ind. Series (1867–77).

Azad-al-Husaini [translated and ed. Jadunath Sarkar]. *Naubahari-i-Murshid Quli Khani* available in Jadunath Sarkar's *Bengal Nawabs*, Calcutta, 1952.

Calendar of Persian Correspondence, Being Letters Which Passed Between Some of the Company's Servants and Indian Rulers and Notables, Vols. I-X.

Datta, K.K., ed. *Some Firmans, Sanads and Parwanas* (1578–1802 A.D.), Patna, 1962.

Farishta, M.Q. [translated by Jonathan Scot]. *History of the Dekkan and the History of Bengal from the Accession of Aliverdee Khan to the Year 1780*, 2 Vols. 1794.

Ghulam Hussain Khan, Sayid. *Seir-ul-Mutaqharin*, Calcutta, 1789, 3 vols.

Karam Ali [translated and ed. Jadu Nath Sarkar]. *Muzaffarnamah* available in Jadu Nath Sarkar's *Bengal Nawabs*, Calcutta, 1952.

Salim, Ghulam Hussain [translated by Abdus Salam]. *Riyaz-us-Salatin* [Bib. Ind. Series] Asiatic Society Press, Calcutta, 1902.

Salimullah [translated by Francis Gladwin]. *Tarikh-i-Bangla* available in *A Narrative of Transactions in Bengal etc*, Bangabasi Press, Calcutta, 1906.

Saqi Must'ad Khan [translated and annotated by Jadu Nath Sarkar]. *Maasir-I-Alamgiri A History of The Emperor Aurangzib-Alaamgiri*, Bib. Ind. Work No. 269, Royal Asiatic Society of Bengal, 1947.

II. Miscellaneous official and semi-official literature available in English

These Records and Literature provide us with the information about the status of Calcutta in the eighteenth century.

Aitchison, C.U. *A Collection of Treaties, Engagements and Sanads (Vols. I. & II)*, Calcutta, 1930.

Broome, Ralph Esq. *An Elucidation of the Articles of Impeachment Preferred by the Last Parliament Against Warren Hastings, Esq. Late Governor General of Bengal*, London, 1790.

Clarke, R. *The Regulations of the Government of the Fort William*, 3 Vols., London, 1853. *The Regulations of the Bengal Government respecting Zemindary and Lakharaj Property*, London, 1840.

Fort William – India House Correspondence, Vols. I-VI & IX.

Guha, Ranajit and A. Mitra. *West Bengal District Records: New Series: Burdwan* (Letters issued 1782–1800).

History of Police Organisation in India and Indian Village Police Being Select Chapters of the Report of the Indian Police Commission, for 1902–03 Published by the University of Calcutta. 1913. [Along with this book

one must read Ranjit Sen, *Social Banditry in Bengal: A Study in Primary Resistance* and Basudeb Chattapadhyay, *Crime and Control in Early Colonial Bengal*].
Hunter, W.W. *Bengal Manuscript Records*, Vols. I & II, London, 1894.
Long, Rev J. *Selections from the Unpublished Records of Government from 1748–1767 inclusive*, Calcutta, 1869. [The 2nd edition of the book has been ed. Mahadeva Prosad Saha, Firma K.L. Mukhopadhyay, Calcutta, 1973].
Marshall, P.J. *Problems of Empire: Britain and India, 1757–1813*, London, 1968. *Minutes of the Evidence Taken at the Trial of Warren Hastings (1788–94)*, Vol. I.
Orme, R. *Historical Fragments of the Mughal Empire*, London, 1805.
Sengupta, J.C. and Sanat Bose eds. *West Bengal District Records: New Series: Midnapore Letters Received 1777–1800*. [Published by the office of the Superintendent of Census Operations West Bengal and Sikkim, 1962].

III. Miscellaneous books and literature in English published in the eighteenth century

These books build up the eighteenth century perspective of Calcutta study. [Contemporary and near-contemporary literature has been considered as primary in the present book]

Bolts, W. *Considerations on Indian Affairs*, London, 1772–1775.
Boughton Rous, C.W. *Dissertation Concerning the Landed Property of Bengal*, London, 1791.
Broome, Ralph, Esq. *An Elucidation of the Articles of Impeachment Preferred by the Last Parliament Against Warren Hastings, Esq., Late Governor-General of Bengal*, London, 1790.
Cornwallis, Lord. *Minutes dated 18 September 1789 and 3 February, 1790* [Firminger ed. *Fifth Report*, Vol. II, pp. 510–515 and pp. 527–550].
Craufurd, R. *Sketches Chiefly Relating to the History, Religion, Learning and Manners of the Hindus*, London, 1790.
Grant, James. *Analysis of the Finances of Bengal* [Firminger ed. *Fifth Report*, Vol. II, appendix 4] *An Inquiry into the Nature of Zemindarry Tenures in the Landed Property of Bengal*, London, 1791.
Gross, T. *Voyage to the East Indies*, 2 vols., London, 1772.
Hamilton, A. *A New Account of the East Indies*, 2 vols [Edinburgh, 1773] ed. W. Foster, London, 1930.
Hastings, W. *Hastings' Review of the State of Bengal*, London, 1786. *Minutes of the Evidence Taken at the Trial of Warren Hastings, 1788–94*, Vol. I.
Hodges, W. *Travels in India 1780–1783*, 2nd edition, London, 1794.
Holwell, J.Z. *India Tracts*, 3rd edition, 1774. *Interesting Historical Events . . . Etc.* Calcutta, 1772.
Keir, A. *Thoughts on the Affairs of Bengal*, 1772.

BIBLIOGRAPHY

Scrafton, L., *Reflections on the Government of Indostan etc*, London, 1763. [Reprinted in Calcutta under the title *A History of Bengal Before and After the Plassey* (1739–1753), Calcutta, 1975].

Vansittart, H. *A Narrative of the Transactions in Bengal* [3 vols., London, 1766] ed. by Anil Chandra Bandyopadhyay and Bimal Chandra Ghosh, Calcutta, 1976.

Verelst, H. *A View of the Rise, Progress and Present State of the English Government in Bengal*, London, 1772.

Watts, W. *Memories of the Revolutions in Bengal*, 1760.

IV. Literature relevant to 18th century Calcutta

Cornwallis, Lord. *Minute* [on the Permanent Settlement] *Dated 18th September*, 1789. [Firminger ed. *Fifth Report*, Vol. II, pp. 510–515].

———. *Minute Dated 3rd February, 1790 [Extract Bengal Revenue Consultations 10 February, 1790]*. [Firminger ed. *Fifth Report*, Vol. II, pp. 527–550].

Firminger, Ven Walter Kelly, ed. *The Fifth Report from the Select Committee of the House of Commons on the Affairs of the East India Company Dated 28 July, 1812*.

———. Vol. I. *Introduction and Text of Report*, Calcutta, 1917.

———. Vol. II. *Introduction and Bengal Appendices*, Calcutta, 1917.

———. Vol. III. *British Acquisitions in the Presidency of Fort St. George, Madras Appendices, Wilkins' Glossary and Index*, Calcutta, 1918.

———. ed. [*Affairs of the East India Company (Being the Fifth Report from the Select Committee of the House of Commons 28th July, 1812)*, Vol. II, Neeraj Publishing House, New Delhi (First Published 1812), Reprinted 1984. The present edition is a reprint from the 19th edition, Vols. I-III are available].

———. ed. *Historical Introduction to the Bengal Portion of the Fifth Report*, Indian Studies Past & Present, Reprinted, Calcutta, 1962.

Shore, John. *Minute dated 18 June 1789, Respecting the Permanent Settlement of the Lands in the Bengal Provinces* [Firminger ed. *Fifth Report*, Vol. II, pp. 1–145].

———. *Minute on the Permanent Settlement of the Lands in Bengal and Proposed Resolutions Thereon*, 18th September, 1789. [Firminger ed. *Fifth Report*, Vol. II, pp. 478–510].

———. *The 2nd Minute, 21st December, 1789 [Extract Bengal Revenue Consultation 21 December, 1789]*. [Firminger ed. *Fifth Report*, Vol. II, pp. 518–527]

———. *Minute dated 12 March 1787*. [Firminger ed. *Fifth Report*, Vol. II, pp. 737–752].

V. Censuses

Census in India 1901, Vol. VII: *Calcutta Town and Suburbs*, Part III, *Tabular Statistics* by J.R. Blackwood (Calcutta: Bengal Secretariat Press, 1902). Censuses of 1872, 1881, 1891 & 1901.

BIBLIOGRAPHY

Census of 1921 *Report on the City of Calcutta*.
'The Population of Calcutta', *Government Gazette*, 8 August 1822; reprinted in Alok Ray, *Nineteenth Century Studies* (Calcutta: Bibliographical Research Centre, 1974).
Report on the Census of Bengal, 1872 by H. Beverly (Calcutta: Bengal Secretariat Press, 1872).
Report on the Census of Calcutta, 1866 by A.M. Dowleans (Calcutta: Thacker, Spink & Co., 1866).
Report of the Census of the Town of Calcutta, Taken on the 6th April, 1876 by H. Beverly (Calcutta: Bengal Secretariat Press, 1876).
Report on the Census of the Town and Suburbs of Calcutta, Taken on the 17th February 1881 by H. Beverly (Calcutta: Benal Secretariat Press, 1881).
Report on the Survey of Calcutta C.E. Consulting Engineer to the Government of India and Director of the Railway Department, Dated 14th August 1850 by F.W. Simms (Calcutta: Military Orphan Press, 1851).
A Short History of Calcutta, Town and Suburbs, Census of India, 1901, Vol. VII, Part 1, by A.K. Ray (1902; reprint, Calcutta: Rddhi India, 1982).

VI. Documents & reports

Administrative Report of the Calcutta Municipality, 1867–1920.
Administrative Report of the Municipality of the Suburbs of Calcutta, 1869–1880. *Annual Report on Architectural Work in India*, 1909–1921.
Barra Bazar Improvement, A Report by Patrick Geddes (Calcutta: Corporation Press, 1919).
Chakravarti, Adhir, ed. *Archives Week Celebrations*, 29 March–4 April 1990: *Glimpses of Old Calcutta* (Calcutta: State Archives of West Bengal, 1990).
———. *List of Documents on Calcutta*, Vol. I: 1764–1800 (Calcutta: State Archives of West Bengal, 1990).
———. *Change and Continuity: Focus on Facts, Calcutta Tercentenary Exhibition* (Calcutta: State Archives of West Bengal, 1991).
First Report on the Drainage and Sewerage of Calcutta (Calcutta: Military Orphan Press, 1858).
Hirst, F.C. *A Brief History of the Large Scale Surveys of Calcutta and Its Neighbourhood 1903–1914 and 1926–27* (Alipore, Bengal: Bengal Government Press, 1939).
Lottery Committee Proceedings, 1817–1821, three bound volumes (manuscript) (Calcutta: Victoria Memorial Hall).
Nicholls, C.G. *Field Book of Survey of a Part of Calcutta* (manuscript) (Calcutta: National Library, 1809).
Report of the Calcutta Building Commission (Calcutta: Government of Bengal, 1897).
Report of the Commissioners for the Improvement of the Town of Calcutta, 1848–1862.
Report on the Drainage and Conservancy of Calcutta by David B. Smith (Calcutta: Bengal Secretariat Press, 1869).

BIBLIOGRAPHY

Report of the Committee Appointed by the Government of Bengal to Prepare a Scheme for the Amalgamation of the Town of Calcutta with the Urban Portions of the Suburbs (Calcutta: Bengal Secretariat Press, 1885).
Statistical and Geographical Report of the 24-Pergunnahs District by Maj. Ralph Smyth (Calcutta: 'Calcutta Gazette' Office, 1857).

VII. Contemporary newspapers and journals

Chaudhury, Pradip and Abhijit Mukhopadhyay. eds. *Calcutta: People and Empire, Gleanings from old Journals* (Calcutta: India Book Exchange, 1975).
Das, Satyajit, ed. *Selections from the Indian Journals*, 2 vols (selections from James Silk Buckingham's *Calcutta Journals*) (Calcutta: FirmaKLM, 1965).
Moitra, Suresh Chandra, ed. *Selections from Jnanannesan* (Calcutta: Prajna, 1979).
Nair, P. Thankappan, et al. eds. *The Calcutta Municipal Gazette, Anthology Number, 1924–1947* (Calcutta: Municipal Corporation, 1990).
Ray, Alok, ed. *Nineteenth Century Studies* (Calcutta: Bibliographical Research Centre, 1974).
———. *Calcutta Keepsake* (Calcutta: Rddhi India, 1978).
Ray Chaudhury, Ranabir, ed. *Glimpses of Old Calcutta* (selections from The Englishman, Calcutta courier, etc.) (Bombay: Nichiketa, 1978).
———. *Calcutta a Hundred Years Ago* (selections from The Statesman and Friend of India) (Calcutta: Nachiketa, 1987).

VIII. Bibliographical supports

Calcutta 1690–1900, A Bibliography (Calcutta: National Library, 1967, 1982).
Nair, P. Thankappan. *Calcutta Tercentenary Bibliography*, 2 vols. (Calcutta: Firma KLM, 1993).
Sutcliffe, Anthony. *The History of Urban and Regional Planning, An Annotated Bibliography* (London: Mansell, 1981).

X. Maps of Bengal in the eighteenth century now available in the national library, Calcutta with their call numbers

A General map from the Ganges to Dacca; being a continuation of route from Jaynagore & Hobbygunge. [no place no pub.] [1765] map (fold)
Scale: 1" to 1 mile, or, 1:63, 360, Inset: Iddyrackpore. M.P. 386. 3/G 286.
India Office of the Surveyor General, Calcutta.
Plan of Calcutta, reduced by permission of the commissioners of police from the original one executed for them by Lieut. Col. Mark Wood in the year 1784 & 1785, Calcutta, Wm. Baillie, 1792, map, Scale : 1" to 800 ft.

BIBLIOGRAPHY

Facsimile plan of Calcutta in the years 1784–85 from an old print in the possession of the Record Commission.
M.P. 954. 15 in 2 pl.
Plaisted, Bartholomew and Ritchie, John, Survr.
A chart of the northern part of the Bay of Bengal [Calcutta], [no pub.], 1772. Map. (fold), Scale; not mentioned. Graduated & engraved by B. Henry. The writing engraved by Whitchurch. Pub. According to Act of Parliament, the 15th September by Alexander Dalrymple.
M.P. 954.1/P 691.
Plaisted, Bartholomew
A Survey of the coast of Chittagag and the river up to Dacca [Chittagang], 1761. Map (part col. Fold.) Scale not mentioned
M.P. 954. 923/P 691.
Plan for the intelligence of the military operations at Calcutta, when attacked and taken by Seerajah Dowlet, 1756. [no place, no pub.] [n.d.] map. Scale not mentioned.
M.P. 954.15/P 692.
Rennell, James. A Bengal atlas: containing maps of the theatre of war and commerce on that side of Hindoostan. Compiled from the original surveys. Calcutta, Court of Directors for East India Company, 1781. 22 maps (part col.) Scale-vary.
M.P. 954. 15/R 294 b
Rennell, James. A general map of part of the Kingdom of Bengall; constructed chiefly from observations made during the course of several surveys.
Calcutta, John Spencer, 1765, map.
Scale : 1" to 20 miles; or 1: 12,67200
M.P. 954–15/R 294
Rennell, James. A map of part of the Kingdom of Bengall, drawn from Surveys made in the year 1762 & 1763. [no place, no pub., n.d.] map (Rennell's collections)
Scale: 30 miles ½ a degree M.P. 351.
Rennell, James. A map; showing the extent of the Late Survey, and its situation with respect to Calcutta likewise a general sketch of the Creeks from the reports of some European passangers and the courtry people; also a comparison of part of M.D. Anville's accurate map with the truth from A to B the extent of the survey. [no place, no pub.], 1764. Map (2 sheets)
Scale: 1" to 10 miles; or 1: 63,3600.
M.P. 954.15/R 294 gan
Upjohn, A. Map of Calcutta and its environs; from an accurate survey taken in the years 1792 and 1793. Calcutta, map. [n.d.] Scale 1" to 1400 ft. (approx.), or 1: 16,900
M.P. 954.15/Up 4
Maps available outside National Library, Calcutta.
Mapping Calcutta: The Collection of Maps at the Visual Archives of the Centre for Studies in Social Sciences (Calcutta: Centre for Studies in Social Sciences, 2009).

BIBLIOGRAPHY

X. Official records available at the west Bengal state archives, Calcutta which help build up the perspective of the formation and growth of Calcutta

Proceedings of the Select Committee at Fort William in Bengal 1752–1770. A calendar of the proceedings for 1752, 1766, 1767 and 1770 is available in print.
Letters to the Court of Directors and *Letters from the Court* (Available in 3 vols.) *Proceedings of the Calcutta Committee of Revenue Volume III, Part I* 6th December 1773–28 December, 1775, *Volume III, Part II.*
2nd January 1776–29th December, 1777, *Volume III, Part III.*
5th January–30th December, 1778, *Volume III, Part IV.*
2nd January–30th December, 1779, *Volume III, Part V.*
3rd January–31st August, 1780 & 4th January, 1781.
Selections from Calcutta Gazette of the year 1784 to 1823 [National Library, Calcutta, Call Number (hereafter referred as NLCN) G.P. 954/C 126 gs *Calendar of Persian Correspondence* (NLCN) G.P. 954/In 2nac
James Long. *Selections from Unpublished Records of Government of India for the Years 1748–1767 with a Map of Calcutta in 1784* (NLCN) G.P. 954. 15/L 852.

Secondary sources

XI. Articles

Archer, John (2000), 'Paras, Palaces, Pathogens: Framework for the Growth of Calcutta, 1800–1850', *City and Society*, No. 12, 1.
Arnold, David (1986), 'Cholera and Colonialism in British India', *Past and Present*, No. 113, November.
Basu, Debashish (1986b, 1987, 1988), 'Sahor Kolkatar Path Naam, Samajik Itihaser Ekti Sutro', *Ekshan*, No. 6, 1–2, 3–4.
Bompas, C.H. (1927), 'The Work of the Calcutta Improvement Trust', *Journal of the Royal Society of Arts*, No. 75, 7 January.
Bose, Amritlal ([1928 and 1990), 'Calcutta As I Knew It Once: Tales of a Grandfather', *Calcutta Municipal Gazette*; reprinted in P. Thankappan Nair et al., eds., *The Calcutta Municipal Gazette, Anthology Number, 1924–1947* (Calcutta: Municipal Corporation).
Bysack, Gaur Das ([1891 and 1978), 'Kalighat and Calcutta', *Calcutta Review*, April; reprinted in Alok Ray, ed., *Calcutta Keepsake* (Calcutta: Rddhi India).
Cohen, A. (1998), 'Jewish Settlement in Calcutta Completes 200 Years', *The Asian Age*, August.
Dasgupta, J.N. (1917), 'Wellesley's Scheme for the Improvement of Calcutta', *Bengal Past and Present*, XV, No. 29–30, July–December.

BIBLIOGRAPHY

Datta, Sudhin (1957), 'The World's Cities: Calcutta', *Encounter*, No. VIII, 6.

Dowleans, Baron ([1860] 1975), 'Calcutta in 1860', *Calcutta Review*, 34, 68; reprinted in Pradip Chaudhury and Abhijit Mukhopadhyay, eds., *Calcutta: People and Empire, Gleanings from Old Journals* (Calcutta India Book Exchange).

'Echoes From Old Chandernagore', *Bengal Past and Present*, No. II, July 1908.

Emerson, T. (1924), 'The Central Avenue: Calcutta's New Thoroughfare', *Bengal Past and Present*, No. XXVII, Part 1, 53, January–March.

Farooqui, Amar (1996), 'Urban Development in a Colonial Situation: Early Nineteenth Century Bombay', *Economic and Political Weekly*, No. XXXI, 40, October.

Finch, Cuthbert (1850), 'Vital Statistics of Calcutta', *Quarterly Journal of the Royal Statistical Society of London*, 13 May.

Geddes, Patrick (1919), 'The Temple Cities', *The Modern Review*, No. XXV, 3 March.

Gupta, Samita (1993), 'Theory and Practice of Town Planning in Calcutta 1817 to 1912: An Apprisal', *Indian Economic and Social History Review*, No. 30, 1, January–March.

Home, R.K. (1990), 'Town Planning and Garden Cities in the British Colonial Empire 1910–1940', *Planning Perspectives*, No. 5, 1 January.

Hornsby, Stephen J. (1997), 'Discovering the Mercantile City in South Asia: The Example of Early Nineteenth-Century Calcutta', *Journal of Historical Geography*, No. 23, 2.

Hossain, Syeed (1908), 'Slavery Days in Old Calcutta', *Bengal Past and Present*, No. II, July.

Kalpagam, U. (1995), 'Cartography in Colonial India', *Economic and Political Weekly*, No. 30, 30, 29 July.

King, Anthony D. (1995), 'Writing Colonial Space, A Review Article', *Comparative Studies in Society and History*, No. 37, 3, July.

Kosambi, Meera and John E. Brush (1988a), 'Three Colonial Port Cities in India', *Geographical Review*, No. 78, 1, January.

Kundu, Abanti (1983), 'Urbanization in India: A Contrast with Western Experience', *Social Scientist*, No. 11, 4, April.

Long, Rev. James ([1852, 1860 and 1974), 'Calcutta in the Olden Time: Its Localities/People', *Calcutta Review*, XVIII and XXXV, December 1852 and September 1860 (reprint, Calcutta: Sanskrit Pustak Bhandar).

Menon, A.G. Krishna (1997), 'Imagining the Indian City', *Economic and Political Weekly*, 15 November.

———. (2002), 'The "Indian" City', *The Book Review*, No. XXVI, 9, September.

Mitra, Ashok (1991), 'Calcutta Diary: On Ending of Tercentenary Celebrations', *Economic and Political Weekly*, No. 26, 4, 26 January.

Mitra, Sarat Chandra ([1889 and 1974), 'Old Calcutta', *National Magazine*, December; reprinted in Alok Ray, ed., *Nineteenth Century Studies* (Calcutta: Bibliographical Research Centre).

BIBLIOGRAPHY

Monro, D.L. (1913), 'Social Conditions in Calcutta, III, City Improvements and Social Conditions', *Bengal Past and Present*, No. 274, October.
Pal, Bipin Chandra ([1930] 1990), 'Civics and the Spiritual Life', *Calcutta Municipal Gazette*, 20 December 1930, reprinted in P. Thankappan Nair et al., eds., *The Calcutta Municipal Gazette, Anthology Number 1924–1947* (Calcutta: Municipal Corporation).
Sengupta, Subir (1989), 'Nagarayaner Itihas', *Desh*, Binodon.
Smith, T. ([1849] 1975), 'Daily Life of a Sahib in Calcutta', *Calcutta Review*, 12, 24; reprinted in Pradip Chaudhury and Abhijit Mukhopadhyay, eds., *Calcutta: People and Empire* (Calcutta: India Book Exchange).
———. (1980), 'Studying the History of Urbanization in India', *Journal of Urban History*, 6, 3, May.
Soltykoff, Prince Alexis (1933), 'Bombay and Calcutta in 1841', *Journal of the Panjab University Historical Society*, No. 2, Part 1, April.
Stuart-Williams, S.C. (1928), 'The Port of Calcutta and its Post-War Development', *Journal of the Royal Society of the Arts*, No. LXXVI, 20 July.
Sykes, W.H. (1845), 'On the Population and Mortality of Calcutta', *Journal of the Statistical Society of London*, No. 8, March.

XII. Books

Ascoli, F.D. (1917), *Early Revenue History of Bengal and the Fifth Report* (Oxford).
Ashworth, William (1954), *The Genesis of Modern British Town Planning: A Study in Economic and Social History of the 19th and 20 the Centuries* (London: Routledge & Kegan Paul).
Baden Powell, B.H. (1892), *The Land System of British India* 3 vols (Oxford).
Bagchi, K. (1944), *The Ganges Delta* (Calcutta).
Bagchi, DR. P.C. (1938), *The Second City of the Empire, The Twenty Fifth Session of the Indian Science Congress Association* (Calcutta).
Ballhatchet, K. and J. Harrison (1980), *The City in South Asia: Pre-Modern and Modern* (London: Curzon Press).
Banerjea, D.J. (2005), *European Calcutta* (UBSPD).
Banerjee, Prajnananda (1975), *Calcutta and Its Hinterland* (Calcutta: Progressive Publishers).
Banerjee, Sumanta (1989), *The Parlour and the Streets: Elite and Popular Culture in Nineteenth Century Calcutta* (Calcutta: Seagull).
———. (2006), *Crime and Urbanization: Calcutta in the Nineteenth Century* (New Delhi: Tulika Books).
———. (2009), *The Wicked City: Crime and Punishment in Colonial Calcutta* (New Delhi: Orient Black Swan).
Banga, Indu, ed. (1991), *The City in Indian History* (New Delhi: Manohar).
Barry, John (1952), *Calcutta Illustrated* (Calcutta: published by author).
Basil, Anne (1969), *Armenian Settlements in India: From the Earliest Times to the Present Day* (Calcutta: Armenian College).

BIBLIOGRAPHY

Baumer, Rechel Van M., ed. (1976), *Aspects of Bengali History and Society* (New Delhi: Vikas Publishing House Pvt. Ltd).

Bhattacharya, Sukumar (1969), *The East India Company and the Economy of Bengal from 1704–1740* (Calcutta: Firma K.L. Mukhopadhyay).

Bhattacherjee, S.B. (1997), *Calcutta, City of Joy* (New Delhi: Sterling).

Biswas, Oneil (1992), *Calcutta and Calcuttans* (Calcutta: Firma KLM).

Blechynden, Katherine (1905), *Calcutta Past and Present*.

Bolts, William, (MDCCLXXII) *Consideration on India Affairs Particularly Respecting the Present State of Bengal and Its Dependencies* (London).

Bose, Nirmal Kumar (1968), *Calcutta: 1964, A Social Survey* (Bombay: Lalvani Publishing House).

Boyd, Kelly, ed. (1999), *Historians and Historical Writings, 2 vols* (London (Chicago): Fitzroy Dearborn Publishers).

Busteed, H.E. (1908), *Echoes from Old Calcutta* (London: W. Thacker & Co.).

The Cambridge Economic History of India, Vol. 1: c 1200-c. 1750 ed. by Tapan Raychaudhury, Irfan Habib, Vol. 2c. 1757–e. 1970, ed. by Dharma Kumar with the editorial assistance of Meghnad Desai. *The Imperial Gazetteer of India*, Vol. XXVI (Oxford: At The Clarendon Press, 1931).

Carry, W.H. (1882 and 1980), *The Good Old Days of Honourable John Company* (reprint, Calcutta Rddhi, India).

Chakraborti, Ranjan, ed. (2013), *Dictionary of Historical Places Bengal 1757–1947* (New Delhi: Primus Books, 2013).

Chakraborty, Bidisha and Sarmistha De (2013), *Calcutta in the Nineteenth Century An Archival Exploration* (New Delhi: Niyogi Books).

Chattopadhyay, Swati (2006), *Representing Calcutta: Modernity, Nationalism and the Colonial Uncanny* (New Delhi: Routledge).

Chaudhuri, Keshab (1973), *Calcutta, Story of Its Government* (Calcutta: Orient Longman).

Chaudhuri, Sukanta, ed. (1995), *Calcutta, The Living City*, 2 vols. (Calcutta: Oxford University Press).

———. (2002), *View from Calcutta* (New Delhi: Chronicle Books).

Chuckerbutty, S.G. (1854), 'A Discourse on the Sanitary Improvement of Calcutta, Read on 8th January, 1852', *Selections from the Bethune Society's Papers*, 1 (Calcutta: P.S. O'Rozario & Co.).

Cotton, H.E.A. (1907), *Calcutta, Old and New* (Calcutta: W. Newman & Co.).

Curzon, George (Marquis of Kedleston) (1925), *British Government in India: The Story of the Viceroys and Government Houses*, 2 vols. (London: Cassel & Co. Ltd., 1925, Vol. I and Vol. II).

Dani, Ahmad Hasan (1956), *Dacca* (Second Revised and Enclarged edition, 1956).

Darian, Steven G. (1978), *The Ganges in Myth and History* (Hawaii, Honolulu: The University Press).

Dasgupta, Biplab et al., eds. (1991), *Calcutta's Urban Future: Agonies from the Past and Prospects for the Future* (Calcutta: Government of West Bengal).

BIBLIOGRAPHY

Dasgupta, Keya (1995), 'Kolkatar Manchitra: Upadan, Samasaya, Sambhavana', *Kaushiki*.

Datta, K.K. (1963), *Alivardi and His Times* (Calcutta: The World Press Private Ltd)

———. (2003), *Calcutta: A Cultural and Literary History* (New Delhi: Roli).

De, Asitkrishna (1989), *Oitihasik Kolkatar Anchal* (Calcutta: Atitihi).

Deb, Raja Binaya Krishna (1905), *The Early History and Growth of Calcutta*, ed. by Subir Ray Chowdhuri Rddhi (India, Calcutta, 1977).

Delwell, H.H., ed. (1963), *The Cambridge History of India, Vol. v, British India 1497–1858* (New Delhi: S. Chand & Co.), Second Indian Reprint.

Dodwell, Henry (1920), *Dupleix and Clive: The Beginning of Empire* (London: Methuen & Co. Ltd.).

Dossal, Mariam (1991), *Imperial Designs and Indian Realities: The Planning of Bombay City 1845–1875* (Bombay: Oxford University Press).

Dutt, R.C. (1906), *The Economic History of India in the Victorian Age* (London).

Eastwick, Edward B. (1882), *Handbook of the Bengal Presidency with an Account of Calcutta City* (London: John Murray).

Eaton, Richard M. (1997), *The Rise of Islam and the Bengal Frontier 1204–1760* (New Delhi: Oxford University Press).

Edwards, S.M. (1920), *The Rise of Bombay: A Retrospect*.

Evenson, Norma (1979), *Paris: A Century of Change 1878–1978* (New Haven and London: Yale University Press).

Fairfield, John D. (1993), *The Mysteries of the Great City: The Politics of Urban Design 1877–1937* (Columbus: Ohio State University Press).

Feldwick, Walter, ed. (1927), *Port Cities of the World* (London: Globe Encyclopaedia Company).

Firminger, Rev. W.K. (1906), *Thacker's Guide to Calcutta* (Calcutta: Thacker, Spink & Co.).

Gaddes, Patrick ([1915 and 1949), *Cities in Evolution* (reprint, London: Williams and Norgate).

Ghosh, Murari (1983), *Metropolitan Calcutta: Economics of Growth* (Calcutta: OPS Publishers Pvt. Ltd., 1983).

Goode, S.W. (1916), *Municipal Calcutta, Its Institutions in Their Origin and Growth* (Edinburgh: T & A Constable).

Gourlay, W.R. (1916), *A Contributions Towards a History of the Police in Bengal* (Calcutta: Bengal Secretariat Press).

Grewal, J.S., ed. (1990), *Calcutta, Foundation and Development of a Colonial Metropolis* (Chandigarh: Urban History Association).

Guha, Ranajit (2009), *The Small Voice of History: Collected Essays* (Ranikhet: Permanent Black).

Gupta, Brijen K. (1966), *Sirajuddaullah and the East India Company, 1756–1757: Background to the Foundations of the British Empire in India* (Leiden: E.J. Brill), photomechanical Reprint.

BIBLIOGRAPHY

Gupta, Narayani (1981), *Delhi Between Two Empires 1803–1931* (New Delhi: Oxford University Press).

Gupta Bahadur, Rai M.N. (1943), *Land System of Bengal* (University of Calcutta).

Hall, Peter (1998), *Cities in Civilization, Culture, Innovation, Urban Order* (London: Weidenfeld and Nicolson).

Hunter, W.W. Sir, *A History of British India*, Vol. I (London: Lungmans, Green & Co.), Printed by Spottiswoode & Co. 1898, Vol. II, 1900 (1875–77), *A Statistical Account of Bengal*, Vols. 20, London.

Huq, M. (1964), *The East India Company's Land Policy and Commerce in Bengal 1698–1784* (Dacca: The Asiatic Society of Pakistan).

Karim, Abdul (1963), *Murshid Quli Khan and His Times* (Daca: The Asiatic Society of Pakistan).

Kellett, John R. (1969), *The Impact of Railways on Victorian Cities* (London: Routledge & Kegan Paul).

Khan, Abdul Majed (1966), *The Transition in Bengal 1756–1775: A Study of Sayid Muhammad Reza Khan* (Cambridge University Press).

Kipling, Rudyard (1891), *The City of Dreadful Night* (Allahabad: A.H. Wheeler).

Knight, Robert (1897), *The Condition of Calcutta* (Calcutta: The Statesman Office).

Kumar, Dharma (1982), *Cambridge Economic History of India*, Vol. II.

La Combe, E.D. (1825), *Book of Reference to the Late Major J.A. Schalch's Plan of Calcutta and its Environs, Compiled from Information Obtained by Enquiries Made on the Spot* (Calcutta: M.D. Rozario).

Long, Reverend James (1974), *Calcutta and Its Neighbourhood : History of Calcutta and Its People from 1760 to 1857*, ed. by Sankar Sengupta (Calcutta: Indian Publications).

Losty, J.P. (1990), *Calcutta, City of Palaces* (London: The British Library).

MacLeod, Kenneth (1884), *The Sanitary Past, Present and Future of Calcutta (Lecture to Bethune Society)* (Calcutta: Thacker, Spink & Co.).

Majumdar, R.C., ed. (1963), *British Paramountcy and Indian Renaissance Part – I*, Bharatiya Vidya Bhavan's History and Culture of the Indian People, Vol. IX.

———. (1967), *An Advanced History of India* (Raychaudhuri and London: Palgrave Macmillan). Datta K.K.

Majumdar, S.C. (1941), *Rivers of the Bengal Delta* (Calcutta).

Manrique, Sebastian (1926–27), *Travels of Sebastian Manrique* (London).

Martin, M.M., ed. (1838), *The History, Antiquities, Topography and Statistics of Eastern India* (London).

Massey, Montague (1918), *Recollections of Calcutta for Over Half a Century* (Calcutta: Thacker Spink & Co.).

McPherson, Kenneth (1974), *The Muslim Microcosm, Calcutta 1918–1935* (Wiesbaden: Franz Steiner Verlag).

Mitra, Asok (1963), *Calcutta, India's City* (Calcutta: New Age Publishers).

BIBLIOGRAPHY

Mitra, Manimanjari (1990), *Calcutta in the Twentieth Century: An Urban Disaster* (Calcutta: Asiatic Book Agency).

Mitra, Radharaman (1980, 1988), *Kolikata Darpan* (Calcutta: Subarnarekha).

Mitra, Rathin (1991, 2009), *Calcutta, Then and Now* (Calcutta: Ananda Publishers).

Moitra, Suresh Chandra, ed. (1979), *Selections from Jnanannesan* (Calcutta: Prajna, 1979).

Moorhouse, Geoffrey (1971, 1983), *Calcutta: The City Revealed* (Harmondsworth: Penguin).

Moreland, W.H. (1920), *India at the Death of Akbar An Economic Study* (London).

———. (1929), *The Agrarian System of Moslem India*.

Mukherjee, Nilmani (1968), *The Port of Calcutta : A Short History*, The Commissioners for the Port of Calcutta.

Mukherjee, Radhakamal (1938), *The Changing Face of Bengal* (Calcutta).

Mukherjee, S.N. (1977a), *Calcutta, Myths and History* (Calcutta: Subarnarekha).

Mumford, Lewis (1961), *The City in History: Its Origins, Its Transformations and Its Prospects* (London: Secker and Warburg).

Nair, P. Thankappan (1984), *Calcutta In The 18th Century Impressions of Travellers* (Calcutta: Firma KLM Private Limited).

———. (1986), *Calcutta in the 17th Century: A Tercentenary History of Calcutta, Vol I* (Calcutta: Firma KLM Private Limited).

———. (1987), *A History of Calcutta's Streets* (Calcutta: Firma KLM).

———. (1989), *Calcutta Corporation at a Glance* (Calcutta: Calcutta Corporation).

———. (1989), *Calcutta in the 19th Century [Company's Days]* (Calcutta: Firma).

Nandy, Somendra Chandra (1978), *Life and Times of kantoo Baboo: The Banian of Warren Hasitngs* (Allied Publishers).

Naoriji, Dadabhai (1901), *Poverty and Un-British Rule* (London).

———. (2004), *South Indians in Kolkata* (Calcutta: Punthi Pustak).

Nilsson, Sten (1968), *European Architecture in India* (London: Faber and Faber).

Oldenburg, Veena Talwar (1984), *The Making of Colonial Lucknow, 1856–1877* (Princeton: Princeton University Press).

Olsen, Donald J. (1976), *The Growth of Victorian London* (New York: Holmes and Meier).

Prakash, Om (2000), *European Colonial Enterprise in Pre-Colonial India* (Cambridge University Press).

Ramachandran, R. (1991), *Urbanization and Urban Systems in India* (New Delhi: Oxford University Press).

Ramaswami, N.S. (1977), *The Founding of Madras* (Orient Longman).

Ray, Mohit (2010), *Old Mirrors, Traditional Ponds of Calcutta* (Calcutta: Municipal Corporation).

BIBLIOGRAPHY

Ray, N.R. (1979, 1982), *City of Job Charnock* (Calcutta: Victorial Memorial).

Ray, Rajat (1979), *Urban Roots of Indian Nationalism: Pressure Groups and Conflict of Interests in Calcutta City Politics 1875–1939* (New Delhi: Vikas).

Reclus, Elisa (1884), *The Earth and Its Inhabitants*, Vol. 3: *India and China* (London).

Richards, D.S., ed. (1971), *Islam and the Trade of Asia* (Oxford).

Roberts, P.E. ([1929] 1961), *India under Wellesley* (reprint, Gorakhpur: Vishwavidyalaya Prakashan).

Ross, R.J. and G.J. Telkamp, eds. (1985), *Colonial Cities: Essays on Urbanism in a Colonial Context* (Dordrecht: Martinus Niejhoff).

Roy, Dalia (2005), *The Parsees of Calcutta* (Calcutta: Sujan).

Rudra, Shankar (1987), *Samakalinder Chokhe Kolkatar Nana Elaka* (Calcutta: New Bengal Press).

Sarkar, Sumit (1997), *Writing Social History* (New Delhi: Oxford University Press).

Sen, Ranjit (1987), *Metamorphosis of the Bengal Polity (1700–1793)* (Calcutta: Rabindra Bharati University).

———. (1988), *Social Banditry in Bengal 1757–1793: A Study in Primary Resistance* (Calcutta: Ratna Prakashan).

———. (1988), *Understanding Indian History* (Calcutta: Firma KLM Private Limited).

———. (2000), *A Stagnating City Calcutta in the EighteenthCentury* (Calcutta: Institute of Historical Studies).

———. (2010), *Property Aristocracy & the Raj* (Calcutta: Maha Bodhi Book Agency).

———. (2010), *1857 Visions Resurrected Shaping Ideas From Oblivion*, Frame Eternity where eternity is framed in knowledge (Calcutta).

Seth, Mesrovb Jacob (1937), *Armenians in India: From Earliest Times to the Present Day, A Work of Original Research* (Reprint, Calcutta, 1983).

Sinha, N.K. (1956, 1962, 1970), *The Economic History of Bengal from Plassey to the Permanent Settlement* (Vol. I, 3rd edition, 1965; Vol. II (Reprint of 1st edition, 1968) *The Economic History of Bengal 1793–1848*, Vol. III (1970).

Sinha, Pradip (1978), *Calcutta in Urban History* (Calcutta: Firma KLM).

———, ed. (1987), *The Urban Experience: Calcutta Essays in Honour of Professor Nisith R. Ray* (Calcutta: Rddhi India).

Spear, Percival, ed. (1958), *The Oxford History of India By the Late Vincent A. Smith* (Oxford: At The Clarendon Press).

———. (1988), *A History of Delhi Under the Later Mughals* (New Delhi).

Spodek, Howard (1976), *Urban-Rural Integration in Regional Development: A Case Study of Saurashtra, India 1800–1960* (Chicago, IL: University of Chicago).

Sreemani, Soumitra (1994), *Anatomy of a Colonial Town: Calcutta 1756–1794* (Calcutta: Firma KLM).

BIBLIOGRAPHY

———, ed. (2015), *Kalikata Kolkata* (Calcutta: Bangiya Itihas Samiti).

Sterndale, Reginald Craufuird (1881), *Municipal Work in India or Hints on Sanitation – General Conservancy and Improvement in Municipalities, Towns and Villages* (Calcutta: Thacker Spink & Co.).

———. (1885), *An Historical Account of 'The Calcutta Collectorate', 'Collector's Cutcherry, or Calcutta Pottah Office', From the days of the Zemindars to the Present Time, with a brief notice of the Zemindars and Collectors of Calcutta, The Ground Tenure of Land-revenue System, Town Duties, Excise and Stamp Revenue* (Calcutta: Bengal Secretariat Press).

Tavernier, Jean (1925), *Travels in India*, Vol. I (London).

Thakur, Kshitindranath (1930), *Kolkataye Chala Phera [Sekal O Ekal]* (Calcutta: published by author).

Thompson, Edward and G.T. Garratf (1962), *Rise and Fulfillment of British Rule in India* (Allahabad: Central Book Depot).

Tillotson, Giles (2006), *Jaipur Nama: Tales from the Pink City* (New Delhi: Penguin).

Tindall, Gillian (1992), *City of Gold, The Biography of Bombay* (New Delhi: Penguin).

Tomlinson, B.R. (1988), *The Cambridge History of India III. 3 The Economy of Modern India 1860–1970* (Cambridge: Cambridge University Press), First South Asian Paperback Edition.

Tripathi, Amales, *Trade and Finance in the Bengal Presidency*.

Vaughan, Philippa (1997), *The Victoria Memorial Hall: Conceptions, Collections, Conservation* (Mumbai: Marg).

Wheeler, J.T. (1878), *A History of the English Settlement in India* (Calcutta: Office of the Superintendent of Government Printing).

Wilson, C.R. (1906), *Old Fort William in Bengal A Selection of Official Documents Dealing with Its History* (London: John Murray).

———. (1917), *The Early Annals of the English in Bengal Being the Bengal Public Consultations for the First Half of the Eighteenth Century* 1895, Vol. I, London, W. Thackers & Co (Calcutta: Thacker Spink & Co. Vol II 1900. Vol. III).

Zilly, Aditee Nagchowdhury (1982), *The Vagrant Peasant Agrarian Distress and Desertion in Bengal 1770–1830* (Wiesbadan: Verlong Fraz Steiner).

INDEX

Abu'l-Fazl 84, 87
Adiganga 84
Ahmedabad 118–119
Ain-i-Akbari 4, 87
Albuquerque 43
Anandamath 170
Anglo-Armenian partnership 98
Ara 110
Arakans 1, 85
Armenian Calcutta 94–105
Asansol 131
Azimu-sh-Shan 101

Bandyopadhyay, Bhabani Charan 53, 238
Basaks 68, 87, 102, 117
battle of Buxar 6, 140, 145, 236
battle of Palasi 6, 9, 46, 56, 113, 123, 124, 139, 140, 151, 152, 232–234, 236, 237
Bayley, W.H. 111
Bengal 111, 116, 119, 121; agriculture and 121; coal 129; silk 39; south Bengal cities, propelling force 121–124; towns 118
Bengal revolution, 1756–1757 149
Bentinck, William 117
Berhampore 123
Betai Chandi 82
Beverley, H. 33
Bhagalpur 110
Bhagirathi river 85, 86, 123, 173
Bhattacharya, S. 111
black zamindar 160–162, 171
Bombay: career, property of English 40–41; comparative understanding, Calcutta and Madras 37–45
Boxer, C.R. 42
Briggs, Asha 32
British Asiatic trade 3
Britons 5, 12, 63, 143, 145
Brown, Percy 50
Burdwan 110, 113–115, 118, 126; case-study 131–133; foreign capital 130

Calcutta: born in turmoil 37–40; comparative understanding, Bombay and Madras 37–45; competition, challenges of 43–45; *see also individual entries*
Calcutta-Madras partnership 150–152
Calcutta Municipal Act of 1863 95
capital deployment 54
Carey, W.H. 99
Cartier, Governor 219
Chakrabarti, Bhubaneswar 179
Chakraborty, Uttara 58
Chakravarti, Mukundaram 173, 174
Chandernagore 125
Chandimangal 173
Charnock, Job 2, 4, 37, 40, 82, 83, 87, 94–98, 159, 176, 233
Charter Act of 1727 160
Charter Act of 1793 13
Charter Acts 159
Charter of 1794 164, 165, 167
Chattopadhyaya, Bankim Chandra 170

INDEX

Chhapra 110
Child, Josiah 39
Chittagong 111, 113, 116–118, 120, 152, 153
Clive, Robert 141, 143, 149–152, 219
Colebrook, H.T. 48
colonialism 95
Communist Manifesto, The 32
cosmopolitan crowd 6–11
Cuttack 110

dacoits 114, 120
Dakha 111, 116, 119, 121
Darian, Steven G. 48
Das, Suranjan 114
de Castro, DeMello 41
de jure Mughal *Subah* 71
de-urbanization 110
Dhaka 11, 93, 110, 112
Dodwell, Henry 150
Dutta, Romesh Chandra 3

Eaton, Richard M. 83, 84
Edwardes, S.M. 41
Edwards, S.M. 43
egoism 146
English East India Company 2–4, 37, 63, 94, 105, 138, 166, 175
English settlement 153
English trade settlement 4
epoch-making theory 32

Farlan, David M. 95
feudal manorial system 31
Fever Hospital Committee 14, 15, 224–231
Fifth Report of 1812 115
Fisher 88
foreign capital 128, 130
Fort William 40, 93, 148, 151, 165, 186, 193
founder, Calcutta 81–109

Ganga river 46–48, 81
Gangetic trade routes 140
garrison town 70–71
geopolitics, operation of 4–6
Goode, W.W. 162

governance: apprenticeship 51–52; regime of 13–17
Grandpre 240
Guha, Ranajit 55, 57
Gunakar, Bharat Chandra Ray 52

Hamilton, Alexander 207
Hamilton, Walter 111
haphazard morphology 199
Harappan civilization 31
Hastings, Warren 15, 89, 91, 117, 142–147, 150, 219
History of Bengal 98
Hugli 11, 81, 111, 117, 122, 125
Hunter, W.W. 128
Hutom Pyanchar Naksha 57

Impey, Elijah 144
Industrial Revolution 32
interior towns: Bengal districts, internal stimulation 129–131; Calcutta and 110–137; challenged interior 110–112; garrison town, journey from 112–114; metropolitan Calcutta and competitors 124–127; occasional growth momentum 116–119; potentialities 127–129
Islam Khan 93

Jagat Seths 52
Jnanannesan 16
judicial pretension 11
jute factories 129

Kalighat 1; antiquity, eighteenth century 173–175; Kali, rallying force 170–171; Kali-worship, eighteenth century 171–172; pilgrim centre 170–183; religious centre, Calcutta 175–178; sacred specialists, absence of 179–181; worship and support 172–173
kalikata Kamalalaya 53, 56, 57
Kalikshetra 175
Kali of Kalighata 103
Khan, Shujauddin 206
Khilji, Muhammad Bakhtiyar 48–49
Kumar, Nanda 144

INDEX

Lancaster, James 44
land legislations 54
Life of Chaitayana 103
Long, Reverend James 221
Lord Wellesley's minute on Calcutta 224–231
Lottery Committee 14–17, 240
Lucknow 110

Madras 138, 140; comparative understanding, Calcutta and Bombay 37–45; competition, challenges of 43–45; foundation of property 38
Magadhan Empire 12
Maghs 1, 85
Maitland, F.W. 32
Malda 111, 120, 122
Malliks 87, 117
Mal Zamini system 60
Manasamangal 87, 173, 174
Man Singh, viceroy 92
Maratha ditch 6, 222, 239
Maratha invasions 6, 115, 153, 235
Marathas 12, 126, 127
Marwaris 87, 88, 117
medical topography 14
Middleton 148
Midnapur 113–115, 126
Mir Kashim 121, 122, 126
Mir Qasim 6, 13, 148, 153
Mirzapur 120
Moreland, W.H. 33
Mughal Empire 46, 52, 149
Mughal-French alliance 236
Mughal rule 10
Munghyr 110
municipal administration 159–169; effective institution 166–167; justices appointment 164; justices of peace, corporate control 164–166; municipal growth, gradual phenomenon 159–164
municipal reforms 205
Murshidabad 11, 110–112, 121, 126, 127, 138, 142, 147, 149, 152

Nadia 49, 51, 85, 90, 124, 127
Nagchowdhury-Zilly, Aditee 127

Navaratna temple 171
nawabs 5, 7, 10, 11, 39, 46, 64–69, 71, 89, 90, 101, 102, 104, 111, 124, 125, 139, 140, 143–145, 147, 149, 161, 232, 234, 235
nizamat 67, 90, 142, 233

O'Malley, L.S. 48

Padma-Meghna system 84
Patna 11
Periplus of the Erythrean Sea 58
Permanent Settlement 54, 124
Peterson, J.C.K. 114
pilgrim centre 170–183
Pipalai, Bipradas 87, 173, 174
Pirenne, Henry 32
Pithasthan (pilgrim centre) 1
Plassey Plunder 151
political revolutions 47
Portuguese 1, 81, 85; removal of 41–43

qasba 101
Quli Khan, Murshid 51, 59, 60, 64, 89, 91, 92, 122, 125, 145, 148, 206, 235

Rahim Khan 37
Raja Radhakanta Deb 14
Ramaswami, N.S. 44
Rangoon 117, 120
Raniganj 117, 128, 131
Ray, A.K. 17, 33, 34, 82–86, 205, 220, 221, 223, 240
real estate boom 116
Regulating Act of 1773 90, 144
religious toleration 103
renaissance 13, 48–51
revenue 190
riverbank, revolution on 46–62
Roe, Tomas 44
Rohillas 12

Sadar Diwani Adalats 11
Sadar Nizamat 11
Salim, Ghulam Hussain 50
Sannyasi, Sevayet 105
Sarhad, Khojah 97
Sarkar, Jadunath 9, 49, 92, 93

INDEX

Select Committee of 1783 146
self-defence 55
Seth, M. J. 96
Seths 68, 87, 102, 117
Shah Alam II 7
Shova Singh 52, 66, 88, 97, 99, 126, 185
Sikhs 12
silk industry 127
Sinha, N.K. 53, 54
Sinha, Pradip 15, 207
social revolutions 47
south Bengal 1, 6
Spear, Percival 144, 148
Srirampur 110
Subeh Bangla 90
Subsidiary Alliance 15
Sunni Muslims 43
Sutanuti Hat 87

Tagore, Dwarakanath 14
Tanda 50
Tanjore 110
Tipu Sultan 13
Todar Mal 51
Tomlinson, B.R. 130
Township and Borough 32
trade boom 86
trade metropolis 3
Treaty of Alinagar (Calcutta) 10
Tripathi, Amales 128

urban growth challenges 184–204
urbanization 1, 2; accidents, avoiding 210; army drill and public work, Spatial expansion 210–211; banditry and reduced 114–116; burial grounds creation 211–212; Calcutta, breakthrough 138–140; civil construction, bricks in 189–191; collaborating humanity 55–58; colonial historiography, uncongenial for 33–34; compact, city 215–216; competent capitalist class 53–55; corridor of power, trade to land 52–53; effective and planned measures, 1805 209–214; eighteenth-century phenomenon, Calcutta's emergence 152–154;

fort-centric growth pattern, private collaboration 187–189; free air circulation 212–213; Ganga river and 46–48; garrison town, planned insulation 184–185; geopolitics of 63–77; geopolitics town planning, stress 65–68; haphazard morphology 199; internal town formation, evolved process 216–218; logic of 138–158, 185–187; mankind necessary for 46–62; mapping pattern of 31–36; mirror from south 197–198; motivation, nineteenth century 208–209; native to imperial city, Calcutta 146–149; political take-off, Calcutta 143–146; political will for 69–70; poor, eighteenth century 205–207; population and 110, 119–121; power, Calcutta 141–143; of property and wealth 53–55; public works, tensions 194–197; river navigation, obstructions removal 210; roads constructions 191–194, 214; seaboard, strategic importance 140–141; security and protection 207; space utilization techniques 208; stagnation, public opinion 221–223; thatched houses removal 210; timber supersession 189–191; town beautification measures 213–214; trade, market, and artisan economy 58–60; unsure identity 31–33; white and black settlements, interpenetration 218–220
urban settlement 8

Vansittart, Governor 219
Verelst, Governor 219
Victorian Cities 32

white zamindar 161, 162
Wilson, C.R. 96, 99
Wilson, Khojah Sarhad 97

zamindars 9, 51, 54, 56, 116, 123, 125, 138, 160, 238